VENI, VIDI, VIDEO

THOMAS SCHATZ, EDITOR

Texas Film and Media Studies Series

Veni, Vidi, Video

The Hollywood Empire and the VCR

FREDERICK
WASSER

 University of Texas Press, Austin

Requests for permission to reproduce material from this work should be sent to Permissions, University of Texas Press, P.O. Box 7819, Austin, TX 78713-7819.

⊗ The paper used in this book meets the minimum requirements of ANSI/NISO Z39.48-1992 (R1997) (Permanence of Paper).

Library of Congress Cataloging-in-Publication Data

Wasser, Frederick.

    Veni, vidi, video : the Hollywood empire and the VCR / Frederick Wasser. — 1st ed.

      p.   cm. — (Texas film and media studies series)

    Includes bibliographical references and index.

    ISBN 0-292-79145-3 (cloth : alk. paper) — ISBN 0-292-79146-1 (pbk. : alk. paper)

    1. Video recordings.   2. Video recordings industry.   I. Title.   II. Series.

PN1992.935 W37   2001

384.55′8—dc21   2001027585

Contents

CHAPTER THREE

76   Home Video: The Early Years

CHAPTER FOUR

104   The Years of Independence: 1981–1986

CHAPTER FIVE

131   Video Becomes Big Business

Acknowledgments

I stepped off the bus in Salt Lake City looking for a job in an independent film company. Within several hours, I was hired to be an assistant editor on a small-budget film that had sat on the shelf for several years, waiting for a theatrical release. It was now being dusted off for the very new and very wide open video market. I felt like a forty-niner stumbling onto Sutter's gold mine. I got more jobs on more films being made in hopes of capturing video profits. I followed the trail of these films down to Los Angeles, and soon I graduated to the big studios.

The small independent companies had a unique culture that attracted filmmakers who loved alternative and cult filmmaking. James Bryan, who had hired me off the bus, acted as a mentor for me, providing in his own career the bridge between older exploitation films and the new cheapies. He instructed me in the poetry of independent film financing, an art form that fascinated me even though I lacked any competency at it. He provided the original inspiration for this study when he pointed out that the video market was turning against the very companies it had initially spawned. I started thinking about the cultural implications of this commercial shakeout.

I was fortunate that Thomas Guback, a leading authority in film industry studies, unstintingly guided my academic research and helped me develop my thoughts on the commercial/cultural nexus. Thomas Schatz was especially important in helping to transform the manuscript into this book. I am extremely grateful for the intelligence and enthusiasm of both men. Also, I would like to thank the anonymous reader and the copy editor, Sue Carter, from the University of Texas Press, whose comments were extremely helpful.

I want to acknowledge Diane Carothers and Ellen Sutton of the University of Illinois Communications Library for their help. I want to thank James

x Carey for his generous efforts and our many talks. My writing was supported by fellowships from the University of Illinois and the School of Journalism at Columbia University, and a residency in the Department of Sociology and Anthropology at Tufts University. Dean June Higgins provided resources from the School of Arts and Sciences at Central Connecticut State University for the completion of this book. I am thankful for discussions I have had with John Nerone, Dan Schiller, Paul Lopes, Ira Robbins, Sheila McBride, Ann Klefstad, Richard Casey, William Megalos, Nancy Salzer, and Shin Mizukoshi. Solidelle Wasser and Henry Wasser have provided continuous support.

Introduction: Signs of the Time

Sumner Redstone had a problem in the fall of 1993. He wanted to buy Paramount studio for his own company, Viacom. Redstone had been in the movie theater business since 1954. In 1987, he took over Viacom, a television company that distributed syndicated shows and ran the MTV and Nickelodeon cable channels. But now he wanted a show biz legend, he wanted Paramount, the studio of Adolph Zukor and Cecil B. DeMille. This was the studio that pioneered the Hollywood film industry, starting in 1914. It was still, to this day, the only major U.S. studio actually headquartered in Hollywood, California. But how could Redstone buy it? He had offered as much as Viacom could afford, but still had not topped the counterbidding from Barry Diller and his allies. In order to enhance Viacom's resources, he contemplated another preliminary merger. This merger was not to be with an old major media business, but with a new force on the American media landscape, Blockbuster, the world's largest video rental chain. Phone calls were made. Negotiations began. In January 1994, Blockbuster was merged into Viacom and on February 14, Viacom acquired Paramount. A film institution had been bought with the cash flow of a video rental business. Home video had now arrived as a mass medium institution.

Another video sign of the times occurred in that same season when William Mechanic was named the president and chief operating officer of Twentieth Century Fox on September 27, 1993. The item on his resume that clinched the appointment? It was Mechanic's nine-year stint leading the Walt Disney Home Video division. He had built on the natural advantages of Disney product to take a dominant market position in the sale of prerecorded videos. Still, there was enough of the old prejudice against the home video division that Disney's chief, Michael Eisner, did not move quickly enough to

2   give Mechanic creative assignments. Twentieth Century Fox decided that it
was time for someone with a video background, now the largest segment of
the movie market, to take charge of the whole works. Mechanic was persuaded to become the first home video vice president to make the switch, to
take charge of another historic Hollywood studio.

This book examines the rise of home video as a mass medium. In today's
world, mass media are woven together in a thick relationship that becomes a
total environment. Every change in one medium affects the balance of the
whole. Studies of media industrial relations reveal more than just the business of media. Media relations must be understood before we can really understand the cultural value of the product itself, be it a mainstream film or an
episodic television show or a pornographic tape. After all, industry practices
determine which shows are made and how they are made. Industry relations
must be understood as a reflection of the audience itself, just as real a reflection of the audience as surveys, ethnographic studies, and other methods.

The worldwide audience's fascination with video ignited the rapid-fire
success of Sony's Betamax videocassette recorder (VCR) after its introduction
in 1975. Sony's VCR competed successfully against various new media "delivery systems" such as Cartrivision and early prototypes of Laservision.
When a competing format, "VHS," came out in 1976 and overtook the "Betamax" format, the video competition became a sporting event attracting the
interest of an international audience. VHS was the result of rivalries within
the Japanese electronics industry and was championed by the biggest electronic manufacturer, Matsushita, now resentful of and aroused by Sony's upstart success. These successive hardware (and ensuing software) wars showed
that no one knew how home video would succeed and that the strongest
manufacturers were not able to impose their version unilaterally on the audience. Well-marketed video products suffered market failure because these
products did not satisfy audience desires. In turn, the audience did not reveal
these desires until they saw the product in the store. Certainly the instant
popularity of the VCR surprised powerful media players and upset quite a few
of them. American pundits and policymakers were particularly chastised by
the fact that both profitable formats belonged to Japanese manufacturers.

In addition to the uncertainty of the format competition, it was not clear
what the audience would do with the videocassette recorder. It could be used
to watch original programming, to watch television shows at times other than
the scheduled broadcast (time shifting), to watch pornography and other non-

mainstream movies, to watch current mainstream movies. Of course, the VCR was used for all these purposes as well as for amateur home recordings. The purpose of this book is to describe which function had the greatest impact on extant media institutions and to describe, in turn, how this impact fueled the growth of "home video" into a major global culture industry. Advertisers and TV producers were very concerned that the VCR would erode the basis of television economics. However, this threat faded as the audience quickly discovered that they could use the VCR to watch movies. The rental of movies became the primary use of the VCR, and certainly the one with the greatest impact on an existing mass medium — the film industry. This historical study focuses on the movie industry, as the VCR becomes widespread by the end of the 1970s and becomes the primary means for viewing movies a decade later. Even if the VCR disappears and new digital players and forms of downloading movies are adopted, its impact on the film industry has been profound and will endure.

The VCR emerges in 1975 and achieves stability by the middle of the 1990s. This time stretch saw a remarkable transformation of the American film and television industries. Among the more significant changes are:

- New styles of filmmaking (a new generation of filmmakers working on expensive blockbusters).
- Hugely expensive advertising and marketing campaigns for films.
- Unprecedented levels of film revenues.
- Global domination of the film industry by the top Hollywood studios.
- The demise of competing independent distributors.
- A buildup of large transnational media conglomerates, uniting film, broadcast, cable, print, records, and new media under one corporation.
- The breakup of oligopolistic networks in the United States and regulated broadcast systems overseas.
- New markets.

The list is not exhaustive or particularly systematic. Among its omissions are changes that require aesthetic judgment, such as the claim that there has been a decline in cinema culture. Nonetheless, there are changes of cultural importance in the above listing. The most striking is that the U.S. film industry has managed to hold onto and expand its global audience while the networks have seen their audience erode. One crucial aspect of the changes has

4   been the relationship between the new market of home video and the mass
audience for film. And whereas it would be unwarranted to claim home video
had an equal impact on each of the transformations, this new medium directly fueled the most basic transformation of all—the increase in revenue
level. The unprecedented levels of film revenues over the past two decades
has been the enabling condition for new filmmaking styles, expensive marketing, global domination, and buildup of transnational media conglomerates. The numbers are staggering. The major studios had revenues of $2.1 bil-
lion in 1975, the year of the Betamax. By 1993, they had $17.4 billion.[1] This
is better than an eightfold increase. In that same time the U.S. consumer
price index—a basic measure of inflation—had less than a threefold increase.[2]

The increased revenues are central to the current media environment, and
the videocassette sales are central to this increase. Home video emerged as a
mass medium in the course of the 1980s, when the combined dollars of millions of video renters and purchasers returned more money to film distributors than either the theatrical or television markets. This milestone was passed
in the period of 1987–1988. Estimates vary after 1987, because annual studio
reports generally stopped breaking out the actual amounts of home video
sales. Nonetheless, it is safe to say that from that time on, sales of videocassettes (to both rental stores and consumers) have contributed about 40 percent of total film studio revenue. There are two ways cassette sales could have
made this impact. The cassette market could have simply grown faster than
the other markets, or it could have weakened the other markets, siphoning
off consumer dollars that would have otherwise gone toward cable and the
box office. This latter process is sometimes referred to as "cannibalization."
The remarkable thing is that home video did not cannibalize the theatrical
revenue. It made its impact the first way. It grew so fast that it was new money,
contributing the bulk of the accelerated studio receipts.

Are video revenues central to every facet of the major film/TV transformations? This question has to be examined in detail. What does video have
to do with the breakup of the oligopoly of the networks? Alternatively, with
the demise of independent distribution? Or with global domination? The answers are not obvious; a historical analysis is needed. A snapshot of any particular moment misses the point. We will see that each stage of video built
upon the previous and that home viewing builds upon older developments
and explorations in the film industry. The long view is the proper study of
video—a view that as yet has not been taken. Previous histories of video have

not been systematic and have not portrayed the phenomenon in context, primarily because they were written too soon, before the full impact of video on Hollywood—and the place of video in the complex weave of film history—could be appreciated.

The American Film Industry before Video

In order to understand the impact of video, it is important to remember the film and television world before home video, particularly in the United States. In the first decades of the century, the film industry was just about the only non-print mass medium in existence. Distributors and exhibitors had discovered they could appeal to a range of audience interests and purse sizes through a tiered releasing system. The first-run downtown movie palaces were built with lavish decorations, showing the newest releases for highly motivated viewers who were willing to spend more money on a ticket. Small, third-run neighborhood theaters accommodated viewers who were neither willing to spend much money nor to go far from home. Radio became a mass medium in the 1920s, but it did little to change film distribution practices. However, the changes that occurred when television came in after World War II coincided with major disruptions in the film industry. These disruptions were caused not only by television but also by the lifestyle changes that Americans were undergoing at the same time. The film industry lost its mass audience.

To be more precise, the postwar film industry could no longer count on its mass audience. Sometimes people came out en masse to see the big movies. Many times, they did not. Boom and bust cycles plagued the movie industry during the 1950s and 1960s. Hits were followed by flops, sustained profits were elusive, and overall attendance continued to decline. It seemed that every time a cycle of hits started up, such as the epics *The Ten Commandments* (1956) and *Ben-Hur* (1959), it ended in a disastrous flop such as *Cleopatra* (1963). The musical cycle that culminated in the hit *The Sound of Music* (1965) was killed off in 1967 by the notorious disappointments of *Dr. Dolittle, Star!*, and others. Stability and growth continually eluded the studios in the postwar period. MGM actually had negative earnings in 1957. Columbia, Universal, and Warner Bros. suffered the same fate in the next year. Twentieth Century Fox had three losing years from 1960 through 1962. Only Paramount escaped such ignominy, until red ink finally caught up with the

6   studio in 1970 and 1971. These old powerhouses were forced to find new ways of making money, from the sale of their real estate and other assets to providing production facilities for the burgeoning television industry. Theaters also suffered, either from the loss of their audience moving to the suburbs or from the loss of product as the major studios cut back on production.

New independent companies started producing and distributing films during those turbulent years. Their earnings were insignificant even compared to the now humbled majors, but their cultural impact was great. These independents gave creative work to new talent. They attracted new niche audiences. AIP (American International Pictures) made exploitation movies such as *Not of This Earth* (1956), *The Little Shop of Horrors* (1959), and similar films for teenagers and young adults. Sunn Classics circulated wilderness films such as *The Life and Times of Grizzly Adams* (1974) to rural families. They imported foreign films, attracting college students and others. They filled the voids. For instance, mainstream studios hesitated to tackle adult themes. Nimbler distributors such as Joseph Burstyn, Walter Reade, Grove Press, and AIP Films imported the new and more daring European films such as *The Miracle* (1951) and *La Dolce Vita* (1960) for the American art circuit. The majors also largely left the development of the drive-in circuit and the summer season to the independents. This season had been written off as a time when the mass audience was away on vacation and unavailable to go see movies. Studio executives watched cautiously as the summer drive-ins screened the titillating and exploitative, such as horror, gang, and biker films promoted by AIP, Roger Corman's New World, et al.

Sometimes a major studio would try to reach this audience. Often, the studio did poorly. One notable lesson occurred in 1971. Warner Communications was distributing an action film with a counterculture/New Age angle, called *Billy Jack,* and was doing very poor business. Tom Laughlin, the producer and star, wanted better treatment. He sued and settled by buying the film back. He distributed it himself in 1973, and grabbed the attention of the industry when he grossed $32 million. Eventually the industry realized that the key to Laughlin's success was his innovative use of saturated television advertising.[3]

Television was also vastly different before the video revolution. Since CBS, NBC, and ABC switched their attention from radio to television programming around 1952, television had been going from one success to another. The dominance of the three networks, particularly CBS and NBC, was nearly complete. In the 1950s, the federal government cooperated with the broad-cast networks by establishing rules that weakened competition from cable programming and Television Theater, and discouraged the movie industry from moving into network distribution. As a result, most American house-holds on most nights were tuned into network programming. By the 1970s, the strength and profitability of the three networks caused the federal gov-ernment to switch course and to promote alternatives to network domi-nance. Cable operators benefited from this new attitude, which was expressed through a series of favorable court decisions and Federal Communications Commission rulings.

The networks were also becoming more competitive with each other at this time. Even popular shows were cancelled if the shows were not attract-ing the audience that the advertisers wanted—young adults. This audience segment was hard to reach, particularly as their schedules were less pre-dictable than those of other groups. In this competition, a question emerged. How would the young adults watch their favorite programs with their long working hours and long suburban commutes? Perhaps they would be willing to buy equipment that would allow them to reschedule their television shows to fit their schedules. Perhaps . . .

Although the movie industry had lost its dependable mass audience, movies per se had not lost their popularity in the United States or abroad. When recent movies were broadcast in prime time during the 1960s, they achieved very high ratings. People were willing to watch the big movies on the small screen in the living room. Perhaps they would buy movies to watch at home whenever they wished. Or perhaps they would rent these movies. Perhaps . . .

The VCR went through a two-stage process in terms of its impact on the mass media environment. People bought their first VCRs to watch television programs when they wanted to. As a critical mass was reached, an infrastruc-ture of rental stores mushroomed, one or more in every neighborhood. People got into the habit of renting movies. Naturally, the movie industry changed as video came in. It was not the same business that had stumbled from hit to flop anymore. It was a new hit-making factory that had made the long pil-grimage back to sustained prosperity. The Hollywood establishment had learned to fight for its audience. It was changing for the second time in the postwar period. This change came to be loosely labeled "New Hollywood."

What is New Hollywood? There are two answers. The first one has to do

8   with a new cohort of directors. The emergence of New Hollywood is often dated from Francis Ford Coppola's *The Godfather* in 1972, and Steven Spielberg's *Jaws* in 1975. The new era is marked not only by the unprecedented earnings of these films and the later phenomenon of *Star Wars* (1977) but also by the arrival of a new generation of filmmakers—most notably Coppola, Spielberg, and George Lucas, who epitomized the influences shaping an entire cohort of new filmmakers. These influences included new ways of training for a directing career, a greater autonomy from old craft guilds, and a willingness to spend more time and money on every aspect of the film in order to make it an "event." Improvements in filmmaking equipment and the popularity of the 16mm film gauge (for amateur and documentary use) allowed these filmmakers to learn their craft in school or on their own, "off the studio lots." Only Spielberg was trained in a studio setting, but even his career started with an amateur self-produced film called *Amblin'*. The others went to film school and learned to appreciate the innovative practices of postwar foreign filmmaking. Their attitude toward the classic Hollywood studio system of the thirties and forties was ambivalent at best. The production discipline of the classic system had severely eroded by the 1970s, but was still prevalent enough to cause Coppola and his fellow film school graduates to dream of working "outside the system."

The irony was that the system was no longer a monolith. It had been beaten down by box office disappointments for several decades. The surprise success of *Easy Rider* (1969) reinforced the studio executives' sense of disconnection with the increasing commercial power of youth culture. They were willing to quickly promote a new cohort into the top ranks of major motion picture directing. After only one or two "apprentice" features, Francis Ford Coppola, George Lucas, Dennis Hopper, Warren Beatty, Peter Bogdanovich, Martin Scorsese, and other relatively young directors were offered big budgets to make high-profile films. Coppola et al. gave up their rebel dreams (to some extent) in order to move up the director track much faster than any group since the original filmmakers of the silent era. These new directors responded to their opportunities with a mixture of awe and contempt for mainstream commercial filmmaking, and their films, such as *American Graffiti* (1973), *Shampoo* (1975), *The Last Picture Show* (1971), and *Mean Streets* (1973), reflected this mixture. As a group they introduced stylistic innovations and yet maintained a high level of conformity to the classic genre conventions.[4]

The new filmmakers liked to tweak every element of the film. This not only pushed up the budget but also reoriented the directors, the crew, and the cast in their careers. Every film became a make-or-break proposition for everyone involved. The new "hotshots" of course had every reason to treat their projects as one of a kind. After all, they were the new generation, not old hackneyed studio directors. Their arrogance and grandstanding was noticed and reported in the news coverage of the time and continues to be a feature of historical and critical writing about the 1970s. What was less noticed was how much the grandstanding fit the new studio emphasis on intensive marketing of individual films. The triumphs of *The Godfather* and *Jaws* were a result of and led to increased spending on advertising and wider releases, which soon became the norm.[5] *Star Wars* led to an increased emphasis on elaborate advertising campaigns and on merchandising toys and other products associated with the film. It was not just film "auteurs" who treated every film as an event, it was the marketing and distribution executives.

Therefore, another key aspect of New Hollywood was the new way of handling a film once it was made. Distributors and marketers made New Hollywood as much as the directors. Marketing departments rebuilt themselves on the big movies the New Hollywood filmmakers gave them. The best example of this was *Jaws*, released by Universal in 1975. Universal had learned the *Billy Jack* lesson. They ran countless television spots with devastating success during the *Jaws* release. They combined the saturated advertising with a wide release of the movie, placing the film in many different theaters at once. They stole another lesson from the independent distributors by opening *Jaws* in the summer. *Jaws* went on to earn $129.5 million in the United States. This was a new record and was the first to break the $100 million barrier in rentals. The summer was not going to be left to the independents anymore. The two paths of mainstream and independent distribution were now merging.

Jaws marked the comeback of the major studios. The trend paid off even further when Twentieth Century Fox's *Star Wars* became a phenomenon in 1977. At this point, it would have been legitimate to suspect that this trend would last only a few years, just as previous cycles of runaway hits had run their course. Previous eras of big-budget movies led to a cycle that usually ran its course in half a dozen years succeeded by a cycle of relatively less expensive filmmaking. The trend launched by *Jaws* might have dissipated, if only because the audience was growing older and there was a noted falloff in movie attendance as people reached middle adulthood. There was some talk

10   that the flop of United Artists' *Heaven's Gate* in 1981 would end the cycle just as *Cleopatra* and *Dr. Dolittle* had ended previous cycles. It did not.

The New Hollywood way of marketing the film paid for itself, as first cable and then home video revenues started to contribute substantial revenues to cushion the added expense. The film itself became a more valuable commodity when the video rental market took off. The isolated successes of *Jaws* and *Star Wars* became the continuous blockbuster parade of the next decade. The string of big blockbusters became possible because the video markets restored some of the dependable audience revenues that the film industry lost after the late 1940s.

The American Film Industry and Video

These developments did not occur all at once. The great irony is that initially Hollywood was still sufficiently old and set in its ways not to recognize the potential salvation home video offered. Video sales and, in particular, video rental developed despite the neglect and hostility of the major studios. New Hollywood marketing and video revenues came together relatively slowly. Independents and newcomers led the way in developing and exploiting the rental market.[6] As the market expanded in the early 1980s, independent production increased, while the big studios hesitated and even cut back.

Why were major studios indifferent or hostile to videocassettes—when they turned out to be a gold mine? First, executive attitudes had to undergo a historical shift. In the beginning of the film industry, distributors determined that leverage and power never come from selling the film, always from leasing it. Leasing ensured that the film distributor knew and controlled every showing of a film. The prospect of millions of global customers owning the film was frightening. How many times would they see it over again? To how many of their friends would they show the tape? Would anyone still attend theatrical reissues, or watch the repeat TV broadcasts? Would the film still be valuable for television programmers? We will see that these questions generated heated debates at the highest levels within the Walt Disney Company. The film industry also expressed concerns about viewers rerecording cassettes. Universal and other studio executives worried that fewer viewers would watch their movies on TV because of home taping. However, these fears turned out to be economically meaningless, as the money from video vastly exceeded expectations. In addition, theatrical income and network TV sales continued on their own record paces, fueled (like the home video industry) by New Hollywood's increasingly blockbuster-oriented production strategy.

There were fears of piracy. In the early days, unauthorized video duplicates started to show up in many markets. The Motion Picture Association of America (MPAA) has spent a lot of time and money to stop video piracy and has been largely successful in the more important developed markets. Piracy has never been on a scale that threatened the emergence of home video as a mass medium in affluent countries.

As fears about home video abated, strategies to maximize returns in every film market emerged. These strategies depended on the big push into the home video, cable, broadcast, and foreign markets, which collectively were known as the ancillary movie markets. As ancillaries became more important, studios redoubled their promotion of the primary market—the theatrical release. This was counterintuitive since the theatrical box office was actually contributing a smaller percentage of the total earnings, but it was a successful strategy. The big theatrical release, with lots of TV advertising, proved to be an effective means of showcasing a film; subsequent publicity drove the successful film through the ancillaries. People would still remember the saturated TV blitz for a particular title when they browsed for films in the video store. Disney became expert at timing the release and withdrawal of videos from the market around past and future theatrical campaigns.

Toy and other product manufacturers contributed to the theatrical campaign in order to push their own merchandise associated with the films. These kinds of associations can be referred to as "branding"—using the elements of a film such as characters to sell toy figures or film music to sell compact discs. Tie-ins with fast food and other retailers became popular ways of maximizing returns from the heavy advertising for the movie. Tie-ins had existed since the silent era but became particularly important in the age of video, when the film itself could be sold as a videocassette, over the counter at local fast food stores.

Video sparked an effort to sell the same film content in various markets. It changed attitudes. Studios no longer wanted to share distribution tasks, as they had in the beginning of the video revolution. They were no longer afraid of selling films outright. The new revenue also emboldened them to trim their profit margins. They wanted to sell every element of their films directly either to the retailer or to the final user. They wanted to benefit from their internal

12   economies of scale, or, as it came to be known, "synergy." However, it took a
lot of corporate power to push a film in every market here and overseas, on
the big and small screens, as a theme park ride and as a music sound track.[7]

The independents' success built the video market. Now the explosive
growth of that market was paving the way for their ultimate doom. Video
wholesalers became a bottleneck. They felt their primary mission was to
stock current big hits, not to provide access to the widest range of choice.
They favored films that had received big theatrical releases. The huge conglomerates used the new video money to finance big releases. Therefore,
video rentals and sales served to facilitate the studio trend toward a few
big blockbusters. Despite their own occasional hits, the smaller distributors
could not keep up. They died off in the late 1980s and early 1990s as home
video stabilized. Vestron, Media Home Entertainment, Cannon, DeLaurentiis, Hemdale, and others went out of business. Orion, Goldwyn, Carolco, and
LIVE were crippled and either disappeared or were radically changed soon
afterward. Miramax, New Line, and other independents survived only by
seeking corporate mergers with major Hollywood studios. Artisan, the successor to LIVE, is the only independent (not yet affiliated with a major studio) to have had a big hit in the last half of the 1990s. There are now far fewer
independent distributors than there were before the video revolution.

It is small wonder that in the era of synergy and branding, there would
be a new wave of corporate takeovers. This wave began when Turner Broadcasting Systems acquired MGM (temporarily) and Rupert Murdoch's News
Corporation acquired Twentieth Century Fox (permanently) in 1985. It
started to crest dramatically in 1989–1991 with the Time–Warner, Sony–
Columbia, and Matsushita–MCA/Universal mergers and is still cresting in
today's headlines of the Viacom merger with CBS in 1999 and AOL's acquisition of Time Warner in 2000. These mergers are a response to the new multi-
market opportunities that were initiated by the video revolution. However,
the calculation in each takeover was somewhat different one from the other.
The most intriguing alliance in the age of video involved the purchase of Columbia Records in 1988 and Columbia Pictures in 1989 by the Japanese manufacturer Sony. These purchases were the direct result of Sony's bruising loss
of the VCR market to the rival hardware format VHS. Sony executives were
convinced by this experience that the future for their various hardware products could be better secured by controlling the content. The alliance of hard-

ware manufacturing and content distribution had not been seen in the movie industry since the days of Thomas Edison. The press expressed concern about the advantages of such an alliance. After all, what would Sony executives know about the vagaries of making movies? Despite these arguments, executives at Sony's competitor, Matsushita, decided to follow Sony's game plan by buying MCA/Universal in 1991.

The purchase of two major studios seemed to augur a major transition. As events transpired, however, the takeovers did little to change American filmmaking. Sony had little confidence in its own ability to participate in film industry decisions and spent excessively for the expertise of Hollywood insiders. Matsushita developed strained relations with the executives at MCA/ Universal and displayed a lack of commitment and vision about the purchase. Matsushita sold the film company to Seagram after four years, while Sony has stuck by its purchases. Although the effects of Sony's ownership have not been stellar for Columbia Pictures earnings, the entry of a manufacturer into the "content" businesses of music and film has been shrewd. Sony has not suffered a format war since its purchases. Industry-wide standards for both digital music and film are being set with Sony's full participation and cooperation. It is unlikely that we will see another rivalry such as VHS versus Betamax in the emerging consumer technologies. Sony's position in the music and film industries has undoubtedly given the company additional power in format negotiations.

A manufacturer's entry into the content-providing business is still rare. Far more typical was the union of content providers and distributors across several different media in order to pursue the multi-market opportunity. Here the exemplary studio is the Walt Disney Company, which was uniquely positioned to take advantage of video. After initial hesitation, the company decided to plunge ahead and rose to dominance. Disney was the one film studio that was not purchased. Instead, it purchased other companies, including Miramax (in 1993) and the network ABC (in 1996), in its rise to the top three of global media corporations.[8] Home video was not the sole cause of Disney's emergence. Walt Disney himself had already set the stage for success in his own lifetime by releasing and rereleasing his animated films for every new cohort of children. He had produced television shows and theme parks that recycled and cross-promoted the content of those films, and his vision bore full fruit when video and cable came into the market more than a decade af-

14   ter his death in 1966. Walt Disney could only have dreamed of the schedules of releasing, rereleasing, and cross-promotions across media that these technologies allowed.

The other big film studios joined or formed huge media corporations such as Time Warner, Viacom/CBS, and the News Corporation. Home video becomes part of the oft-told story of media and film industries concentration. If we focus on its effects within the film industry, we can clearly assess how the proliferation of media technology and concentration of media industries are linked. It is my argument that the film industry has learned how to retain a mass audience for a narrow range of products, with, not despite, new media technology. This argument has important implications for even newer technological developments. Home video confirms a point made by media theorist W. Russell Neuman. Technologies that can lead to new audience formations will not do so if institutional economics are strongly structured toward mass distribution and if audience habits are too ingrained.[9]

While video revenues contributed to media concentration, we should not assume that power flows have been one way. We have episodes of resistance to corporate power in this history. I have mentioned the triumph of Sony over the MCA/IBM Laservision alliance and RCA, and the transitory flowering of independent video distributors. In addition, there was the mushrooming of video rentals despite the efforts of the film studios to control and limit these operations. These were barriers and limits to corporate power. The audience had needs that no one could anticipate. Corporate practices had to harmonize with these unarticulated needs before success could be achieved. Although the result was enhanced corporate power, the narrative is one of surprises and improvisations. The media landscape today is largely a result of media corporations trying to be flexible enough to outflank the surprises of video technology. This is also how they hope to negotiate the coming digital age, with the lessons learned in video distribution. A study of how film distribution practices adjusted during the first decades of video will be suggestive of the challenges the audience may set in the digital future.

The Political Economy of Distribution

This is a history strongly informed by concepts developed in the study of the political economy of film. Political economic studies of communication are driven by concerns for cultural power. Who gets to produce? What? For whom? These questions go to the heart of the elusive relationship between film distribution and film production. That is because these questions are answered on a regular basis by distributors. They are the ones who ultimately secure the funding for production and determine which types of films to make.

Studio heads may spend a good part of their day meeting with stars and directors and the agents who represent these glamorous, creative people. They say yes, they say no, and the results are hashed over in the magazines, newspapers, and TV talk shows. Nonetheless, these meetings are far less important than their meetings with the marketing executives. It is those meetings that form the framework for why studios decide to make movies, which movies, and how many.

Political economists have described the power of distributors by making the distinction between allocative and operational control. Filmmakers formulate the story, develop the look and feel of a film, cast the stars and supporting players. These are operational decisions made on a day-to-day basis. The activities of distributors are mundane by comparison to the filmmakers' creative efforts. The distributor has to decide how many prints to make, what deals to cut with movie theater owners, whether to price the videocassette at a high price for rental or a low price for sell-through, how to package a bunch of films together for a sale to cable. The sum of these decisions determines whether the studio will make $100 million fantasy epics or $2 million slashers (that may not even be released in the U.S.). These are allocative decisions. This is because the earnings that the distributor can put together determine the overall allocation of production resources. It is only as secondary players that the writers, directors, set designers, et al., can make their operational decisions in terms of actual filmmaking.

The allocative power of distribution companies is primary and therefore sets the limits to the operational power of the producing team. It is also of fundamental interest to the social theorist because allocative power derives directly from the audience. I am not arguing that distributors have any great personal insight into the audience. After all their relationship with the audience is strictly limited to dollars and cents. The meaning and intelligibility of any particular revenue stream is severely limited. The distributors themselves can be rather inarticulate about the audience's use of their product. Nonetheless, over a period the structure of distribution will accommodate the lifestyle of its audience. Otherwise, the structure collapses.

16   The relationship of distribution to cultural production leads to another political economic concern—the health of independent distribution and its importance to cultural diversity. Independent filmmaking is important to cultural diversity. Independence, though, is often in the eye of the beholder. People refer to the political independence of the message of a film. They also talk of an independent film style that avoids the various conventions of realism. Independence has also been defined in terms of financing or originating the film outside the studio system. Non-studio financing may be very difficult, but it occurs frequently. Often mainstream studios encourage it as a way of lessening their own risk. If the studio likes the finished product, it will contract to distribute the film ("negative pickup"). Therefore, independence in this arrangement becomes a rather technical term. The various filmmakers (Soderbergh, Smith, et al.) who have emerged at the Sundance Institute or at the Park City film festival (a premier showcase for independently financed films) fit this definition of independence. The independently financed films are often made as apprenticeship pieces, intended to catapult the director and other contributors into the "big leagues," to enable these participants to go on to make large-budget mainstream movies.[10]

In this study, "independence" is defined in terms of distribution, rather than content or financing. There are good cultural reasons for studying the relative levels of independent distribution in order to evaluate the social impact of video. The rise and fall of independent distribution is a proper measure of independence and diversity within the film industry. It is the independent distributor who, in the constant search for a market, explores unknown genres and new ways of putting together a profitable audience. Today we have very few independent distributors. Along with Artisan (the sole surviving veteran of the once-new video companies) we have Roger Corman, who operates at a lower profile than in his earlier periods, as well as Trimark and Troma. Practically all other boutique operations we think of as independent, such as Miramax or October, are parts of larger studios. They may be operationally independent, but ultimately allocative resources reside in the larger studio. Their autonomy in operational matters is tentative. At any moment, those who control the company may reallocate their resources to mainstream films and cut off their funding of quirky little projects. Independent distribution is a shadow of its former self. In comparison to the handful of such survivors, there are many independent film producers and directors, who struggle from project to project.

Video and the Audience

Another theme of this book is to use home video to look at the evolving sociology of the audience. My arguments build upon the book-length field research conducted by Ann Gray[11] and the various ethnographic articles collected in Mark Levy's and Julie Dobrow's anthologies,[12] and in various journals. These publications report direct research into various viewers' behavior. They describe how sample groups actually use the VCR. In my political economic study, the method is to see how media institutions anticipated and determined the way viewers use their products. It is not a direct look at people using the VCR. Nonetheless, my study has to consider how audience behavior was changing in order to explain the new opportunities and limits for film distributors.

The VCR is merely the latest phase in a continual struggle of film distributors to accommodate its audience. We can look throughout film history and realize that the audience, particularly in the U.S., has oscillated between two modes: "staying in" and "going out." "Staying in" should be interpreted loosely to mean not just literally staying home to watch movies, but also watching movies in convenient neighborhood locations with little or no preparation, casually, without much regard to the specific movie playing, at any time of the day, on any day of the week. "Going out" refers to more of a theatrical experience of going to watch the movie in a central public space, such as a downtown movie palace. In general, it means sacrificing convenience for the sake of a heightened experience, such as going to a movie theater far from the neighborhood, in order to see a relatively limited release movie or a theater that features better sound and/or a wider screen, and so on. It can also mean that audience members will strive to see a widely publicized movie as soon as possible in order to participate in the current conversations about that movie.

The age of video seems to represent a severe swing of the pendulum, one where staying in approached a collective autism. Listen to this rather sour assessment of early VCR users, offered to us by an anonymous electronics sales clerk:

They don't want any network or even a station to tell them when they may watch or any radio station to tell them when to listen. They don't trust anything that they can't control, and they feel that they have no

18   control of government, the press, and organized religion. The kind of
people who make the big buys here are two $30,000-a-year computer
programmers either married or living together and not planning to
have children. You start talking to them about city schools, budget, supply side and defense and they turn up their Walkaman [*sic*] to drown
out the noise.[13]

This colorful caricature of home video users has a glimmer of truth. Such
shut-ins are a new audience, perhaps massive in numbers but resenting collective actions. Home video is the story of movie industry triumph despite
rampant agoraphobia.

Although these two modes are always present in every period, the balance
between them shifts historically. The successful film distributor will try to fit
the balance most appropriate to the times. The distributor has such an opportunity because film is such a plastic form. It has a great capacity to be all
things to all people, perhaps even more so than other cultural products. This
is why it is so interesting to do an integrated study of the movie industry, using both economic and cultural analysis. Movies are both pastimes and highly
expressive works of art. They can be simultaneously the products of a single
vision and a collective collaboration. Their presentation is well suited to both
staying in and going out. The history of movie distribution is the story of the
constant negotiation between the two.

Structure of the Study

Therefore the story of home video has a "prehistory" that dates back to the
first industrialization of film distribution and the earliest negotiations between staying in and going out. The first chapter briefly reviews this prehistory. It summarizes misguided attempts to screen films in the home just the
way record players had become home entertainment at the turn of the century. The more enduring organization was the tiered release system, which
did strike a practical balance between those who wanted to go out to the
movies and those who just wanted to sit in the local theater and watch whatever. Television finally did place movies in people's living room and set the
groundwork for the acceptance of home video.

Chapter 2 turns to the technological history. Because of the economics of
broadcast networks, the radio industry was slow to adopt improved recording

techniques. Magnetic recording, for either audio or video, was not available until after the adoption of television. After video recording was finally invented in 1956, manufacturers started to explore mass market uses for it. Over the next two decades various formats and systems were developed. The American companies miscalculated and decided to follow the model of the record player. They built and marketed machines only capable of playing back prerecorded material. Consumer interest was lackluster. Sony not only had a better idea, they stuck with it until it succeeded. They advertised that their video recorder should be used to rearrange television programs to fit the consumer's schedule, and the global market responded.

How and why did the consumers respond to the VCR? Chapter 3 begins with changes in the way the audience members worked and lived that might help explain their need to shift programming. However, film companies were not yet recognizing the value of video in reaching an increasingly mobile population. Universal and Disney sued Sony, and the case went all the way to the Supreme Court. The American film companies lost the case. The VCR formed a symbiotic relationship with pornography. The "adult" market built up the necessary infrastructure for the sale and exchange of prerecorded tapes. Later, Twentieth Century Fox became the first major studio to take a hesitant dip. It allowed a small Michigan company to manufacture videocassettes of its older movies. Soon, rental stores appeared all over the country like so many nickelodeons. The next chapter of video as a mass medium had arrived.

Now, the Hollywood studios wanted to resist the rental stores. They tried to impose leasing plans. They went to the U.S. Congress to seek exemption from the "first sale" doctrine, which effectively allowed renting. Their strategies did not succeed, except in creating a void for new distributors to enter the field of video distribution. The bulk of Chapter 4 is concerned with these struggles and, in particular, with the rise of independent distribution in video in the period through 1986.

Chapters 5 and 6 are paired sides of a single argument. Chapter 5 is about business practices emerging during the maturity of the video market. The more important ones are two-tiered pricing, "breadth versus depth" inventory strategies, wholesaling and retailing consolidation, and the refurbishing of movie theaters. Some of these business practices worked against independent distribution, and their struggles after 1986 form the narrative of the next chapter. Chapter 5 covers the rise of Blockbuster Video while Chapter 6 covers the demise of the independents and the resurrection of Disney. The

20 majors were not expanding production. They were using their new ancillary revenues to increase their advertising budgets. Video retailers and wholesalers were demanding that cassettes have heavy theatrical exposure. The independents could neither keep up with the expense of a theatrical release nor avoid it. Vestron, Carolco, et al., faltered and disappeared. In fact, costs became so high that even the majors started to worry about their own declining profit margins.

The concluding chapter reviews the changed media environment and the purchases of the major film studios by highly capitalized, transnational media empires. It is at this point that we can finally assess the importance of video in creating the new film industry. Particularly since in absolute terms, Hollywood films are making more money than ever, all over the world. Video accounts for much of the increased global revenues. In the response of the film industry to video there have been changes in the ways it treats the audiences and in the way it makes movies. Elements of film style have changed to compensate for the loss of medium specificity, in other words, to enhance the movie experience, be it on the big, small, or computer screen. Any video study also has to tackle the question of the audience and why they choose to use the VCR the way they do. It seems that the answer here is that the audience is experiencing stressed leisure and that Hollywood used video to learn how to market its products in this time of less free time.

The lasting hallmark of the video age is the total integration of film studios within the larger mass media industries. These media conglomerates have special needs for the maximum sale of their product. Every film is under pressure to be an instantly sellable commodity. Opening weekend grosses have become very important since they determine how much more effort the distributor will make in pushing the film to other markets. One film critic, Timothy Corrigan, has noted that in response to this pressure the movie is now "an advertisement of promises it usually cannot possibly keep."[14] The 1990s saw one film after another break budget barriers, in an effort to become an opening weekend event. This reached a high watermark with the 1997 release of *Titanic*, which was so huge that Twentieth Century Fox and Columbia Pictures shared the expense in a coproduction deal. Soon after, the renewed popularity of low-budget films encouraged some movement back toward smaller films. Nonetheless these are relative terms; small films are big by yesterday's standards and most films are still expected to be instantly popular. This is the lasting effect of the ancillary markets. International films continue to be a very hard sell in the United States, the largest film market. Theater time is just too valuable to give over to the limited appeal of a typical foreign film. In both the United States and overseas, theaters respond to the power of the big distributors, whose power derives from handling films that earn large ancillary revenues. For the foreseeable future, there will not be much room for independent distribution.

The future fate of analog magnetic tape, the underlying technology of the VCR, is less clear. Digital video, probably in the DVD format, may well supplant the videocassette. There is continuing speculation that downloading films from central computers through a fiber-optic line to the home will create a major market. This time the major media corporations will not just stand by and watch these markets develop. The need for time flexibility has become a defining feature of present-day life. The VCR was one of the first technologies to reveal the strength of this need, particularly among the international affluent classes, who use the computer and the internet in pursuit of efficiencies in work, shopping, and leisure. Media corporations now understand this desire. They are already taking steps to ensure that they are fully involved and that the lessons they learned from home video will be applied. They now know that only institutions that can bear the cost of marketing across several time-flexible media have a chance of thriving. They seek alliances in order to outflank and be ready for new technologies of distribution.

It is hard to overemphasize the importance of home video as the opening of a new chapter in the media industries. Gerald Levin, the cerebral chair and CEO of Time Warner, confirmed it on *The Newshour with Jim Lehrer* broadcast when he discussed the announced purchase of Time Warner by America Online (AOL).[15] He asserted that the media industries needed to formulate strategies right now to deliver their products to an increasingly active audience. He was able to pinpoint his view of audience power by referring explicitly to the VCR. The audience wants to ingest media on its own schedule, and people want to stop and start their viewing at their own pace. He promised that those future delivery systems that AOL and Time Warner develop will preserve the flexibility and audience conveniences of the video rental store. When the VCR is used to justify the motivation of the largest media acquisition to date, we know its legacy will endure beyond its actual technology. It is the time to examine in detail video's history and its impact on the film industry.

22   However, it is important to choose a point in this history that serves as a stop point, when the legacy was clearly established. Since the stem of my arguments centers on film distribution, I have used 1993 as a cutoff point. This is not just because of the events described at the beginning of this introduction. It is also because the fate of independent distribution was fully understood at that point. The purchase of Miramax and New Line in that year are the coda to the era. In that year, the New Hollywood revolution had been going for a generation. The next generation was being recruited on an incremental basis. A hundred years of cinema had come to terms with twenty years of video.

CHAPTER ONE

Film Distribution and Home Viewing before the VCR

When the audience adopted the VCR, they had already experienced several historical evolutions in film showings. The VCR was not sui generis. It was another evolution, triggered perhaps by a technological breakthrough, but definitely flowing out of extant relationships. The examination in this chapter of the prior histories of film and broadcasting is necessary in order to understand these relationships. We will see that the VCR was only the latest manifestation of home viewing of movies. There were premature attempts to rent movies to individual households in the second decade of this century. There was the earlier convergence of movies with broadcasting, as far back as the early days of radio. There were also the protracted negotiations that led to movies playing on prime time network television. In neither case was the convergence straightforward or entirely satisfactory to the film industry interests.

I follow the political economy model by analyzing these relationships from the industrial side. The question here is not so much why the public wanted to see a new movie every week or even every day, but how an industry organized itself to give them a new movie every week. I do not ask whether people wanted to see movies in their neighborhood or in downtown palaces. I do describe how exhibition circuits were set up to provide both options. The American film industry strategies were highly successful, so we can make the sociological assumption that these strategies reflected the predilections of the mass audience.

The industry took two decades before it coalesced around the production of relatively expensive feature-length films (over an hour in length, typically one and a half hours long). The expense of these films necessitated an efficient nationwide distribution system. Efficiency was achieved by the control

24 distributors had over both the production and exhibition schedules. This control was successfully exercised within vertically integrated movie studios. Indeed the film industry was so successful that the studios that emerged seventy to eighty years ago are still the powerhouse studios of today. However, this chapter also describes the serious challenges the film industry strategies faced in the postwar era.

Lifestyles changed first in the United States and then in other industrialized countries after the Second World War. In the U.S. these lifestyle changes coincided with and facilitated the widespread adoption of television. The audience lost the habit of going to the movies. The economic stability of movie exhibition eroded. Yet, the popularity of feature films remained high as evidenced by the high ratings films attracted when they were shown on television. Meanwhile new, independent distributors sought opportunities in this era. They introduced new promotional schemes and new themes to attract the audiences to the movie theaters. The chapter concludes in the mid-1970s with the marriage between home viewing (i.e., television) and film only half consummated and with an increasing synthesis between independent practices and major studio financial power. This heady brew becomes a new Hollywood and inaugurates the new era of blockbuster moviemaking.

A Brief Review of the Early Days of the Movie Industry

The cinema was introduced to the public in 1894–1895. The film manufacturers had great hopes for the new medium but little certainty on how to realize its potential as a mass medium. A decade of starts and stops ensued after the introduction, with movies popping up at amusement parks, the various World's Fairs, downtown arcades, as part of live vaudeville acts and in traveling lecture shows. It was not until the Spanish-American War of 1898 that movies even got beyond the novelty stage (where audience interest goes beyond the demonstration of the moving image) in the United States. The war enthusiasm sparked Americans' interest in any film depicting the war. Filmmakers were learning to lure viewers with attractive content.

A critical mass started to build. By 1903, there were storefronts devoted exclusively to showing movies. These theaters (often referred to as "nickelodeons") soon mushroomed. They were omnipresent—in centralized downtown locations, in small farming towns, in residential neighborhoods, in shopping districts. It is estimated that by 1908 there were 6,000 movie theaters.

The number more than doubled in the next five years.[1] Russell Merritt estimates that approximately 28 percent of the total U.S. population attended the movies every week in 1910.[2] The American audience was, from the start, the largest in the world, although the Western European film industry was also developing and sometimes surpassing American rivals.[3] The largest film producer and distributor at this time was the French Pathé Frères. In 1907, Pathé decided to stop selling film prints, which had been the normal way for producers to make money from their films. Instead of selling, Pathé would only rent prints for limited periods in order to gain power over exhibitors by controlling the circulation of its films. Many vendors were astonished and called this new practice a coup d'état.[4]

The theater boom had made the movies a big business. It was too big to waste energy on squabbling over key patents. In September 1908, Thomas Edison and other patent holders rationalized the movie industry by organizing the Motion Picture Patent Company (MPPC). They organized a closed system of production and exhibition. Member theaters were not allowed to buy films from non-members of the MPPC. One MPPC member was the American subsidiary of Pathé. The MPPC members were undoubtedly impressed by Pathé's leasing program because they soon introduced the practice into their own rules. They agreed that no film print was to be sold, but only to be leased at a fixed rate per foot of the film's length. Leasing thus became the sole basis of film exchange for seventy years, until the arrival of the videocassette.

The leasing provision was one of the defining moments of the formation of the film industry. The lessor, otherwise known as the distributor, became the primary broker between the audience and the filmmaker. The distributor now exercised leverage over the theater owner by setting conditions of guaranteed minimal payments and often arranging to split the box office take. The theater owner had little to say about the scheduling and circulation of prints. The distributor became the only one who could coordinate the advertising and promote the film for its entire run. The film producer stepped back from such activities. It was the distributor who collected and redistributed the film profits from the film to the producer, after deducting distribution expenses.

Leasing was one enduring legacy of the MPPC. Another legacy was a fully rationalized national distribution system. A loose system of local exchanges had emerged spontaneously during the boom. Film exchanges had operated

26 just as their name suggested; to circulate and exchange film prints in order to feed the local theaters' perpetual hunger for new shows. In 1910, all of the MPPC members joined to form the General Film Company. General Film quickly became a central nationwide distributor for the MPPC producers and theater owners, by buying up the various local film exchanges. The company set up forty-two outlets throughout the country to facilitate the rapid circulation of prints.

Many vibrant film companies were frozen out of the patent pool. Carl Laemmle, a prominent Chicago film exhibitor, and others who found themselves on the outside, soon formed their own independent centralized exchanges. The MPPC and General Film started to lose power due to rivals such as Laemmle (who went on to create Universal Pictures) and to a court suit filed and successfully litigated by William Fox (another legendary founder of a movie studio which still bears his name). However, even though the MPPC and General Film faded away after 1915, the leasing and national distribution systems remained intact.[5] The only difference was that new alternative independent companies were distributing.[6]

From Universal Audiences to Feature-Length Films

Movies with story lines proliferated and the audience soon started to patronize storefronts and theaters that did nothing else but show movies. Although audiences were seeking out story lines and other special content, they were not going to great lengths to do so. The theater owners took maximum advantage of the low cost of reproduction and transport of film prints to make it as easy as possible to see a movie. Unlike the live theaters, the movie theaters were not confined to downtown but sprang up in various locations. The movies went further than even vaudeville in charging the customer less and thereby appealing to all classes, to a mixed audience of men and women, and to adults and children. Movie houses tried to play seven days a week, often lobbying against local Sunday restrictions. If circumstances permitted, they showed films at all hours of the day and evening. These theater owners wanted everyone to attend, from shoppers to workers on their lunch break, to kids, to those out on the town for the evening.

The technology lent itself to this universal appeal because it was relatively easy to put together shows with films on every subject. A reel of film could only hold slightly more than fifteen minutes of images. Most films were even shorter. Therefore shows of a half-hour or longer consisted of several different films with several different subject matters. This type of viewing tried to offer something for everybody.

There was one other requirement for film shows in addition to universal appeal. The audience instantly learned to avoid seeing the same thing twice. Therefore, shows had to be changed at least once a week or even more often. The exhibitors did this even if the new films were hackneyed or formulaic. Many theaters reported that even their most dedicated regulars disappeared when they repeated reels or could not get a new program in. Theaters had to exchange their prints in order to change their shows. Elaborate distribution was necessary because it was so easy to use up the inventory of films lying around. Rapid circulation of prints became easier with the practice of leasing and the rationalization of national distribution systems.

The MPPC members favored shorts mounted on one reel, which lasted no longer than fifteen minutes, because production costs were easy to control. Italian and French filmmakers were already making multi-reeled historical films. These films lasted from one to two hours. An American, Adolph Zukor, was convinced that expensive multi-reelers were the future and that distribution systems were capable of handling longer shows. He raised his own money to get the American distribution rights to the French film *Queen Elizabeth* in 1912 and earned great enough profits to form his own production company. Ambitious filmmakers such as D. W. Griffith also longed to make such "feature" films. In 1915, Griffith released his own epic-length *Birth of a Nation*, destined to become the most famous if not the most profitable feature film of the silent era. Now, more and more film producers turned to multiple reelers, contributing to the obsolescence of General Film single-reel distribution.

Zukor and Griffith can be credited with the first American "event" movies. An event movie creates its own momentum through word of mouth. So many people are interested in the movie because so many others are talking about it. *Birth of a Nation* drew tremendous attention, inspiring comment from President Woodrow Wilson and protests from the NAACP since the film praised white supremacy. Nevertheless, the "event" nature of the film was not just due to its racist message. It also derived from Griffith's mastery in conveying meaning through the cinematic means of editing, composition, and pacing. Zukor was also creating events, such as paying Mary Pickford the highest salary in the country so that she would star in his high-priced movies.

28 When the American public showed a willingness to pay higher prices to see the films of Griffith and Zukor, they demonstrated a new appreciation of film as something special, not just a pastime but a mythic art form. Audience members were quite willing to "go out" to see this new art.

Movies at Home

Thomas Edison was one of the first inventors of cinema, introducing it in 1894. His first claim to national fame (he was soon to be dubbed "the wizard of Menlo Park") came after he invented the phonograph in 1877. It had taken two decades before the phonograph found a consumer use as the playback device for prerecorded music. Although he had not anticipated this use, Edison became fascinated with the prerecorded music and eagerly took a hand in selecting the music. The inventor's interest was remarkable since his hearing was poor. On the other hand, film content did not seem to engage his interest much. His actions and comments treated film as secondary to recorded sound, particularly his attempts to market film as if it was a phonograph. Even after the development of feature films, Edison continued to treat film as a pleasant pastime for a "stay-in" audience.

The primary markets for phonographs were the arcade and the home. Edison explored both venues for filmed entertainment. He made small viewing machines suitable for arcades and did not build theatrical projectors until others demonstrated their popularity. Even after the triumph of theatrical films, the Edison Company did not encourage feature-length filmmaking. Edison's people just were not tuned in to larger-than-life showmanship or to film as a theatrical epic. The Edison Company's corporate culture was such that they rarely held on to producers or directors interested in higher ambitions of creative expression.[7]

In 1912, the same year Zukor started importing big expensive films, the Edison Company developed and introduced the Home Projecting Kinetoscope for domestic and other noncommercial spaces. Edison was interested in selling portable projectors that teachers and traveling salesmen could use in their demonstrations. The business model tried to follow the phonograph. The home projector was priced only somewhat higher than the phonographs. However, the cost of the hardware was not as much of a problem as the cost of content. Even short films were expensive to print and sales cost far exceeded the cost of selling prerecorded music. Therefore, the home projecting system offered home viewers the option to rent short films. Rental films would be shipped and returned through the post office.

The home projector failed. Only 500 machines were sold. Rentals of films added considerably to the already high cost of the projector. Cost alone seems sufficient to explain the disappointing lack of customer interest. There were the additional factors of the skill and energy needed to set up a screen and operate a projector and the lack of films available on the narrow gauge that the projector used.[8] Edison abandoned the home projector in 1914.[9]

Edison was not the only one interested in home viewing. There are testimonials from successful film entrepreneurs as early as 1906 about the potential of home viewing of films, for entertainment and the dissemination of news and political discussion.[10] Pathé Frères had some success with a home projector that it introduced in the same year as Edison's. Pathé had the advantage of offering its home viewing customers its own larger library of films. It also moved more adroitly than the Edison Company into the school and church film markets.[11] However, the parent company's position eroded dramatically in the next few years, due both to the world war and to a corporate fight with Eastman Kodak. The Pathèscope slipped from view during WWI. Kodak developed the 16mm film gauge in 1924 and that system achieved relative market success (in industrial, educational, and some home usage), but still as a tiny fraction of the film market.

Home viewing as a mass medium stalled until the development of broadcast television and home video. This was not just due to technological obstacles. People were simply more interested in going out to the movies than in staying in, during this phase of mass entertainment's history. We can speculate that although people were use to staying at home to make music and therefore to listen to prerecorded music, they were still in the habit of going out for their theatrical entertainment. Edison had made a false analogy between home viewing and home listening. He would not be the only one.

Tiered Releasing

By 1915, the U.S. film industry was prospering with the elimination of foreign competition because of the First World War, the elimination of the rigid monopoly of the MPPC, and the triumph of *Birth of a Nation*. Zukor, in particular, had found a profitable niche. He was now producing his own films and rolled over his rivals by outspending them. However, he did not feel safe.

30   With high overheads, he needed guaranteed support from a powerful distributor. He felt that he could not rely on the business arrangements he already had. He had to take over a big distribution company. When he acquired such a company, he renamed it Paramount, a simple statement of his
imperial wish fulfillment. He was now at the top of the film industry.

The other producers imitated his actions in an effort to keep up. William
Fox, Carl Laemmle, Marcus Loew, the Warner brothers, and others were expanding by building their own vertically integrated movie companies. In
other words, what the MPPC tried to do for the entire industry, they did for
themselves. They tied together production, distribution, and exhibition divisions together into one studio. This way they were not beholden to any other
company for product, theatrical outlets, or distribution. Loew's MGM, National Theaters and Warner Brothers, Twentieth Century and Fox, RKO and
Laemmle's Universal emerged in the 1920s as fully integrated as Zukor's Paramount. Each had national distribution, centralized production studios in
Southern California, and ownership of key theaters in various big cities. Columbia and United Artists were two of the few significant film companies that
did not own movie theaters. However, they both had formidable distribution
arms. From this point, some seventy years later, it is truly remarkable how
many of these companies are still the most powerful film studios in the world.
These constituted the American film oligopoly that would respond to the
home video.

A rising middle class had disposable income to treat itself to the occasional
evening at the most expensive movie theaters for a special film. On other occasions, these same audience members would just want to pop into the local
theater for a more modest fee to watch whatever was showing. The film industry used the flexibility of film to try to accommodate every one of those
motivations. The studios produced films for all audiences and relied on a mix
of the occasional big-budget spectacular, general interest films, drama and
genre films, and "cheapies" and short films to keep the theaters filled all year
round. The potpourri offered something for everyone—those who wanted
something special, those who wanted the safe and routine plot, and those who
wanted something in between.

"Tiered" releasing was another effective way of enticing the various
moviegoers on a range from the "big spenders" down to children with a few
spare dimes in their pockets. This system was based on the classification of
the theater and time "windows." If the theater was in the first-run circuit, it

would receive the film as soon as the film was released. The distributor would guarantee that the theater had the film on an exclusive basis in its locale during the first run. No other theater could run the film at that time. In turn, the theater would guarantee the distributor that its ticket prices would be set at a high rate and the two parties would negotiate their split of the box office. The publicity effort was timed for the first-run release and the momentum from that release would hopefully drive the film through for its subsequent runs. Many first-run theaters were directly owned by the studios. Many were also highly ornate "movie palaces" so luxurious in décor and appointments that the box office rarely covered the overhead. These first-run theaters served as lost leaders.

After a few weeks or months the film would be released to second-run theaters. These second-run venues would charge correspondingly less per ticket than the first run. After a set period, the film would be leased to third run and subsequently to any theater willing to lease the film. Those viewers who were patient or indifferent enough to wait for a third-run showing paid very little to see the movie.

The tiered release system got America hooked on going to the movies regularly. In 1922, an average American went to the movies three times every eight weeks. Attendance leaped forward after the introduction of sound films in 1927, and fell back during the depression. The historic high point of this system was from 1946 to 1948, when it was estimated that the average attendance was five times every eight weeks. The system maximized revenues in the domestic market so that most movies earned profits even before they were exported to other countries. For this reason, Hollywood's priority was to capture the American audience. Distribution executives viewed the rest of the world as found money, although they did quite well with the global audience.

Broadcasting: The Other Entertainment Medium

The 1920s was a time of growth for other forms of commercial entertainment. Radio networks were emerging and transforming radio into a mass medium of entertainment. Radio's popularity did not harm moviegoing. Nonetheless, the introduction of a new mass medium will always change the strategies and logic of other mass media. Film executives started thinking about broadcasting. What was it revealing about the mass audience? Was it logical for film companies to get into the radio game? Were film stories appropriate for an aural medium? Was the audience for radio different from the movie audience? If the two audiences overlapped, how should film companies utilize the radio?

The film companies tried to buy into radio to create the first media conglomerates. Zukor knew from his own experience that the most powerful position in mass culture was that of the distributor. The most powerful distributors in radio were the national networks such as NBC and CBS. Zukor arranged for Paramount to extend credit to CBS in exchange for a future merger of Paramount and CBS stock. The intervening depression drove Paramount stock down while CBS stock rose. The head of CBS, William Paley, was able to buy out of the agreement. The film industry had been effectively frozen out of the radio distribution business.

The studios, nonetheless, used radio to promote their films in a way that was a true first step toward home viewing. They were early pioneers in the use of radio as an advertising medium in 1922.[12] A decade later, various radio shows started presenting audio enactments of Hollywood movies. These shows included "Screen Guild Theater," "Warner Brothers' Academy Theater," "Academy Award Theater," and the very successful "Lux Radio Theater." A further integration occurred as radio stars started their own movie acting careers (Will Rogers, Eddie Cantor, Bob Hope, Bing Crosby, Abbott and Costello, et al.).

The American audience appreciated the media crossover from radio to film and back again, and yet the film studios could only benefit from radio in a peripheral manner. They could hire radio stars to appear in the movies. Their music publishing divisions increased sales due to radio and movie exposure of their copyrighted music. They could give the home audience a taste of the upcoming movies through the film on radio shows. Nonetheless, they were frustrated in their attempt to earn directly even a part of the millions of advertising revenues passing into network coffers. The Hollywood studios became even more frustrated when the networks switched their resources to television programming and distribution in the period 1948–1953.

The frustration was twofold. The development of television as an extension of radio ensured that the film studios would be in a subordinate position despite the close fit between film and television. The networks seamlessly transformed their distribution operations from the aural to visual medium without competition. At the same time, the U.S. government forced the Hollywood studios to change their way of doing business. The Department of Justice had received numerous complaints, over the decades, about the collusive behavior of the major movie studios in the field of exhibition. They investigated how "tiered" releasing, with its promises of exclusivity and its pressure on independent theaters to accept disadvantageous contracts, had amounted to a conspiracy to behave as a trust. The specific onerous practices were block booking (forcing an exhibitor to take an entire slate of films, not just the popular ones) and blind selling (forcing exhibitors to bid on films that they had not had the opportunity to view). The crisis of the depression and WWII had forestalled drastic action. After the war, the department decided that the proper cure was to force film studios out of the theater business altogether. In 1948, the Paramount et al. consent decree stipulated that the five majors had to sell their theaters. It was anticipated that this would force them to deal with independent theater owners on a more equitable basis.

In this atmosphere, the film studios' pursuit of power in the nascent television industry seemed predatory. The Federal Communications Commission (FCC) took the view that such pursuits would only renew Hollywood's conspiratorial practices. Wayne Coy, the chairman of the FCC in 1948, told motion picture company representatives that he opposed motion picture–television ownership tie-ups.[13] The Justice Department obstructed the Paramount/DuMont partnership from forming a profitable fourth TV network, and discouraged other studios from purchasing stations.[14]

In hindsight, it seems that the government was unfairly coddling the networks, helping them avoid sharing power with the movie studios. American broadcasting was an advertising medium. In order to attract an audience to the advertising, broadcasters used the popular entertainment values established by Hollywood films. American filmmakers realized that their films had paved the way and they wanted to share in television's riches. Christopher Anderson has shown that even David Selznick, the producer of the biggest Hollywood movies, was eager to reach the audience in their living rooms. He went on to produce one of the early big television shows, *Light's Diamond Jubilee*, in 1954.[15] The fact that even the maker of *Gone With the Wind* wanted to produce for the stay-at-home viewer suggests that mainstream film producers did not disdain the small screen, as some film historians have argued. Current film histories have thoroughly debunked previous explanations that film executives purposely ignored or were instinctively hostile toward this home medium. If they were hostile, it was because they had been kept out of

34   the TV market by the combined strength of RCA and CBS and by overt government action.

In this situation, the major studios could only act as program suppliers to television (not as distributors or exhibitors). By the mid-1950s, major and independent studios were shooting TV shows on their lots. One film studio, Disney, was able to take full advantage of its role as a program supplier. Walt Disney had decided to seek an investor in the theme park that he was building called Disneyland. This was his condition for setting up a television show. ABC decided to accept it since they were the weakest of the three networks. Disney was able to use the show to promote his films and his theme park. His vision was to sell many different products to his core market—parents—in an atmosphere he called "total merchandising." [16] His business plan enhanced the company's power to the point where its products became a central stem of American popular culture. As we shall see, Disney's idea was far reaching enough to bear even fuller fruit with the advent of the VCR, almost two decades after his death. However, the Disney TV show did not show films in their entirety. Major theatrical films did not appear on regular network programming until 1961.

In the first decade of TV, CBS and NBC had their own reasons not to lease films from Hollywood. There were also symmetrical reasons for the studios to resist broadcasting their recent films. The primary reason for such hesitancy was that the networks simply did not wish to spend the amount of money it would cost to lease recent feature films. There were also a few strategic motivations to keep Hollywood movies off the air. In the early years, the networks were anxious to establish that television offered something different from the movies. This would build prestige for the new medium and an added purpose for the networks, since they would be the only experts in TV's unique power. Television promoters subscribed to a rhetoric of "live"ness as the best feature of television. [17] ABC was more willing to get away from live shows; its weakness relative to the other networks led it to explore all possibilities. Even NBC's and CBS's rhetoric on this matter faded as networks built up an inventory of programs and developed economic interests in recording and repeating broadcasts.

Network executives had other considerations for not wanting the audience to view television as a primary medium for movies. One reason was that movies could be leased by stations directly from the film studios or their sub-distributors. Therefore, a station could use a film as an inexpensive substitute and turn down network offerings, or use the movie as a counterprogram against network shows. Executives wanted to discourage station owners from thinking that film programming would attract as many advertising dollars as network offerings.

Advertisers were also hesitant about movies on TV. A movie is a single program appealing to a singular audience. Some movies draw a large audience only once. Others take a long time to build an audience. Television thrives on repeat audiences week after week. Advertisers want predictable, regular ratings. One director of programming stated that films are a "stopgap, . . . They don't represent a direction that is fruitful for us, and they don't give us consistent ratings either." [18] TV programmers may have some ability to predict a film's appeal, but the room for error is far greater than that for episodic television. The length of feature films also ran counter to programming philosophy. In 1946, an unnamed communications attorney warned that the hour-and-a-half-long feature film will not hold the attention of the television audience. [19] Although subsequent practice proved the attorney wrong, the two-hour slot for a feature film in prime time unbalanced the hours of evening programming.

Despite these institutional hesitancies, films were broadcast from the beginning of television. The first instance was in 1933, when W6XAO (the future KTSL of Los Angeles) experimentally broadcast a World Wide production of *The Crooked Circle* (1932). [20] As TV matured, individual stations sought more movies, but film distributors were reluctant. For one thing, they did not want to anger their principal clients, the movie theater owners, by selling films to television. They also were uncertain about the claims of composers, actors, and writers to additional payments if movies were shown in a new medium. The old contracts rarely broached the subject of exploitation in a new (ancillary) medium. The fiery Petrilli, leader of the American Federation of Musicians, and other labor leaders were demanding a share of any television sales of movies.

If the studios were to face such exhibition and union headaches, they wanted adequate compensation from their television sales. Such compensation was not forthcoming. As late as 1952, Paramount reported that a national broadcast of a first-quality film would bring in, at most, $55,000. This was a pittance compared to the $1.4 million that the average film cost to produce, or even to the $125,000 to $750,000 a film often earned in a rerelease. [21]

Foreigner distributors and bankrupt studios without much concern for fu-

36   ture relations with exhibitors and unions were the first to lease their libraries. The first major film sale was in 1948 when the unaffiliated WPIX of New York acquired twenty-four films from Alexander Korda, the British producer. RKO was in trouble and was sold to General Teleradio in 1955. This company owned the WOR station in New York and used the RKO library (740 features and 1,100 shorts) for its *Million Dollar Movie* series. Other sales were made to television distributors by such "poverty row" studios as Republic and Monogram. They had reached an agreement with the American Federation of Musicians. Important unions also allowed sales of pre-1948 films. The Screen Actors Guild (SAG) continued to pressure producers for additional compensation (residuals) to its members for television sales of later movies. It finally won a comprehensive settlement regarding residuals in its 1960 contract with all major American producers.

The settlement was fortuitous for the Hollywood studios. They had lost their habitual audience in 1948 and had had varying luck over the next ten years. By 1958, whatever luck the top nine film companies had had was running out. In the period from 1958 to 1963, only Paramount did not suffer a losing year. Some of the others had huge losses, and the television sale of their libraries meant the difference between corporate life and death. It is instructive to see how the studios came to this reversal of fortune at this time.

Postwar Film Exhibition

The dichotomy between "staying-in" and "going-out" is useful in understanding the dynamics of media rivalries from the early time of the MPPC through the maturity of television. The tiered releasing system that flourished from the 1920s through the 1940s was an attempt to balance both impulses. In the 1940s and 1950s the balance was breaking down, first because of the extraordinary situation of the war and then because of the radical changes in the media environment following the war.

Through the classic studio era, the pendulum swung between big and medium-size films, although both always coexisted. Big-budget musicals were prevalent in the early thirties. In the thirties and forties, the Hollywood studios scaled back on "event" movies (increasingly referred to as "blockbusters").[22] As the depression took hold, exhibitors increased their use of adding a second "B" grade film to the featured film. "B" movies are defined by their use of extremely limited budgets, formulaic plots, and a lowest common denominator appeal to the general audience.

There were exceptions. In the middle of this period, filmmaking ambition flared up again; 1939 was a year of the extraordinary with the releases of several large-budget films, most notably Selznick's *Gone With the Wind*. However, as America entered a war economy (even before our entry in December 1941), the film industry had less and less competition for the consumer dollar. Hollywood responded with medium-sized films. This continued, after the war, as the film industry earned record profits with only modest efforts. The films themselves could have serious ambitions as dramas. This was the period when dark urban thrillers, subsequently labeled "film noir," became a mature genre. Serious adult issues were dealt with in such Academy Award winners as *The Lost Weekend* (1945), *Best Years of Our Lives* (1946), and *Gentleman's Agreement* (1947). Filmmaking in these years was not a high-budget search for breathtaking technical breakthroughs. These films did not need expensive promotional campaigns. There was little motivation to dazzle the audience, since the patrons were already attending in record numbers.

This situation soon changed dramatically, partly due to television, which itself was symptomatic of a larger change. People had more money to spend and more time and things to spend it on as the economy shifted from a war to a postwar footing. It would be too simple to say that the postwar suburbanization led to a stay-at-home audience. We must realize that film was now competing with longer vacations and other outdoor leisure activities, as automobile ownership became universal, with education and other non-work pursuits available to an increasingly affluent public. In these circumstances, the habitual film going of the depression and war years was due for a decline. Affluence did not immediately return to the rest of the world and for that reason, Hollywood films continued to export well. Nonetheless, this was of little consolation for the loss of the American audience. The foreign audiences had less money and therefore paid far less, and many countries placed restrictions on the repatriation of American film earnings.

The major film studios were finally motivated to go back to some old show biz razzle-dazzle as they suffered a 32 percent decline in domestic attendance from 1946 to 1952.[23] They concentrated on the going-out audience by cutting back on the number of productions and trying to turn away from routine moviemaking. Actors, writers, and other employees on long-term contracts

38   were let go and became freelancers, moving from project to project. The studios also reduced risk by forming alliances with independent producers, who took on more of the financing responsibilities. In the short run, focusing resources on a few big movies worked. The decline of the revenues was temporarily reversed. Combined profits for the major studios had an annual increase of 50 percent, to $35.3 million, in 1954 and a further increase to $37.4 million in 1955.[24] It was hoped that film could maintain its economic health by producing spectaculars, blockbusters, and other out-of-the-ordinary movies. In short, films should be everything that television was not.

The movie producers adopted the two major technical innovations of color and widescreen. Previously, the expense of color cinematography had limited its use. Now, in the age of black-and-white television, there was a rush to color. Eighteen percent of movies were shot in color in 1949. A decade later that figure had risen to over 50 percent.[25] The widescreen lens and the multiprojector system had been around since the 1920s, on a limited basis. Starting with *This Is Cinerama* in 1952 and other widescreen formats such as Cinemascope, Todd-AO, and VistaVision, various studios switched to widescreen filmmaking. They also resorted to the fad of three-dimensional films. Both the widescreen and color represented a deliberate attempt to make film going a more exciting and unique experience than television. We can label this the "if you can't join 'em, lick 'em" approach.

Another bigger-than-life strategy came about from the combination of necessity and opportunity. American film companies decided to use their blocked foreign earnings to finance foreign productions. European locations and crafts personnel were a bargain compared to U.S. counterparts. Labor was so cheap in Italy and Spain that Hollywood went ahead and made films that were particularly labor intensive in these countries, such as various costume epics with "casts of thousands." These epics became an additional source of blockbusting moviemaking. A postwar cycle of biblical and historical epics began with *Samson and Delilah* (1949), peaked with DeMille's 1956 *The Ten Commandments*, and dramatically declined with the money-losing *Cleopatra* (1963). The use of relatively cheap exotic locations continued through the 1960s.

The profit level of 1955 proved to be temporary. The audience lost interest in widescreen movies per se. A particularly bleak year was 1958, with profits of only $12.6 million.[26] The studios now needed the television money. They switched back to "if you can't lick 'em, join 'em." The 1960 resolution of the residual dispute paved the way for wholesale leasing of the various libraries to network television. The first network regular prime time film program was NBC's *Saturday Night at the Movies* in 1961. ABC followed with a Sunday movie program the next year and CBS started a Thursday series in 1965. The video display of movies was now an established part of the American landscape.

Distributing Films to Smaller Audiences

During this time, independent film distributors found and exploited market niches and product shortages in the movie theaters. They wanted to become alternatives to the majors, not just adjuncts. Their stories, while economically miniscule, were important because these independents became one of the catalysts for the current "new" Hollywood. Their history began with the postwar disappearance of the "poverty row" studios, such as PRC, Monogram, and Republic, that had churned out B movies during the depression. The newly freed employees of these companies formed new distribution outlets such as Allied Artists. Another important independent eventually became famous as AIP (American International Pictures). These companies exploited several new market developments. Unlike the poverty row studios, which made low-budget films for a general audience, the new independents directed their efforts at the emerging teenage market. They were aggressive in tackling sensational and violent themes. Their topics were precisely those that would never be shown on television.

Theaters were also changing in response to the new media landscape. They were now suffering product famine as the major studios cut down production in search of big blockbusters and as B movies dried up. These theaters encouraged the new independents to make "exploitation" films. In addition, outdoor exhibitors had taken advantage of suburbanization by quickly setting up "drive-ins" on cheap land on the fringe of developments. These exhibitors discovered that an important audience was teenagers seeking the slightly subversive pleasures of horror, scandal, or titillating looks at girls and juvenile delinquents in trouble. Because of the tie-in between drive-ins and exploitation, the summer season (which the majors ignored) was important for independents.

Exploitation films nurtured a new generation of filmmakers and sensibilities about the relationship between the audience and the film. Exploitation

40   films were different from B movies since they were not fillers on a feature program. If they were double billed, it was with other exploitation or specialized
films. In this manner, exploitation films formed an economic continuity with
the Euro-art film (despite their disparity in formal experiment and narrative
ambition). The theater circuits that used either of these film genres were not
trying to attract everybody. They were targeting those groups of spectators
who wanted to go to the movies to see something outside the mainstream.
By the late 1950s and 1960s, various European production centers had re-
emerged, helped in part by Hollywood's overseas spending on the exotic locations.[27] Rossellini, Fellini, DeSica, Bergman, Kurosawa, et al. made films
that were regularly released in the U.S. One quantitative measure of the importance of foreign films at that time is their percentage of all releases. Imports were 20 percent of all U.S. film releases in 1946. Twelve years later, they
were 50 percent. They remained above 50 percent of total releases until 1969,
when imports started dropping sharply.[28] These films sometimes received
major distribution but often just played major cities and college campuses. To
a large extent, independent distributors introduced foreign films here, although major distributors stepped in as the trend continued.

The older Hollywood film studios followed the independent development
of "niche" audiences and occasionally imitated them. For example, in 1952,
the U.S. Supreme Court allowed the independent distributor Joseph Burstyn
to import Rossellini's *The Miracle*, despite the banning of the film by the New
York State Board of Censors. The next year, Otto Preminger and his Hollywood distributor, United Artists, decided to release the film *The Moon Is Blue*
without a seal of approval from the major studios' own censorship board, the
Production Code Administration. They were able to distribute the film successfully without the seal. Independent distributors made money from foreign films because American audiences were interested in the way these films
treated sex and other adult topics. This put pressure on the major film studios to emulate sophisticated European themes. The MPAA finally scrapped
the Production Code and substituted a ratings system in 1968. The majors
ventured into producing and distributing the adult films that independents
had pioneered.

This was a time of eliminating the final remnants of the old system. A
watershed of sorts was reached with the runaway successes of big movies
such as *Dr. Zhivago* and *The Sound of Music* in 1965. However, the aftermath
of these big-budget triumphs was a string of big-budget flops such as *Dr.*

Dolittle, Hello, Dolly! and *Star!* The general audience was fickle, again. Box office volatility lowered the value of the studios to the point where they became attractive acquisitions. Gulf + Western took over Paramount in 1966. United Artists was purchased by Transamerica in 1967, and Warner by Kinney National Services in 1969. These companies gave the film distributors deeper financial resources and coincided with a shift in management to a new generation. However, this wave of conglomerate takeover did not, in itself, change film industry practices.

The brightest spot in the major distributors' ledger sheets was leasing to television. During the wave of conglomeratization, movies shown on television achieved consistently high ratings. Table 1.1 charts the rise and fall of films on television as measured by their hit ratings. The chart is compiled from *Variety*'s listing of movies that have drawn a rating of 24 or better on network television. The second column counts those movies made for theatrical releases that were subsequently shown on television. The third column counts the high-rated movies made directly for television. This type of production originated in 1966 with the NBC broadcast of *Fame is the Name of the Game*. A comparison of the second and third columns shows that the popularity of made-for-television movies paralleled the popularity of theatrical movies. The window between a theatrical showing and a network showing narrowed over the years until it stabilized at approximately three years in 1975. Networks leased films for an average of $2 million. At times, they would go much higher for individual titles.

Showing movies on television became very popular after the start of regular network showings in 1961. Early in 1966, the advertising agency BBDO issued a report stating that feature films on television were the best buy for advertisers. Six months later, *The Bridge on the River Kwai* broke all records for a broadcast film, with a 38.3 rating. This was a watershed, particularly since ABC paid $2 million to Columbia for the broadcast. Feature film showings became part of the arsenal used to seduce audiences to stay with one network. When one network programmed a very popular special, another network was sure to program a box office hit. The network sales force could also count on getting a high-powered corporate mix of advertisers for the feature film, companies that were less interested in direct sales and more interested in building corporate awareness. IBM, Citicorp, American Express, Coca-Cola, Pepsi, et al. were the prominent advertisers during feature films.[29]

The movie industry could now rely on television sales as an important rev-

TABLE 1.1 Number of High-Rated Movies on Television, 1962–1989

Year	Hit Theatrical Movies	Hit Made-for-TV Movies	Total Hit Movies	Average Years between Theatrical Release and First TV Showing
1962	3	0	3	8.0
1963	4	0	4	5.5
1964	3	0	3	10.0
1965	10	0	10	11.0
1966	11	2	13	7.0
1967	45	2	47	5.5
1968	21	3	24	6.0
1969	18	1	19	4.3
1970	14	13	27	7.0
1971	21	24	45	6.5
1972	22	19	41	5.8
1973	18	14	32	4.3
1974	13	18	31	6.3
1975	9	9	18	3.3
1976	26	17	43	6.1
1977	14	21	35	2.0
1978	11	12	23	3.8
1979	11	6	17	2.6
1980	6	9	15	2.5
1981	4	7	11	2.8
1982	2	6	8	2.5
1983	3	6	9	2.7
1984*	2	9	11	5.0
1985	0	2	2	n/a
1986	0	7	7	n/a
1987	0	2	2	n/a
1988	0	3	3	n/a
1989	0	3	3	n/a
Total	295	214	509	

*1984 results are skewed because *Star Wars* finally made it to network after seven years.

Sources: *Variety*, October 7, 1981, pp. 176–177, 186; *Variety*, January 24, 1990, pp. 166–170.

enue center. Nonetheless, feature film marketing practices remained relatively untouched by the television release. Since the films were leased for flat fees and often in packages of several titles bundled together, the individual film distributors had little economic incentive to be concerned about the share of the television audience that watched a specific film. The window between theatrical release and broadcast was several years. This furthered the lack of influence the TV market had on financing and production practices. On a title-per-title basis, there was minimal "marginal" incentive for the film distributor or producer to worry about the television success of the film. Television remained a truly secondary market.

Despite television's afterthought status in film distribution, the high ratings demonstrated that the public had not abandoned feature films. Yet, the post-1965 big-budget failures led to the major studios feeling disconnected and bewildered by the elusive movie theater patrons. This disconnection was part of the general social atmosphere. The late sixties were a time of ferment. The ferment was hard to characterize since it was a new mixture of political and cultural. It was not specific either to the struggle for racial equality or to the anti–Vietnam War movement, although both political stances were part of the ferment. Another important component was a sense of a community by generation. Influential segments of the youth audience definitely wanted cultural products that were different from those of the adult audience. This was most clearly expressed in music and rock's radical separation from other music formats.

The radical separation was also percolating in American films. Warner Communications' *Bonnie and Clyde* in 1967 celebrated an earlier generation of young outlaws. In 1968, MGM produced Stanley Kubrick's altered-consciousness space fantasy *2001,* and the independent company Avco Embassy had a hit with Mike Nichols' *The Graduate.* Exploitation films, in particular, were exploring the young side of the "generation gap." These films expounded rebellion, sexual liberation, and alternative senses of community. However, films did not seem to interest the youth audience as much as music did. Several producers had the obvious idea to combine the two. Festival movies such as a documentary on the Monterey Pop Festival earned modest sums. In 1969, Dennis Hopper combined a wall-to-wall rock sound track with a narrative about drug-dealing bikers in *Easy Rider.* This film made box office history when it earned $19 million for Columbia Pictures. The majors were now inspired to pursue the young "counterculture" audience.

Dennis Hopper and the other principal contributors to *Easy Rider* had worked for Roger Corman, who started as a producer for AIP and was now distributing his own exploitation films. The surprise success of *Easy Rider* was a harbinger that the future key to health for the studios was somehow combining their own strengths as major distributors with the sensibility of a

44   new generation, coming up through the independent ranks. At first, studios issued a bunch of "copy cat" movies directly catering to the counterculture. These rarely ignited the box office.

The more lasting legacy of *Easy Rider* came when Hollywood (a notorious closed shop industry) opened its doors to a new cohort of filmmakers. Steven Spielberg, George Lucas, Francis Ford Coppola, Brian DePalma, and Martin Scorsese got their first big studio assignments around the time of *Easy Rider*. This new generation had cut its collective teeth by working for Corman or other independent distributors (with the notable exception of Spielberg). They aspired to combine European "art" filmmaking and "counterculture" ideas. Thomas Schatz argues that Francis Ford Coppola's 1972 film *The God-father* was the first major success of this new group.[30] Coppola's film absorbed some of the themes and techniques of contemporary foreign directors. The other members of this new wave, American style, also showed interest in new hybrid forms of moviemaking, breaking boundaries between different genre conventions and taking a looser approach to storytelling. Another example was *American Graffiti* (1973), coproduced by Coppola and Lucas and directed by the latter. This new cohort was already achieving success in combining new sensibilities and old-time studio distribution power. Their achievements were still tentative. It was not until Spielberg and Lucas reached full stride with *Jaws* (1975) and *Star Wars* (1977) that the majors would have a distribution formula that reunited the stay-at-home viewer with the going-out audience. Before this happened, the major distributors had to learn two more lessons from the independents.

Television Advertising and *Jaws*: Marketing the Shark Wide and Deep

Tom Laughlin was angered when he read the 1971 box office statement from Warner Communications about *Billy Jack*, the film he wrote, produced, and starred in with his wife. The studio distributors did not understand how to handle such a special project. The film combined kung fu action with Native American spirituality and counterculture sincerity. Nonetheless, the executives were positioning it as a typical genre piece. Laughlin demanded to know what Warner was going to do about the low figures. Dissatisfied with the answer, he decided to handle the film himself.

The Warner people were not prepared to let the movie go. Laughlin went to court and finally got the film back. What he did next was distribution history. He took the film print from town to town, rolling the first town's profits over into the marketing and advertising for the next town. In order to maximize the power of his advertising, he put most of his money into local television spots. The audience came out to see the film and the campaign gained momentum. By the time he was done in 1973, his company had pocketed $32 million.

Major film distributors had been curiously circumspect about using television advertising. From 1970 to 1972, MPAA members together spent $4 million per year on network television advertising, about 2 percent of their total movie advertising budget.[31] There was no change for those three years. Executives did not like the expense of TV advertising since they viewed TV as a rival medium and TV audiences as separate from their own. Perhaps they also did not like the shotgun nature of television promotion, with its broad range of who sees it and when. In contrast, newspaper advertising can be run precisely on the day and the week the movie opens, and radio advertising can be targeted at specific groups. Nonetheless, the power of the TV medium could not be ignored forever. At the same time Laughlin was rolling out *Billy Jack*, Lester Persky at Columbia was achieving success for several movies by running TV spots.[32] The other studios now had two examples of TV power. They increased their network advertising by 50 percent in 1973, and by 73 percent in 1974. By 1974, network advertising was 4 percent of the total advertising budget.[33]

Steven Spielberg's second feature film, *Jaws*, released in 1975, eventually earned $129.5 million in the North American market for its distributor, Universal. The earnings were unprecedented. It was the launch of the "New Hollywood." It confirmed large changes in the industry's production and distribution practices. It was released in the late spring and played during the summer, a season previously reserved for cheap drive-in movies. In content and marketing practices, it can be argued that *Jaws* combined major studio clout with exploitation thrills. *Jaws* was a movie about a shark terrorizing a beach resort community. The community displayed ambivalence about publicizing the danger. The movie ended with a final successful hunt for the shark that only one of the original three crew members survives. *Jaws* may hint at Ibsen and Melville, but its real pleasure is the terror of shark attacks on vulnerable teenage swimmers and anything else that gets in the way. Neither the ad campaign nor the opening of the movie missed the opportunity

46   to present the innocent female swimmer taken by the huge shark. It was definitely exploitation material.

Spielberg worried about being typecast as an exploitation director. His consolation was that he would make it better than any low-budget thriller. He spent more and more money—on the mechanical shark, on the sets, by shooting in a real ocean rather than in a tank, and on the crowd scenes. The movie was initially budgeted at $3.5 million. It came in at over $10 million.[34] The producers and Universal reluctantly put up with this kind of overage. Dimly, without much discussion, the executives realized that they could pull in a bigger audience, beyond the traditional appeal of the thriller or other action genres, with the added production values of a big budget. The big budget enticed a wide audience to look at a hitherto narrow genre such as horror, or comic book films such as *Superman* (1978), previously only attended by young males.[35]

The high budget reinforced the distributor's decision to spend heavily on television advertising, since the added money paid for spectacular visual, audio, and music effects that, in turn, could be featured in the television advertising. Universal decided to push the new post–*Billy Jack* importance of TV advertising. It opened *Jaws* simultaneously in 464 theaters.[36] This wide release took maximum advantage of the television campaign, which featured, in graphic terms, the movie's ability to terrify. The final budget for Universal's promotion campaign was a high $2.5 million. *Jaws* became an event film, which is to say that the success of the movie fed upon itself. Infrequent moviegoers felt as if they were missing something if they did not go to see *Jaws*.

The ability of the new Hollywood cohort to make and market an event movie was confirmed when *Star Wars*, directed by Lucas, came out in 1977. Previously science fiction had a following limited to the Saturday matinee audience. In 1968, Kubrick's *2001* used the genre to explore metaphysical themes and drew attention from a more cerebral audience. Nevertheless, it was *Star Wars* that found the right balance between formulaic action and mythic concerns to draw in both adults and children. The plot of *Star Wars* was action driven, although Lucas was skillful in publicizing his use of mythic devices borrowed from mythologist Joseph Campbell. Critics noted the mythic elements and labeled the film a sophisticated space epic. Heavy marketing, critical acclaim, and hybrid appeal made *Star Wars* an event film. It combined big-budget special effects with a wide release, heavy advertising, and exploitation of the film through merchandising products associated with the film's characters. It was made for $11 million and earned rentals, in its initial release, of $193.5 million. It was the top box office earner of all time for five years and then briefly regained the honors in its rerelease in the 1990s.

The film industry had made two advances at once. The directors had fashioned hits by combining a new sensibility with traditional matinee genres. The distributors had learned to market and effectively advertise the new blockbuster. The advertising was increasing in expense, and there was an upper limit. After all, not every film was *Jaws* or *Star Wars*. Lesser films could not justify expensive advertising if they did not make money in their initial theatrical run. Theatrical advertising could not really boost the sale price of film to television since there was a three- to four-year gap between the theater run and the network broadcast. From the audience's perspective, there were technical drawbacks. Theaters only showed the movie several times a day, not necessarily at convenient times. Indeed, what was a convenient time to take the children to the movies if both parents were working?

The new practices set the stage for the twenty-plus year boom in major motion picture production. It created a global audience that was now eager to watch recent movies, if not at the theater, then at home. The year of *Jaws*, 1975, was also the year of the first satellite transmission of Home Box Office (HBO), a cable channel devoted to showing movies. Finally, it was the year when Sony introduced Betamax.

The old Hollywood had balanced its distribution and production practices for both the going-out audience and the neighborhood viewers. Television and suburban living had ruined the tiered releasing system in the U.S. Distribution practices initially responded to television by targeting separate segments of the moviegoing audience. They did this with widescreen presentations, with exploitation films with the drive-in, midnight cult, and art house circuits. By the late 1970s the new Hollywood was reuniting these segments. This sets up the argument that will be developed below about the role of home video in sustaining the New Hollywood. Home video restored the audience—which Hollywood had to share with television. It also restored the economic power of the old studios because the audience was willing to spend money to watch movies at home on the VCR. Indeed, Bruce Austin argues that home video restored the old tiered releasing system of the studio system.[37] In any case, we will see too that the video market would also change the relationships between the independent distributors and the majors. The next chapter turns to the technological development of video.

CHAPTER TWO

The Development of Video Recording

David Sarnoff, the head of RCA, was already a media legend when he joined the service, where he rose to the rank of brigadier general during World War II. After the war, General Sarnoff often exercised a military style of command and strategy as he redirected huge resources to tackle seemingly insurmountable problems. When, on September 27, 1951, RCA staged an elaborate celebration of Sarnoff's forty-five years in the radio business,[1] the general directed his engineering staff to present him with three more breakthrough inventions in the next five years. One of the breakthroughs he wanted was a "videograph," a video playback unit using magnetic tape.[2] He got his wish. Unfortunately for Sarnoff, it was RCA's rival, Ampex, that achieved the breakthrough by demonstrating a practical videotape recorder in 1956. The irony deepens since Bing Crosby was one of the financial backers of Ampex. The popular singer had left Sarnoff's NBC in 1946, after the general turned down Crosby's request to broadcast recordings of his radio show.

This chapter is about the development of video recording technology and the creation of a mass market. This is not just a chapter about inventors, it is also about manufacturers, broadcasters, content providers, and content distributors, and, finally, the audience. Technology is not an autonomous pursuit, it is the conjunction of scientific opportunity, corporate vision, and marketplace struggles. The relationship of technologies of communication to culture is a fascinating one. It is not a task for the fainthearted to explain this relationship. The landscape is littered with abandoned theories that have tried to reduce this relationship to a single cause or a single moment. The evolution of any communications tool shows that different institutions will facilitate or hinder development depending on the entire media mix at the time.

For example, broadcast institutions initially invested in circulating cultural products (i.e., radio shows) in "real" time. Many radio executives deplored the use of recordings until the advent of television. We can therefore ask the question: Is it sheer coincidence that the phonograph stagnated and the magnetic recorder never emerged while broadcast institutions had this attitude? History is merely suggestive on this score. We have the story of Sarnoff driving Crosby away from NBC over the recording issue and then seemingly having a change of heart, four years later, when he asked his engineers to develop video magnetic recording. The argument is that Sarnoff's change parallels changes in the media environment, changes that no one could anticipate, not even Sarnoff himself.

Magnetic recording, which is the underlying principle of video recording, was invented at roughly the same time as radio broadcasting. While radio quickly captured the public imagination, fifty years would pass before the average citizen would even hear of magnetic recording. What factors had to fall into place before magnetic recording could become a consumer item? To answer that question we have to review the tangled history of broadcasting and recording media up to 1951. Only then can we ask what further factors had to line up for the home video machine. Assumptions are embedded in technology. Sometimes these assumptions doom the technology. Ampex, RCA, CBS, Avco, MCA, Philips, IBM, and even Sony suffered failures as they tried, over the course of a decade, to move video recording from professional use to consumer use. The American companies suffered disproportional losses because they were not nimble enough in adjusting their attitudes about the audience. The relatively small Japanese manufacturer Sony was the one to finally unlock the market, only to lose it again to its big Japanese rival, Matsushita.

In the previous chapter, I showed how film distribution changes as it tries to negotiate a balance between the stay-ins and the going-out viewers. In this chapter, we shall see how inventors and manufacturers have their own relationship with the media audience. Their relationship is mitigated by their concurrent relations with content distributors. The VCR arose not as the result of one company's vision but as the result of a three-way relationship; between manufacturers, content distributors, and customers.

The VCR is one of the great success stories of consumer electronics. Nonetheless, its rapid rate of adoption can be exaggerated—not unlike the vaude-

50   ville comic who worked thirty years to become an overnight success. VCR adoption has been compared to television's rate of adoption. Television was introduced by RCA as a ready-to-use machine (unlike the early radios, which were sold as kits), and it encountered few obstacles as it became the most ubiquitous piece of hardware in the world. The only major change in the first four decades was the switch to color TV sets, although we are now on the verge of several more major changes. In contrast, the VCR was the result of a series of intermediate stages. It was only after a series of incremental advances that the rate of VCR adoption approached that of television. Each one of these stages fulfilled one of the potential uses of the machine and built a market appropriate to that use.

There are four stages in the development of home video recording machines.[3] The first stage dates from the 1956 Ampex machine. This technology led directly to the industrial market and indirectly to future visions of an expanded consumer market. The second stage was reached a decade later when both business and educational professionals starting using the ¾-inch U-matic. But hopes for general consumer adoption of the U-matic fizzled, and Sony went to work on the time-shifting capabilities of ½-inch tape cassette that Sony and its rival VHS manufacturers started selling in 1975, which became the third stage of home video development. Sony sold the Betamax home video recorder as a tool of consumer empowerment. This claim must be taken with a grain of salt; nonetheless it succeeded in making the VCR a global mass medium. This market led without further technical developments to a fourth stage around 1979, which was characterized by the increasing use of prerecorded material, preponderantly adult programming at the beginning and subsequently mainstream feature films. Sony's Betamax system had already lost ground to the VHS by 1978, but still maintained a healthy market share. The development of the prerecorded market eventually led to the demise of Betamax by 1988. We are still in the fourth stage.

Throughout this multistage process there was the alternative technology of laser disc. In the early 1970s many thought the laser disc would be more important than the video recorder. Even a year after the introduction of the Betamax, the U.S. media continued to emphasize disc over tape.[4] I will describe below how alternatives to videotape failed to find a mass market during this period. In 2000, the rollout of recordable videodiscs signaled perhaps yet another stage when the video recorder becomes united with laser disc technology. The market has yet to make that decision.

Broadcast Networks and Recording Technology

The career of David Sarnoff is illustrative of the issues involved in early recording technology. He was not an inventor, nor was he a cultural producer.
He was not even a distributor. Yet, he helped create an integrated company
that was a leader in all these activities. The Radio Corporation of America
(RCA) under the guidance of Sarnoff took up the gauntlet of home entertainment where Edison left off. As a young executive, Sarnoff announced his
vision of radio as a national music box, maybe as early as 1916.[5] In order to
realize this vision, he proposed that RCA, at that point still just a company
making radio sets, start a radio entertainment network. Sarnoff argued that
radio could attract the finest music by building a national audience listening
to various stations networked together by the same broadcast signal. He was
more vague when asked who would pay for this programming. The question
of who would pay puzzled most observers.[6] The British provided one answer
when their government set up the British Broadcasting Corporation (BBC)
by charging radio owners an annual license fee. U.S. policymakers rejected
the BBC model. American political and social conditions favored the rise of
commercially sponsored broadcasting.

Advertising financed the national network for the distribution of radio
programs. AT&T, the telephone company, had already networked a few stations in 1922 by sending broadcast signals through its telephone lines. AT&T
stations were accepting advertising. In 1926, they accepted a bid of $1 mil-
lion from RCA for their network. RCA renamed the old AT&T network
the National Broadcasting Company (NBC), and stations rushed to affiliate
with NBC.

One of the reasons AT&T decided to sell illustrates the relationship between radio networking and recording technology. The radio networks did
not want to rely on records; they wanted to distribute their programs live.
The radio signal degraded significantly after short distances, and AT&T supplied the telephone lines that would allow radio programs to be carried long
distances. The cost of leasing these lines from AT&T was very high, and the
telephone executives realized that this was the best way to make money from
the emerging radio industry. They got out of owning stations and networks in
order to lease their lines to other networks such as NBC and its upstart rival,
the Columbia Broadcasting System (CBS).

Despite the high cost of leasing lines and other expenses, NBC was prof-

52   itable by 1928. CBS also quickly earned profits and both were the boom
growth companies of the period despite the onset of the Great Depression. In
contrast, the record industry was deteriorating as more people decided to listen to the music on the radio. From 1923 to 1925, record sales fell by almost
50 percent, from $238 million to $125 million. They were already weak when
the economic downturn set in; sales had almost disappeared by 1931, down
to $17 million.[7] One survey done at that time found that in North Carolina,
many people kept the radio on all the time, and that the Victrola (record
player) only got used when the radio static was too harsh.[8] Radio proved se-
ductive. It was "free" and it had a large selection of music. It also had a tech-
nically superior quality since the equipment provided a wider range of sound
than the records, although, as surveyors noted, the static was a weakness.

As a result of the record crisis, RCA bought Victor, the largest record company, in 1929. Victor had suffered as the phonograph market softened with
the advent of radio as a mass medium. RCA's primary motivation was to acquire more manufacturing plants, such as Victor's facilities in Camden, New
Jersey, and to take advantage of Victor's distribution system in order to sell
radio sets. RCA was not concerned with the record business or with improving the technology of recording sound. Recording scholars lamented that "the
management of RCA had no real interest in the talking machine."[9] After the
purchase, RCA changed over Victor's Camden factory to make radio sets, with
some activity in manufacturing combination sets of radio and record players.

RCA's lack of interest in the declining consumer record market paralleled
NBC's hostility toward the use of records on the radio. The explanation of
network hostility toward records goes beyond the record market decline,
however. The national networks possessed power for two reasons. The first
was the rather straightforward fact that NBC and CBS owned the best radio
stations in the largest cities. The second was their ability to deliver a national
audience to the advertisers. The networks are not content distributors in the
same way that film studios are content distributors. The networks are audience distributors, selling listeners to the advertisers. This understanding
helps us pinpoint some of the key differences between the broadcast industry and other cultural distributors. For example, during the interwar years of
radio, advertisers originated and produced many shows for their clients
directly. They did not just buy time for advertising, they bought the entire
fifteen- or thirty-minute network time block. Therefore, advertisers and their
agencies often had the leverage to demand when their show should be aired.

Network programmers were only relayers. Their power came from their power over radio stations. If advertisers started to contact radio stations directly, they would need the networks less. However, the networks had the superior equipment and the AT&T lines.

NBC and CBS executives did not hesitate to disparage the alternative means of circulating radio shows, which was by making records and sending these records out to the individual stations. This campaign was directed mostly against the use of popular music records. Merlin H. Aylesworth, the president of NBC, expressed this attitude in 1930. He regretted that stations were using records out of economic considerations and stated: "If radio is to become a self-winding phonograph, it would be better to discard radio entirely and go back to buying phonographs and records than to waste the all too few wave lengths available for living speakers."[10] Hostility of networks was measured by the stigma that came to be attached to recorded programs. Eric Barnouw notes that the term "transcriptions" was substituted for "recordings" in order to avoid the stigma.[11] Despite technical improvements, the stigma remained. As late as 1946 the Federal Communications Commission was writing: "Through the years the phonograph record, and to a lesser extent the transcription, have been considered inferior program sources."[12]

There was some improvement of recordings and several obscure experiments with magnetic tape before World War II. Lee DeForest's invention of the "audion" tube in 1913 initiated electronic amplification of sound. Western Electric, a subsidiary of AT&T, bought his patent. Eleven years later, in 1924, Bell Laboratories, owned by AT&T, unveiled electrical recording. Electronic amplifiers improved both the sensitivity of the recording microphone and the amplitude of the playback. These improvements were part of the technological campaign that resulted in sound film, which became an instant smash hit with the public in 1927. Electronically amplified record players were adopted at a slow pace, with a modest impact on the market.

Magnetic recording developed at an even slower rate. An American, Oberlin Smith, published a suggestion for this method for recording in 1888.[13] In 1898, the father of magnetic recording, Vladimir Poulsen, a Danish scientist, built a prototype, the "telegraphone," that recorded varying magnetic impulses on a piece of steel to convert sound into electricity and back again. He demonstrated it at the 1900 Paris International Exhibition. This exhibition brought the method to the attention of AT&T executives. Poulsen started manufacturing telegraphones in Europe and the United States, but

54   prospects were poor and he shifted his attentions to radio improvements. U.S. research and development into magnetic recordings was sporadic and short-lived. Bell Laboratories did devote some resources to investigating the use of magnetic recording for a telephone-answering device. By 1937, executives had decided to suspend these efforts. There is no written evidence that Bell feared that the use of magnetic recordings would bypass the distribution of radio programs over telephone lines. Historian Mark Clark has found internal memos indicating that AT&T suspended the magnetic recording program because it might have sparked consumer fears over the privacy of phone conversations.[14]

Whereas Bell Laboratories lost interest in alternate recording techniques, the radio engineers never had any to begin with. Radio transcriptions were a cheap fix to be used as "bridge" music on the radio, as a source of secondary radio programming, and to distribute prerecorded advertising. CBS and NBC engaged in the business of producing and selling transcriptions to radio stations. In 1938, RCA controlled 26 percent of the transcription business.[15] Barnouw describes network control of the transcription business as a preemptive move against competitive uses of recordings. He writes that the networks "virtually controlled the phonograph field and through it the making of transcriptions. Transcribed programs were potential rivals to network programs; control could inhibit such competition."[16] Although both CBS and RCA owned record companies (Columbia and RCA Victor, respectively), they did little to further recording technology until 1946.

From the start, European radio favored the use of recordings to a much greater degree than American broadcasters. It is thus not surprising that work on magnetic recorders continued on the continent while it stagnated in the United States. Austrian and German inventors were able to improve the magnetic recorder in the 1930s. Fritz Pfleumer invented a process for coating paper tape with magnetic powder, which became the basis for modern magnetic recording. American engineers, unaware of these developments, became puzzled as they monitored German radio during World War II. The Americans noticed that the same recitals were broadcast on different days. These recitals must have been recorded. However, their duration was longer than the capacity of the familiar disc transcriptions. The secret was not discovered until the occupation of Germany, when the U.S. military uncovered long-playing magnetic tape recorders at German radio stations.[17]

After the war, the U.S. broadcast industry became more accepting of the development and use of professional recordings, both for record sales and for broadcast purposes. They wanted to do more to expand their consumer record divisions to capture postwar leisure dollars. CBS' Columbia Records financed Peter Goldmark's successful effort to create higher fidelity records with longer playing time by using 12-inch vinyl platters, introducing the resulting "LP" to the market in 1948. RCA quickly followed with its new 45-rpm disc.

The use of records for broadcast purposes also started to gain wider acceptance, although NBC continued to resist. In 1947, singing star Bing Crosby failed once again to convince Sarnoff and NBC to record his radio program and to use the recording for retransmission. He was tired of having to do the show twice, once for the east coast time zone and again for the western time zone. Crosby was also tired of the general's anti-recording bias. He switched to another network, the American Broadcasting Company (ABC),[18] and another sponsor that year. ABC allowed the show to be transcribed onto recording discs. Although audience members complained, detecting the loss of quality due to the transcription, Crosby was not about to give up and return to the daily grind of dual performances. In June 1947 he had attended a demonstration of the war-confiscated German tape recorder "Magnetophon" in San Francisco. The singer decided to take a chance and adopted tape technology for his show.[19] At the same time, he invested in a small California electronics firm, Ampex, because it was engaged in improving magnetic recording technology.[20] Crosby's gamble paid off. With the improved sound, the complaining subsided, and Ampex was soon a major player in magnetic recording.

Crosby turned out to be prescient because television changed everything. As the networks switched their attention and their most popular shows from radio to television, radio stations had to adopt new survival techniques. They relied heavily on programs featuring music records. The higher fidelity of the new LPs and 45s eliminated sound quality complaints. The new record formats were part of a sea change in American leisure habits and a new focus on home entertainment. The new acceptance of using recordings in radio would now work itself into television, but not without a detour.

Television and Recording

It is a truism in media history that new media pioneers promote their systems with reference to other media that the public already knows. Sometimes it is

56 a positive reference, as in this new "x" does it bigger and better than the previous "y." Just as often it is a negative one: "x" does what "y" could never hope to do. Early television pundits used both strategies. They proclaimed television as a positive improvement over radio since it added picture to sound. They also compared television positively to film by noting that the new medium brought moving pictures into the home. More often, they made a negative reference to what the movies could not do that television could. The proudest claim that television executives, from Paley and Sarnoff at the top through the middle- and low-level ranks, made was that television was "live." The viewer received the representation of the event in the very instance that the event transpired. In 1937, Paley predicted that TV would be most interesting when it presented current events as they happened. A decade later, David Sarnoff was less specific on the charms of the new medium but was equally sure that they would be unique:

> A first-class radio program is unlike any theatrical or motion-picture presentation. It is a new thing in the world. Similarly, it is quite likely that television drama will develop in novel directions, using the best of the theater and motion pictures, and building a new art-form based on these.[21]

In 1949, Hollywood executives became very interested in rumors that Sarnoff had met with Nicholas Schenck, the head of MGM studios, to discuss a partnership.[22] They wondered if the general wanted to fill the NBC schedule with filmed programs rather than the live shows coming out of New York. Perhaps he had learned his lesson from Crosby's desertion two years previously. In actuality, nothing happened and Sarnoff continued to openly support NBC's president Sylvester "Pat" Weaver's strategy of programming as much live material as possible.

 The general rule of thumb in the late 1940s and early 1950s was that live shows were cheaper than filmed shows. Film had the considerable cost of film stock, laboratory processing, editing, and printing. In addition, the use of a film camera necessitates lighting and production techniques that were more expensive than the equipment needed for a live show. As late as 1955, a live "upscale" hour-long drama was budgeted at $45,000; its filmed equivalent ran to $125,000.[23] In order to match or undercut the budget of live shows, independent film producers improvised low-budget techniques.

Film gained a permanent advantage when an after-market developed in the mid-1950s. In 1951 the *I Love Lucy* show was filmed rather than broadcast live. The network now had the possibility of using reruns during summer, the off-season. The production company, Desilu, made the film process pay for itself when it started reselling the episodes after the network run. In 1955, the British government allowed the development of commercial television in Great Britain, after an intense lobbying campaign by advertising interests. Other countries expanded their television services and were desperate for a source of programming. American producers started to export their filmed programming. In the U.S., there was also a continuing hunger for programming, even of shows that already been aired. Film producers easily syndicated their shows to individual stations after a network airing. The network interest in the after-market for television shows became substantial and corresponded to decreasing network interest in nonrecorded live shows. This was a sea change in broadcasting. However, the networks were interested in a cheaper electronic recording alternative to film.

Back in the 1920s, several inventors realized that some kind of scanning process could generate the electrical impulses appropriate for broadcasting and recording the image. John Logie Baird (1888–1946), a British inventor, recorded electronic images on a videodisc in 1928. He sold discs to a curious public for seven shillings apiece. One surviving copy is now on display at the New York Museum of Broadcast as an archaeological curiosity (it cannot be deciphered).[24] Baird's mechanical system was an inventor's dead end, since it produced a very poor image. The entire approach was abandoned when Philo T. Farnsworth (1906–1971) invented the "image dissector," which used electronic scanning. Farnsworth's machine vastly improved the transmitted image. At the same time it complicated the problem of recording. A stopgap solution known as the kinescoping process allowed films to be made off the image on the TV monitor. The resulting photographic image was high in contrast and suffered other degradations in image quality. Nonetheless, it was used extensively in retransmissions of television shows before the development of coast-to-coast co-axial lines by AT&T in 1951 and afterward by networks and stations that did not have access to the lines. Even the major networks relied on kinescoping for syndication and reruns in the early fifties.

Broadcasters still promoted the excitement of live television, even as their hostility to recordings lessened. The tremendous popularity of television secured network power. Advertising revenue levels were rising to the point

58   where filming scripted television shows had become profitable. Profits would rise even further if engineers could come up with a cheaper, more flexible method of recording. By 1951, General Sarnoff had a vision of the economic advantage of video recording. He could anticipate several advantages to recording electronically over filming. The electronic recording would eliminate kinescoping. The electronic recording would not need developing or other processing. There would be no need for chemicals. Video recording would be available for instant use, particularly for popular sports broadcasts. Sarnoff could also anticipate that the preservation of the image as electronic data would facilitate creative uses of the image that were difficult and laborious when the image was manipulated as a photograph in film technology.

When Sarnoff urged his staff to go forward and invent video recording, we are not sure if it was only for professional broadcast purposes. Perhaps the general was also anticipating home usage. Business historian Margaret Graham speculates that RCA's interest in video always had a consumer component. In 1939, Sarnoff already had "a picture of a population which may increasingly center its interest once more in the home; a population with ample leisure time . . . in individual small houses which they will be able to afford because of the development of low-cost construction and increased income."[25] He had taken a visionary risk by directing RCA to put $50 million into the research and development of television in the 1930s and 1940s, gambling on its successful adoption in the postwar years. RCA won twice in the success of TV—in the sale of TV sets and in the increased profits of NBC. This success could be amplified by an increasing stream of new products. By 1950, Sarnoff was actively promoting color television, though it would still be another decade before color TV sets earned significant profits. The general lavished more and more resources on the different RCA laboratories and even allowed the Princeton facility to explore projects without an immediate goal. He was encouraging RCA to continue to introduce new products and to maintain its manufacturing momentum after the maturity of the television market. Perhaps the videograph would be another consumer item.

Graham wonders whether RCA's home video system was "the fulfillment of a promise RCA made long ago to its public. In a sense it was the product that David Sarnoff . . . had imagined would free television viewers from commercial broadcasting, the part of the entertainment electronics industry he himself had helped to create but had long despised."[26] In contrast to CBS'

William Paley (running his operation five blocks away), Sarnoff never fully embraced the commercial support of broadcasting. His interests, as head of RCA, were in manufacturing and selling the technology of the future, not in serving as America's pitchman. The general may have anticipated that video would redirect television away from its worst excesses. Graham's speculation introduces a continuing theme in the development of video: giving control back to the audience. This theme was reintroduced in the 1970s, when Akio Morita at Sony and Kenjiro Takayanagi of JVC openly articulated video recording as a corrective to commercial television.

We will never fully know Sarnoff's motivations for the videograph. But we do know that he was frustrated in his desire for RCA to be first. After Sarnoff's 1951 announcement, the still-tiny company Ampex, having profited in the field of audio recording, plunged into a video research program that paralleled RCA's. Direct application of audio recording techniques led to cumbersome and unworkable tape lengths since video information was so much greater than audio information. Ampex solved this problem by recording diagonally on the tape with spinning recording heads, rather than vertically. The company was able to introduce a practical video recorder at the National Association of Broadcasters' conference in 1956. RCA was chagrined not to be first, but it was not standing still, either. RCA's own research led to the development of color video recordings in 1959, and so both companies controlled vital patents to the emerging video technology. The first video machines cost over $50,000 and were large units suitable only for studio work. The early video did not lend itself to editing. Its use was initially confined to tape-delayed broadcasts. A string of inventions improved the video recorder to the point where it could take on more production functions. For instance, in 1965 CBS used a magnetic disc machine built by Magnetic Video Recording to provide stop action and instant replay during football games.[27]

By 1960, many research and development teams were actively exploring the possibility of building video machines for the consumer. I group the various approaches to home video into two technological categories. The first group is those technologies that did not feature home recording capabilities. This promised several advantages to the manufacturers of these systems. They could enjoy dual revenue streams, from the playback machines and from the discs and tapes that provided the content for those machines. They could more easily negotiate with content providers (such as the film studios) since

60   these providers did not have to worry about unauthorized home recordings of their products. Of course, these advantages could only develop if a large enough market adopted the system. American manufacturers, by and large, decided to offer the consumer playback-only machines without a recording capability.

The second group consists of the home recorders, a Japanese effort. European manufacturers explored both options but did not succeed with either. The most successful television manufacturer, RCA, hesitated through the critical 1960s decade. It explored both playback-only and recording systems for awhile, and only in the late 1970s did it opt for the former.

Home Video 1: Playback-only Systems

EVR

Peter Goldmark at CBS was looking around for the next great thing after his triumphant invention of the long-playing record. He decided to initiate one of the earliest video projects for the consumer market. In 1960, he asked Paley and the leadership of CBS for $75,000 to develop a way of recording onto miniaturized film for the purposes of home playback.[28] Paley was the first man in America to demonstrate a clear understanding of the logic of selling broadcast audiences to advertisers. He had refined the whole business of affiliating stations with the network in a way that allowed a small upstart, CBS, to challenge the NBC leviathan. In order to stay ahead, NBC was forced to imitate his tactics. Now well into the television age, Paley had pushed CBS into the number one spot, beating out NBC and the perennially weak sister, ABC. He listened to Goldmark with intense skepticism. He already had doubts about the man, and he certainly did not understand why CBS should finance a machine that would give an alternative for the time viewers already devoted to watching CBS.

Goldmark went away empty-handed, but he kept the project going by receiving an exploratory grant from the U.S. military. In 1964, he approached his superiors again with the playback unit, now labeled as electronic video recording (EVR).[29] Frank Stanton, president of CBS, supported the project and overcame Paley's objection by framing the device as a tool for schools and other educational purposes. The EVR was unveiled to a sympathetic press in 1968.[30] But the transition from prototype to manufacturing was too difficult for the delicate system. By 1970 CBS had sunk $14 million into EVR and it still was not suitable for the market. Two years later Paley killed the project.

EVR was the first high-profile home video unit, and it stimulated key institutional players to think through the logic of their positions regarding the consumer application of such technology. Paley had gone back and forth on his support of the EVR, since neither did he want to miss a potential moneymaker nor did he want to destabilize network dominance of the television receiver. At this stage, Paley's concern was whether the TV set should be used for anything else but the display of broadcast shows. His ambivalence caused him to call off research before the EVR received a market test. His decision was correct. Subsequent players would find out that the development of home video required tremendous investments, and even the most tenacious program did not result in commensurate success. CBS got off with relatively light losses. Paley would get back in the game when home video was an extant technology, this time not as a manufacturer but as a distributor, when he signed a deal with Twentieth Century Fox in 1982.

Jack Gould, an influential critic for the *New York Times*, had become excited over the possibilities of home playback systems for the very same reasons that made Paley hesitate. He had been an early vocal supporter of live drama on television. His columns were increasingly hostile as the networks turned toward filmed television shows and away from innovations. For Gould, television had become what Newton Minow famously called that "vast wasteland." But what technology imposed, more technology could possibly cure. The EVR promised a new positive use of the TV set. Gould wrote in 1967, "By far the most interesting aspect of the innovation is its promise to introduce into the television medium the element of individual selectivity that up to now has been lacking."[31] He even anticipated that educational and other new programming would be created for the playback system and would be available through rental.[32] A video machine would finally break the monotonous pattern of television. It would redeem it from the wasteland. But salvation had to wait, and enthusiasm began to wane as technical difficulties continued to plague the system.[33]

The demise of EVR research and development not only dashed hopes for TV redemption, it also forestalled any attempts by a television network to provide programming for the home machine. Other manufacturers would have to find their own source of video programming. The next system did try to come to grips with these issues, but not in a satisfactory way.

CARTRIVISION

The Cartrivision video system was an interesting American hybrid of a record/playback unit, introduced to the marketplace for a brief year in 1972. It was a magnetic video recorder/player that substantially looked and performed like the future VCR. Its developers took the software question seriously and designed Cartrivision to give program providers, particularly the film studios, maximum control of sales and rentals. In retrospect, Cartrivision executives wondered whether the anti-piracy design might have actually contributed to market failure.[34]

Playtape, Inc., the developers of Cartrivision, formed a company called Cartridge Television, Inc. (CTI). They went to obtain both manufacturing and cash support from Avco Industries. Avco was diversifying from its aero-military background by acquiring an insurance company, real estate, and several entertainment companies, including television stations and Avco Embassy, primarily a distributor of independent motion pictures, but also a producer. Avco executives agreed to supply cash to manufacture the system. In exchange, Avco received 32 percent ownership of CTI.

CTI wished to market Cartrivision both as a recorder and as a playback unit for prerecorded movies. In order to get the rights to Hollywood movies and to maintain control over prerecorded tapes, Avco manufactured two different tapes: an ordinary cartridge for recording and playback and a non-rewindable red-coded cartridge for viewing a prerecorded movie once. After the viewing was complete, the consumer would return the cartridge to a rental dealership. On this basis, several studios made their product available, and Columbia Pictures became an actual partner in the rental network. The non-rewind function led to consumer complaints. In addition, rental dealerships were hard to line up.

The system was a marketplace failure. Cartrivision suffered fatally from being introduced before engineers and distributors had worked out the technical and marketing flaws. Customers lost patience. Before these flaws had a chance of being reduced to less than disastrous proportions, Avco decided to stop funding, and CTI went into Chapter XI bankruptcy in June 1973. It was never revived, and Avco wrote off $48 million.[35] Avco soon lost interest entirely in the entertainment sector and sold off the broadcasting stations and record company in 1975–1976. It sold off the film distribution/production

arm in 1981. One spinoff, Embassy Pictures, was destined to have an interesting afterlife as a video distributor and producer.

TED

The German company Telefunken and the British Decca were the first to introduce a disc system, in March 1975. Their technology was an application
of phonograph technology to the reproduction of images. The disc resembled
a long-playing record with grooves cut into it, and the machine featured
a needle that rode up and down in the grooves. Of course there were many
modifications, since the amount of information needed for visual reproduction was several magnitudes greater than that for audio. Instead of audio's
33⅓ rpm, the TeD (Television Disc) speeded up to 1,500 rpm. The TeD never
was able to give more than ten minutes worth of playing time per disc. Telefunken and Decca were never able to get much programming for the system.
They brought it to the market, but it was rated a failure after a year of slug-
gish sales.

DISCOVISION

One major Hollywood studio, MCA, the owner of Universal Studios, entered
the home entertainment market with its own disc technology, three years after TeD. This technology was not based on magnetic recording or on needle
vibrations, but on laser technology that recorded an electrical pattern on
photosensitive emulsion sandwiched in a plastic disc. Retrieval of these patterns by a playback unit was translated into a video image on the TV screen.
MCA publicly demonstrated the laser system at the end of 1972, dubbing it
"DiscoVision."[36] This technology paralleled similar research being conducted by Philips, the giant Dutch electronics firm. The two companies
formed a partnership in September 1974. Philips would manufacture and distribute players, while MCA would manufacture and distribute the software.

MCA continued to search for a disc manufacturing partner and even approached Sony.[37] However, by this time Sony had introduced its own Betamax magnetic video recorder and was already defending itself against an
MCA lawsuit. It did not appreciate the irony of an alliance with a legal ad-
versary. MCA eventually found two partners: Pioneer of Japan in early 1978

64   and IBM in September 1979. The film trade journal *Variety* reported the rumor that IBM invested $70 million. If this was true, MCA had neatly recouped its own research and development costs.[38] The MCA/Philips laser disc player was brought to the market in 1978, selling at $695 per player, and MCA priced discs in a range from $6 to $16.

The manufacturing of laser discs was a very delicate affair and the Carson, California plant had an excessively high rate of rejected discs. This put pressure on the price, and in 1979 most feature films on laser disc went up in price to $25.[39] Competition from both magnetic recorders and another incompatible disc system introduced by RCA in March 1981 slowed sales and eliminated profits. Among the various maneuvers to counter sluggish sales was a name switch to "Laservision" in 1980. Although rejection rates improved, sales did not improve enough, and the MCA/IBM partnership called Disco-Vision Associates (DVA) closed Carson in February 1982. MCA was out of the disc business (although it continued to make money from patent royalties). Philips went on to successfully launch the compact disc for audio playback in 1983, using the same technology with some modification as the laser disc.

Sony's U-matic (1969) and Betamax (1975) magnetic recorders had already changed the market by the time Laservision entered the field. These recorders gave the consumer additional options, and MCA had to compete by providing satisfactory programming. MCA rejected the cumbersome rental plan of Cartrivision. Because MCA owned Universal Studios and was a major owner of films, it was not timid about selling feature films. Universal supplied almost 25 percent of the initial 202 offerings in the Laservision catalogue. Paramount, Warner, and Disney also supplied a few feature films but confined their offerings to shows that had been out for at least six years. The studios were satisfied that laser technology eliminated home recording (although the more adventuresome owners could transfer a laser disc to a magnetic tape). However, this control of content proved to be a double-edged sword. MCA had to provide enough new titles to inspire the potential Laservision owner to buy the system. The catalogue might not seem large enough to prospective adopters.

An interesting drawback for discs was corporate policy on pornography. A major American corporation such as MCA could not be seen as a smut peddler. Therefore, it refused to transfer X-rated material to laser disc. Since anyone could set up to record on the VCRs, hard-core and soft-core pornographic shows soon became available on VHS and Betamax. This gave another edge to the competing magnetic recorders. VCR owners were perfectly willing to pay high prices for these shows and to arrange for rental networks that circulated X-rated material.

Pioneer of Japan was left to continue laser disc manufacturing, as it does to this day. One of the first changes Pioneer introduced after the departure of MCA in 1982 was to press movies with "X" ratings and eventually even hardcore titles.[40] The company found niche markets for Laservision, which is particularly popular in East Asia and Japan because of its use in karaoke bars and clubs.[41]

The final entry in the first group of playback-only systems was RCA. As the last arrival, RCA had the full benefit of learning from other companies. It also had the ultimately insurmountable challenge of competing with a quickly maturing video recorder market.

SELECTAVISION

RCA made a heavy investment in home playback systems that ultimately culminated in its "Selectavision VideoDisc." In the spring of 1964, the RCA labs decided to develop a practical and low-cost video recorder that would lead to a mass market. RCA accelerated its efforts to reach the consumer market when it heard rumors of CBS' EVR.[42] Meanwhile the original video leader, General Sarnoff, retired in 1969 and died two years later. The 1960s had been good, with consumers finally buying color TV en masse. At the end of the decade, after the departure of the general, RCA started to experience its first major market failures. For example, the success of transistor radio imports from Japan had alerted RCA to a new generation "on the go" for audio products. They became successfully involved with audio magnetic recorders and became part of a four-way deal to put eight-track audio cartridges into Ford and other American cars in 1965. Eight-track had a short but profitable life. In the 1970s, the eight-track cartridge steadily lost market share to the audiocassette tape. RCA also overreached with a heavy investment in audio quadraphonic sound in 1973, a format that appealed only to audiophiles and that was phased out five years later. The pressure was on to make another successful consumer item, hopefully a home video system. However, the video project suffered from the lack of the firm hand of David Sarnoff. There was now a degree of drift and lack of focus as RCA committed resources to

66   various magnetic tape recording systems and nonrecording disc systems, including both lasers and a capacitance reader.

During the various stops and starts that characterized the separate research programs, RCA executives told their researchers that the company
wanted effective control of the video machine. They wanted distribution of
the machines, and they wanted control of the content to be sold for use in
those machines. This strategy was a traditional component of RCA culture.
For instance, RCA did not introduce pieces of television piecemeal and did
not seek development cooperation from other research teams.[43] The company had been vindicated in its total approach when it introduced and sold a
complete television system ready for average consumer use.

RCA wished to make a similar complete system entry into home entertainment. However, complete system manufacturing was getting out of date,
since competitive electronic development was accelerating on a global basis.
The days when one company sold both the player and the content exclusively
were disappearing. Not only was the competition fiercer, the consumer was
more demanding, particularly about flexibility. Even record players featured
both LP and 45 formats within the same machine. In the realm of video,
RCA's internal surveys were revealing consumer resistance to playback-only.
In the late sixties, RCA executives could already read focus group summaries
saying that "respondents showed a strong preference for tape over records
because of its recording capability."

Despite the surveys, executives did not want a consumer video recorder.
The RCA development team could not work out the problems with their recording prototype: Magtape. When Sony was able to demonstrate to the public a recorder that was far more advanced than Magtape, internal company
support for developing recorders evaporated. Other executives cited new
studies that showed strong consumer interest in prerecorded material, and
downplayed recording systems.[44]

The gem of the RCA empire was consumer electronics, and the gem of
consumer electronics was the distribution system. Above all, the company
wished to keep feeding the distribution pipeline. The distribution outlook
colored the marketing outlook. RCA developed the comforting delusion that
the stores would make the added effort to convince their customers that playback-only was better than the VCR. They would do so in order to promote
their sale of video records. There was no compelling reason to assume that

store clerks would have such influence. Nonetheless, this belief sustained RCA's effort to introduce "Selectavision."

Delays had stretched the research program for years after General Sarnoff's demise, into the late 1970s. In addition to dropping work on magnetic tape, RCA also abandoned work on an optical system when the rival Laservision was revealed. By 1978, RCA had problems that they did not have at the start, particularly the strong presence of actual VCRs in the stores. How would they regain market advantage against the existing Betamax and VHS? RCA executives decided to compete on a price and convenience basis. The VCRs were retailing above $1,000 at this time. RCA established a target price of $400. RCA focused its efforts on a cheap yet reliable "capacitance" system that would be stored (similar to but not compatible with Laservision) on a plastic disc. All programming would have to be manufactured by RCA or its licensee.

The decisive points of competition for the Selectavision system would be the RCA distribution network, simplicity of operation, pricing, and finally, a wide selection of software for the system. In 1968, RCA estimated that an adequate library of software would cost at least $9 million. Within three years RCA scrapped the original planning as inadequate and announced that it would devote $50 million to purchase rights to film and other programs.[45] By the time Selectavision was in the final stages, cable, the VCR, and Laservision had raised the cost of programming further. As an example, in 1981 a package of eleven James Bond titles was estimated to cost RCA $2 million.[46] Nonetheless, RCA, like MCA, rejected advice to put non-mainstream "adult" material on its discs.

RCA finally began marketing Selectavision in March 1981. VCRs were now selling above $900. Selectavision was priced at $495 and was further discounted within two months.[47] Video recorders started coming down in price to cut into Selectavision sales (see Table 2.1, column 4). RCA's huge advertising campaign did not help Selectavision sales, although it was credited with raising consumer awareness of the video industry. The other systems were too well established and Selectavision could not sufficiently distinguish itself. Dealers complained that the 100 titles RCA was able to provide (priced from $15 to $28)[48] were not enough for the rollout in an already established market. The consensus was that it was too late. RCA struggled on until it closed Selectavision in April 1984, taking a total loss of $580 million.[49]

TABLE 2.1 Growth of U.S. Home Video, 1978–1992

Year	Cumulative manufactured VCRs* (thousands)	Cumulative VCRs purchased by U.S. dealers (thousands)	U.S. VCRs as percentage of U.S. TV households	Average wholesale price per unit of U.S. VCRs (dollars)
1978	2,232	402		811
1979	4,431	877		819
1980	8,872	1,682	2.40	771
1981	18,370	3,043	3.10	828
1982	31,504	5,078	5.70	640
1983	50,030	9,169	9.90	528
1984	79,464	16,785	17.60	471
1985	112,108	28,121	27.30	368
1986	148,624	40,126	37.20	331
1987	183,013	51,828	51.70	294
1988	219,970	62,576	62.20	259
1989	257,244	72,336	67.60	270
1990	296,182	82,455	70.20	241
1991	337,009	93,173	73.30	231
1992	371,109	105,502	75.60	239

*The production figures are global totals for U-matic, Betamax, and VHS.

SOURCES: Column 2–Electronic Industries Association of Japan, _Facts and Figures on the Japanese Electronics Industry_ (Tokyo, 1993). Columns 3 and 5–Electronic Industries Association, _The U.S. Consumer Electronics Industry in Review_ (Washington, D.C., 1993). Column 4–Motion Picture Association of America, _U.S. Economic Review_ (Encino, Calif., 1995).

At least the RCA distributors hedged their bets during the various delays of Selectavision. Feeding the pipeline was so important that RCA agreed to distribute the JVC/Matsushita Video Home System (VHS) magnetic recorder to the U.S. in 1977. This turned out to be quite fortuitous, as Selectavision flopped. Nonetheless, RCA was demoralized by a string of product failures, of which Selectavision was the last straw. Within two years, in 1986, General Electric took over the Radio Corporation of America.

There are several observations to be made about the failure of Selectavision, Cartrivision, and the weak sales of Laservision. American corporations had invested in playback-only systems. They were not naïve, as they proved by arranging to provide software even before their machines went to market. They were inspired by the thought that they would sell visual products the way record companies sell LPs and 45s. However, consumers wanted the greater flexibility of recording their own programs.

The straitened situation of the playback-only manufacturers resulted from the unique circumstances of the media scene in the United States. The various developers had different alliances with program suppliers. MCA owned Universal, a major film studio. Avco owned a minor one. CBS and RCA owned broadcast networks. All the American manufacturers operated in an environment where they were very sensitive to the needs of program suppliers and copyright owners. Peter Guber, early in his long career as a powerful Hollywood producer, articulated the creative community's feelings when he linked RCA's and CBS' fears of piracy and prime time audience erosion with their interest in playback-only video.[50] American media companies were torn between their anticipation of a new market and the loss of control of programs.

Magnetic technology had already subverted control in the music industry. While bootleg vinyl records had been a small-scale problem in the early years of rock'n'roll, unauthorized taping and selling of illegally copied audiocassettes grew along with the adoption of cassette recorders. By 1970, Jack Smith of Warner–Reprise Records was complaining that tape bootleggers were netting $130 million in U.S. sales.[51] His estimate was considered high. In any case, not all bootlegged tapes displaced legitimate sales. Nonetheless, copyright holders were concerned that piracy hovered at around 5 percent of U.S. recorded music sales. The film community knew that the public played music over and over again, whereas they generally went to a movie only once. But the film community could not predict whether this difference would safeguard video from the piracy that was occurring in music. Therefore, there was a general Hollywood inclination to maintain control and to take a "go-slow" approach to transferring films from the theater to the home. Film distributors had become cautious. If they had to change technologies of distribution, they should at least favor a technology that would not bestow recording capabilities.

But as we have seen, playback technology was not adequate for success in the American market. Both Japanese and American consumers favored recording machines, and this gave recorders a global advantage since these countries were the most influential. Playback-only machines might have had greater success if Northern Europe had been the largest market. In Northern Europe, audience members wanted machines that expanded program choices beyond the limited fare offered by their public broadcast systems. They were

70   less interested in time-shifting than in prerecorded tapes. The Dutch Philips and the German Telefunken responded with videodisc machines. Philips also came to the market with a magnetic video machine called the V-2000, and established a market share in Europe. However, even Northern Europe embraced the Betamax/VHS juggernaut as the Japanese firms gained global ascendancy.

Home Video 2: Japanese Recorder System Development

Many companies decided to try various approaches to home video recording machines after the Ampex demonstration of 1956. In 1958, the Japanese Ministry of International Trade and Industry (MITI) initiated coordinated talks between various national firms on developing video recording.[52] Toshiba improved the video recorder by introducing helical scanning in 1959. Ampex tried to maintain its invention by pursuing both legal suits and cooperative agreements with its Japanese competitors. Sony signed one such agreement and was able to introduce a video recorder in 1961. Ampex did not show the same sustained interest in the mass market as the Japanese firms, although it did place a "consumer" recorder on sale in the Neiman Marcus department store for $30,000 in 1963.[53] The Sony/Ampex agreement soon dissolved.

Sony plunged ahead, introducing the first ½-inch recording system in 1965. It was called the Portapack and used open reel tapes that cost $60 for an hour. The unit itself cost $995; the camera cost another $350 and was only capable of black-and-white recording. The Portapack was designed for personal and home taping. Because of this intended usage, it ran into direct competition from the Super 8mm film system that had just been introduced by Kodak. The familiar technology of photography and the lightweight camera made Super 8 popular. Despite the advantage of easily marrying sound and image, the Portapack had limited sales. It was more expensive than Super 8. It was not very portable due to its backbreaking weight. It was hard to edit, and its black-and-white image was a further deterrent, as color television had become standard by this time.

Sony switched to cassette packaging and to color for its next video product: the ¾-inch cassette U-matic system in 1969. The U-matic was the result of an agreement between Sony, Matsushita, and its independent subsidiary, the Japan Victor Company (JVC), to cooperate on the specifications of the machine. The price tag of $2,500 in 1969 prohibited many consumer sales. Sony succeeded in marketing the unit to broadcasters, some educational and industrial customers. This marked the second stage of the video market. The market grew slowly and Sony dominated the modest pace of sales. Matsushita and JVC grew to resent Sony's success, since they were not enjoying comparable sales. These frustrations would come back to haunt Sony when Matsushita and JVC decided not to cooperate with Sony on the Betamax in the third stage of VCR development.

Both JVC and Sony kept trying to expand U-matic sales by positioning it as a source of entertainment. They hoped that production would be specifically undertaken for the new video medium, but in the short run they realized that a video system would not be adapted unless preexisting programming was made available. Time–Life, which had a film division at this time, started marketing cassettes in 1972.[54] Sony had some half-hearted talks with Hollywood studios about licensing their films for the U-matic format, but these talks were not fruitful.[55] Commentators questioned whether customers would ever buy prerecorded U-matic tapes since the blank tapes alone cost $12–$26. Sony responded with the idea that the customer reuse the same tape by bringing it back to a dealer who would erase the original program and record another selection. However, that system was not implemented. One development, which undoubtedly Sony was not publicly aware of, was the increasing use of U-matics for pornography arcades. Noel Bloom, working in California, as well as other operators, found U-matics easier than film loops to run in these arcades. Bloom's company would emerge into a major independent video distributor in subsequent stages of the VCR.

As Sony kicked around these ideas for video programming, it developed the idea that a video recorder could be used as a complement to the television, as a "time shifter." The video recorder could be programmed to record a program from the television when the owner was not present. The owner would then possess the recorded program and could play it back at a more convenient time. Sony decided to introduce this novel feature in a new 1/2-inch version of the U-matic recorder, to be called the Betamax.

SONY AND BETAMAX

The corporate culture at Sony was conducive to the relentless search for a video mass market (the third stage of VCR development). The company was founded in the aftermath of World War II as a newcomer seeking a foothold in the devastated Japanese electronics industry. Sony gained strength by concentrating on the consumer market, particularly by emphasizing miniaturization. Its first product was a small audiotape recorder. It was so cheap that the tape was made from paper. It went on to achieve global prominence with the transistor radio. After this breakthrough the company accelerated. By the time of the video developments of the sixties, it had captured substantial market shares in color and portable television set sales.

Sony's very definite ideas about how to pursue the consumer market were articulated by its spokesperson and leader, Akio Morita, in his autobiography:

> In the fifties and sixties, popular programs in the United States and later in Japan caused people to change their schedules. People would hate to miss their favorite shows. I noticed how the TV networks had total control over people's lives and I felt that people should have the option of seeing a program when they chose.[56]

Engineers at Sony's rival, Japan Victor Company, also cited dissatisfaction with the control of monopolistic television programming as inspiration for their video systems. At JVC, the senior engineer was an early television inventor, Kenjiro Takayanagi. He regretted the path that television had taken and disliked network broadcasting. Although he had little to do with the day-to-day development of JVC's recorder, his insistence that the consumer be able to record his or her own images drove JVC's consumer video recording engineering.[57]

Sony went ahead to create the Betamax. They basically shrank the U-matic down to a $\frac{1}{2}$-inch format. Morita was convinced that a key to success was a cassette the size of a pocketbook. This cassette could hold about one hour's worth of recordings. Sony sought the same cooperation from Matsushita and JVC that the three companies had had on the $\frac{3}{4}$-inch VCR, but they were not forthcoming. JVC plunged ahead in a deliberately competitive development project that it called "VHS," for "video home system." Under pressure from JVC, Sony increased the capacity of the Betamax cassette tape to two hours to try to win the format battle. Matsushita, the largest Japanese electronics firm, nonetheless decided to back JVC's VHS. It was now a format war.

Sony went to the market first, introducing the Betamax to the world in 1975. It sold 55,000 Betamax units to American dealers in 1976 with a $1,300 suggested retail price. But VHS was breathing down its neck. Matsushita sought out a powerful U.S. distributor and went into talks with RCA. RCA had previously rejected a Sony offer because Sony refused to let RCA put its name on the machines and because Sony wanted too much money.[58] Matsushita was flexible on both points and, in turn, RCA made a small suggestion that turned out to make a key difference. Since time shifting was the selling point and a major consumer frustration was the inability to watch sports games in their entirety at scheduled times, why not adjust the machine accordingly? RCA told Matsushita that a four-hour tape would nicely cover the length of a televised football game.[59] Matsushita went back to JVC, which obliged with a four-hour VHS cassette. In 1977, RCA started marketing the VHS in the U.S. at a price $300 less than the Betamax. Other distributors handled the global rollout of the VHS in that year.

Although Zenith, the U.S. distributor of Betamax, quickly matched the price cut, Sony had lost market dominance in both the U.S. and worldwide to VHS by 1978. In that year 402,000 VCR units were sold to U.S. dealers. There were 1,470,000 units manufactured in Japan. At this point, the struggle between VHS and Betamax was waged by distribution strengths and the perceived value of VHS's four-hour tape length. Betamax still had a viable market share. The introduction of Laservision in 1978 led to further decline in prices for both VCR formats. Laservision tried to compete based on price, availability of feature films, better freeze frames, and random access, but the lack of recording was decisive. VCR prices started to creep up again because of pressure on the Japanese yen, but the 1981 rollout of Selectavision forced another wave of price slashing for the VCR in the following year.

Sony had successfully introduced the video machine to consumers all over the world, initiating the third stage of home video. Sony had made the breakthrough for video when it became the first manufacturer to make the time-shifting function the central focus of its promotion campaign. Morita claims that the term "time shifting" was his own coinage. Was Sony the very first to realize that time shifting would motivate consumer video sales? Philips had announced in 1971 that it would install a timer in its recorder to facilitate such usage. Even earlier, Cartrivision had the capability of recording broadcasts off the air. However, these companies only mentioned recording broadcast shows as one feature among many. When Sony introduced the Betamax in 1975, Morita made sure that "time shifting" was prominently featured in a hard-hitting advertising campaign.

However, Sony's success was not complete. The format war between Beta-max and VHS became a "winner take all" situation, and its aftermath haunted the electronics landscape in the following decades. The media industry had seen format competition before, such as in recorded music between Edison's waxed cylinder and Berliner's disc in the first part of the century and between 45s and LPs more recently. In the first case, the two formats managed to coexist profitably for a least a decade. In the latter case, the formats were more complementary than competitive. Video formats, on the other hand, had great trouble coexisting. The Betamax survived only as a professional tool, while the laser disc never rose to even 6 percent of the VCR market (in either machine or content sales) for any year from 1978 through 1993.

The popular media portrayed Sony as a loser in the Betamax / VHS fight, although the irony is that Betamax helped the company immensely. Sony's video profits were considerable. For example, VCR sales contributed 41 per-cent of Sony's 1981 earnings.[60] The video revenue financed the company's dominance in portable cassette players ("Walkman") and compact audio discs markets through the 1980s. Despite the profits, Sony decided Betamax was no longer viable after about eight years. The last growth year for both Beta-max and VHS was 1984. By the end of that year, 68 million households in the world had either one or the other format.[61] Together, both formats earned $8.8 billion that year.[62] However, Sony's share was only one-fifth of the market.[63]

In 1985 Sony started cutting back and phasing out production of the Be-tamax. By 1988, mass manufacturing of the Betamax had stopped, although it continued for professional and semiprofessional uses. The conventional wisdom was that Sony would not be able to find a stable market and coexist, but would face sales that would soon dwindle to nothing. This was not be-cause of inherent qualities of the machine. After the initial period, Betamax could match the VHS features on length, price, and so forth, and many ex-perts argued the Betamax was superior in technical qualities, particularly image reproduction.

VHS took over the entire market when the purchase and rental of prere-corded tapes became as important if not more important than recording pro-grams off the television. Sony tried to license unique prerecorded programs for the Betamax format such as music videos (see Chapter 4), but this effort was meaningless. New purchasers would naturally select the format that gave them the widest access to prerecorded tapes in addition to time shifting. Because VHS was already the biggest, all new programs were sure to be offered in that format, while only the companies that could afford additional Betamax duplication would bother to do so. The customer therefore chose the VHS system on the basis of external considerations, not intrinsic ones. This type of competition is called "network externalities." It defines the fourth phase of the home video revolution. The fear of "network" competition has shaped new media products since the 1970s. The VHS–Betamax format war was the last one fought out in the marketplace. Manufacturers have sought industry-wide cooperation on every audio and video innovation offered since. Network competition continues to be a determining factor in computer software economics.

The history of home video technology was a succession of cultural shifts that started with the abandonment of network hostility toward recording technology. Gould, Goldmark, and perhaps Sarnoff had early visions of home video as an extension of and a corrective for television programming. Another vision was of home video as an extension of the movie theater, and this motivated Laservision, Selectavision, and Cartrivision. However, Akio Morita of Sony and Kenjiro Takayanagi of JVC stayed with the original idea that home video would sell on the mass market as an extension of television. Nonetheless, the competition between Betamax and VHS was decided on the basis of video as an extension of the movie theater.

This technological history raises legitimate questions about the audience's evolution. Why did affluent classes, in America and throughout the world, pick the VCR over its rivals? It seems that the audience demanded video as both a TV extender and as a movie player. They were driving the media convergence between film and television. This opened up new institutional opportunities. In the next chapter, we will look at the possible sociological explanation for audience preferences and the slow response of the film industry to the audience desire to rent prerecorded videocassettes.

CHAPTER THREE

Home Video:
The Early Years

The success of the VHS was a revelation about the evolving U.S. audience. Unfortunately for several corporations, U.S. executives did not accurately predict audience response to the VHS. For example, RCA executives swapped contradictory or inconclusive focus group summaries as they tried to build a consensus for the playback-only Selectavision. The fact that they dismissed some summaries as inconclusive shows how hard it is to know the audience before the fact. As it turned out, the audience embraced the VHS despite contrary predictions. Indeed, the development and eventual success of the VHS provides as good a controlled experiment as is possible in media history. After all, VHS and Selectavision both shared the same mighty RCA distribution system within the U.S. If there was any hometown advantage, it should have favored the American playback-only machines. Yet, the recording machines won out.

The media historian is obliged to ask why one technology was favored by the public despite institutional backing for another technology. The answer lies with the evolving behavior of the audience. American viewers had been watching television for two decades. Their global counterparts had been doing so almost as long. After two decades they were willing to spend money in order to get beyond the mere passive viewing of whatever was on the set when they turned it on. They wanted to be able to choose when to see the program, where to see the program, and/or which program to see. The consumer's willingness to buy a technology of "choices" was undoubtedly driven by changes emerging as the affluent classes struggled to maintain their increasingly suburban lifestyles. In other words, broad macrosociological factors tipped the format competition in favor of the VCR. The most important of these factors was and continues to be "harried" leisure, a function of changing work and family schedules as the labor force grew.

Choice, "Harried" Leisure, and New Technologies

There are two arguments that link harried leisure and choice. The harried leisure phenomenon emerged in most affluent countries during the last two decades of the twentieth century. The emphasis on consumer choice coincided with a rise in the perception that even prosperous America was losing its battle for more free time. Indeed in the late sixties, economists Gary Becker and Staffan Linder argued that consumer choice contributes to time loss. Linder coined the term "harried leisure" to denote the time squeeze caused by rising affluence.[1] There were too many interesting activities competing for the few hours of leisure one had each week. People felt that their leisure was stressed because they had too many toys to play with. At this point, harried leisure was a problem of abundance, not of shrinking time.

Juliet Schor makes another argument linking choice to lost leisure time by turning the Becker/Linder thesis on its head. It is not that we have too many "toys" to play with. It is that we spend too many hours working in order to afford to buy the toys. We are working more than ever because we feel obliged to keep up our seemingly "affluent" consumerist lifestyle. Our notion of affluence becomes self-defeating since we have sacrificed our time and health in order to achieve it. She states that in the U.S. the average number of hours spent at work have been increasing since 1969.[2]

This is an oversimplification of her argument. There are several reasons (in addition to buying leisure technology) for more people working longer hours since 1969. The American and other leading economies had to readjust to successive shocks of the early 1970s such as oil price hikes and rising inflation. The most radical readjustment was the growth in the number of families with two working parents. For these and associated reasons, leisure time became a precious commodity.

The percentage of Americans working increased by slightly more than one-fifth from 1960 to 1985. The most dramatic change in leisure was the rising percentage of women working in the paid labor force. It had been rising since 1950 and accelerated after 1960. Table 3.1 shows that between 1960 and

TABLE 3.1 Trends for Women in U.S. Labor Force (in thousands), 1950–1993

Population	1950	1960	1970	1980	1985	1990	1993
Total population	152,271	180,671	205,051	227,738	238,740	248,239	259,364
Female population	76,422	91,352	104,697	116,864	122,579	127,258	132,730
Total labor force	65,178	73,171	87,222	109,872	117,167	123,869	129,525
Female labor force	18,433	23,243	31,845	45,743	51,200	56,030	58,563

SOURCE: International Labour Office, *Economically Active Populations: Estimates and Projections 1950–2025* (Geneva, 1985, 1990, 1993).

1970, 8.6 million more women started working out of the home. Table 3.2 indicates the percentage of women working by 1970 was 20 percent greater than ten years before. The feminization of the labor force and other sociological trends increased the nomadization of the U.S. audience. Family routines were changing. Suburban lifestyles featured decentralized activities that necessitated more time in the car. Having two working partners within a marriage, if it did not change the division of household labor, at least changed the timing and ways of doing domestic chores. The audience was mobile.

Schor based her arguments on two measures, the number of people working and the number of hours worked. While the first measure is uncontroversial, some observers have disputed the absolute decline in leisure hours that Schor has measured. The most vigorous disputants are Robinson and Godbey, whose studies show leisure hours have been increasing even since the 1970s. However, even they have to report that, in 1992, the number of Americans who *felt* that they had less free time was up 22 percent from 1971.[3] A 1995 Lou Harris poll asked how much time people had for themselves in 1995 compared to the 1970s. The respondents reported a decline in the number of weekly leisure hours, from 26.2 in 1973 to 19.2 in 1995.[4]

The strict measurement of the dichotomy between work time and free time does not capture the subjective experience of leisure, however. People report that time-saving appliances are anything but time saving, such as the washer/dryer that makes washing more convenient and therefore we wash

TABLE 3.2 Women in the U.S. Labor Force, 1950–1993

Population	1950	1960	1970	1980	1985	1990	1993
Labor as percentage of total population	42.8	40.5	42.5	48.2	49.1	49.9	49.9
Female labor as percentage of total female population	24.1	25.4	30.4	39.1	41.8	44.0	44.1
Female labor as percentage of total labor population	28.3	31.8	36.5	41.6	43.7	45.2	45.2

SOURCE: International Labour Office, *Economically Active Populations: Estimates and Projections 1950–2025* (Geneva, 1985, 1990, 1993).

more often, exhausting the saved time. Simple tasks such as going to school, picking up a quart of milk, or playing a neighborhood baseball game now involve the logistics of driving longer and longer distances. More single people have to perform individually tasks that only one member of a large household needs to do. Therefore the decline of the domestic household size—from 3.33 persons per unit in 1960 to 2.63 in 1990—is another reason for the decline in an efficient division of household labor.[5] It is to be expected that people will report the subjective reality of losing control over their free time. In terms of social impact, Robinson and Godbey, Harris, and Schor all agree—we are used to a level of efficiency in the use of our work time, and we regret that our leisure time does not have the same efficiency. It is surprising to desire efficiency in leisure, and yet that is what we are expressing when we complain about time squandered rushing here and there without enjoyment. Whether Americans are actually experiencing the loss of free time or just think they are, there are important consequences for media usage. There is a direct connection between the subjective experience of harried leisure and the consumer desire to own a VCR.

The VCR promised choice, which has been one of the key selling points of contemporary retailing. Choice can be between more products (TV shows, rented movies), but choice can, in the case of the VCR, also be between now and later—when to watch these media products. Product choice has been a central tenet of American marketing strategies. As the postwar lifestyle matured, brand proliferation accelerated. Companies put increased efforts into coming up with different brands to inspire consumer curiosity and to capture increased shelf space in retail stores. In the five years from 1968 to 1972, there

80   was a 34 percent increase in the number of advertised brands.[6] A 1993 study
found that a typical supermarket stocked twice as many items in 1989 as it
did in 1979.[7] Both the VCR and the playback-only systems promised prerecorded movies or, in retail terms, more movies on the shelf, paralleling brand
proliferation in other items. Home video could be viewed as part of a seam-
less effort to increase the "channel capacity" of the average home, alongside
cable and satellite systems.

However, the emphasis on product choice misses an important point of
Morita's time-shifting campaign. The reason Sony's campaign worked while
Laservision and Selectavision failed was that the Betamax gave two kinds of
choices at once. It gave not only *more* choices over what movies and television shows to watch but also over *when* to watch the shows. This was a new
and decisive form of consumer control over TV programming. This is why
the VCR did not become a mere transition instrument as the market moved
toward a cheaper and better videodisc system. The combination of product
choice and time flexibility was sufficient to make it ideal for a new lifestyle of
more work and shifting schedules. It was also an instrument of flexibility for
household members to watch their own programs in their own time, separate
from the other members of the household.[8] The VCR fit in with the new, fragmented patterns of family life.

We should have these distinctions in mind as we examine the interwoven
histories of cable and home video. Concurrent with the rise in home video
entertainment was the opening up of cable television. There were subtle but
crucial differences. Cable promised greater choice of product than conventional TV, although the reality of more programs took a while to catch up with
the promises during the early 1980s. Cable was less suitable than video for
those seeking control over their time. Cable, of course, offered many repeat
broadcasts. However, it could not approach the convenience of popping in
the videotape precisely when one wanted to or stopping the tape in order to
attend to other errands. Many also found the continuing cost of a cable subscription to be a burden, while video involves only a cost per viewing after
the initial hardware purchase. For these reasons cable became an "also ran"
behind video. By two different measures, the rate of consumer adoption and
the amount of money program suppliers (i.e., the film companies) earned
from cable, cable had fallen behind the VCR by 1984 and has since stayed
behind.

The Emergence of Cable

The commercial application of cable has been around since 1950. In those earlier days, a cable operator charged subscribers for the relay of an improved television signal. It was usually set up in hilly regions suffering from poor reception, such as Eastern Pennsylvania or Southern California. Cable systems had excess capacity beyond just relaying the local station signals, and soon there were attempts to send additional programming, even if it just consisted of a camera trained on a news ticker tape. Community access television, as cable was known in that period, did not fit easily into the jurisdictional categories of telecommunications policymakers. Were these companies mere relayers of a broadcast signal or the commercial distributors of copyrighted material? The Federal Communications Commission displayed its own mixed feelings by issuing regulations that treated cable alternately as a common carrier and as a broadcaster.

The additional programming became a policy challenge and a source of a twenty-year struggle. In the beginning of the television era, the FCC felt under some pressure to protect the "fledging" broadcast networks. As late as 1966 the FCC was still faithful to this motivation and therefore bowed to pressure from broadcasters and the movie industry to limit the cable distribution of programming from distant areas. An FCC ruling also effectively stopped cable programmers from showing current movies. Various groups opposed FCC policies because they wanted more from television than the "wasteland" of the three networks. They called for more access to more stations, and for increased diversity in programming. It was these groups that achieved the creation of a public broadcast network in 1967 with modest federal government support. On the non-broadcast side, access and diversity advocates embraced new technologies such as cable. Some of these hopes were embodied in the 1971 Sloan Commission on Cable Communications report.

In the aftermath of the Sloan report, various government officials felt compelled to open cable up to be a source of more programming. The FCC began some deregulating with a new set of cable rules in 1972. In 1977, the District of Columbia appeals court struck down FCC restrictions against cablecasting current movies in the *Home Box Office v. FCC* case. These were the years when cable matured into a mass medium, in large part due to the changed policy environment. The industry attracted the enormous invest-

82   ments needed to build more systems and gain a wider audience. There were
       6 million subscribers in 1972; by 1978 the number of subscribers had more
       than doubled to 13 million.[9] The pace of cable construction also accelerated
       from $126 million per year in 1975 to $1.2 billion per year in 1980.[10]

       The film community made little response when Charles Dolan initiated
       Home Box Office (HBO) in 1972 for a cable system owned by the publishing
       giant Time, Inc. As the pace of cable development accelerated in the next few
       years, HBO grew rapidly. In September 1975 HBO became the first program-
       mer to distribute its signals by satellite when it showed the Ali–Frazier box-
       ing match live from Manila in the Philippines. Ted Turner, the owner of At-
       lanta television station WTBS, also decided to distribute his station's signal
       via satellite to cable systems throughout the country at this time, creating
       the first "superstation." Satellite distribution proved to be a tremendous ad-
       vantage for both HBO and WTBS, making both national centers for the
       distribution of filmed entertainment, sports, and other programs. Nineteen
       seventy-five became the year of the VCR, and satellite distribution of cable
       movies. Cable and home video were now in direct competition for audience
       and for programming.

       The VCR entered a media landscape that was already in flux due to the
       large-scale commitment to build up cable capacity. Both technologies became
       part of an American ethos of consumer choice. The challenge for the Holly-
       wood majors was to make sure that consumer choice meant new revenues for
       their products. This was a simpler task in cable than in home video, since
       Hollywood did not lose control of its films in the cable market. In the cable
       market, the studios leased their films for a flat fee, a per-viewer rate, or a
       combination of the two.

       ### The Universal Lawsuit

       The mantra of the VCR was "giving choice back to the people." The defini-
       tion of "choice" changed according to geography. The United States and Ja-
       pan had a relatively greater variety of television programming than the rest
       of the world. In Western Europe, the state-controlled systems often had aus-
       tere selections of various forms of popular entertainment. In other regions,
       government censorship frustrated the desires of local residents to see the
       kinds of movies and programs they had become familiar with on their trav-
       els. Therefore, the choice these purchasers sought with their VCRs was a

larger selection of programs. Japanese and American locals suffered relatively 83
less from these frustrations; rather, they suffered from time constraints. In
these two countries—the largest markets for the VCR—video publicists
pitched the VCR as a corrective to the rigid schedules of television and a
challenge to the status quo. Certain members of the status quo decided to answer the challenge.

Sony's advertising agency, Doyle, Dane, and Bernbach (DD&B), fulfilled
Morita's desire to promote the Betamax as a "subversive" machine that would
take control away from programmers and give it back to the consumers.
DD&B had revolutionized Madison Avenue with the so-called creative revolution of the 1960s. This revolution asserted that advertising was an art form
that could appeal to the consumer by upsetting conventional beliefs and associations. The agency was famous for selling products such as the Volks-
wagen automobile and Levy rye bread by emphasizing nonconformity. DD&B
had fun with its themes of customer empowerment. DD&B staff constructed
a similar campaign for the Betamax, featuring a big "x" over a TV schedule
in the visual and the copy line "What in the world are we doing to ourselves?
Our lives are being governed to too great an extent by TV schedules."[11]

MCA's number two executive, Sidney Sheinberg, the president of the Universal division, had read the Betamax ads and was not amused. MCA decided
not to accept the Betamax revolution passively. On November 11, 1976, Universal City Studios, Inc. (the wholly owned film-distributing subsidiary of
MCA) filed a suit against Sony Corporation of America; Doyle, Dane, and
Bernbach; several Betamax retailers; and one Betamax user. Disney Productions was the co-plaintiff. DD&B would go to the Supreme Court as a reward
for its wit.

The lawsuit, essentially, was an attack on home taping. The plaintiffs did
not consider the rental of videotape, which was not a prominent activity in
1976. As the court case continued for the next eight years in tandem with
the growth of video rental, Universal and Disney did not and could not cite
rental activity. The 1976 Copyright Act was clear on the legality of renting
copyrighted material; the only redress for such activities was legislative (see
Chapter 4). The plaintiffs' argument in this case was based primarily on time
shifting.

Why had Universal, of all the MPAA members, taken the lead position
against Sony's promotion of time shifting?[12] MCA/Universal collected far
more revenue from television in 1976 than its rivals. It received $213.4 mil-

84   lion—27 percent of its total revenues and 46 percent of its filmed entertainment revenues. Columbia came in a distant second with $87.1 million in that same year.[13] Disney's motivations had an added element. The company had built itself up by producing a full library of children's shows, ranging from cartoon shorts to full-length animations. Films for young children are uniquely timeless because they can be renewed every seven to ten years for a new generation of children who have not yet experienced the originals. In the media of theatrical films and television, Walt Disney Studios had developed an expertise in timing the theatrical rerelease or repeat broadcast of its shows in order to ensure maximum profits. A new generation of children could always discover—after their parents purchased the price of admission—the timeless appeal of *Snow White and the Seven Dwarfs* (since its 1937 release), etc. If people could now tape and own cassettes of these movies or of the repeat episodes of the Disney television offerings, how would these titles retain their value in rerelease or repeat broadcasts? Disney executives were naturally concerned over a technology that eroded their ability to release and withdraw products from the market in order to wait for the next generation.

The chronology of the Universal lawsuit is as follows. The November 1976 initial filing was in the Federal District Court of the Central District of California. Judge Warren Ferguson heard the case and ruled against Universal et al. in October 1979. Universal appealed and won a relatively quick reversal from the U.S. Appeals Court for the Ninth Circuit in October 1981. Sony went on with the case, and on January 17, 1984 the U.S. Supreme Court reversed the appeals court and sustained Judge Ferguson's original decision, with five justices voting for Sony, and four dissenting.

Although the final decision now seems to have an air of inevitability, the judicial history shows that Universal had launched a formidable challenge that nearly succeeded. It is reported that after the first hearings the majority of the Supreme Court was inclined toward Universal; but Justice Stevens raised several objections.[14] Justice Brennan switched to Sony's side and the undecided also rallied around to give the manufacturer the edge. The Sony win is one of the rare instances when the government or the court did not take the opportunity to extend copyright protection in the current era of new technologies.

The Universal/Disney team chose their plaintiffs in order to direct their attack on the manufacturer of the VCR rather than the users. While Sony was an easier political target than the average U.S. television and movie viewer, this focus weakened their argument just enough to ruin their case. After all, Sony was not systematically engaged in taping Universal or Disney shows, although Universal did manage to find several Sony dealers doing just that in their showrooms to demonstrate their VCRs. These dealers became defendants in the lawsuit. The final defendant was an individual who had taped Universal shows off the air and was willing to testify that he had been inspired to do so by the Sony advertisements promoting time shifting.

Universal streamlined its argument to two principal points. The first point was that home taping did not pass the "fair use" test for exemptions from infringement. The second point was that Sony was contributing to the infringement by making reproducing machines. The plaintiffs argued that actual damage from copyright infringement did not have to be proved in order to seek redress, only potential damage. The Universal argument went beyond home video. It was an opening round in reformulating copyright for new media. If only for that reason, we need to examine the concept of fair use and contributory infringement.

FAIR USE

Fair use as an exemption test had existed in case law since 1841.[15] This means that it was a concept judges stated and elaborated as they wrestled with the conflicting claims of copyright, free speech, and privacy over the years. It was not written into actual law until the 1976 revision of the Copyright Act, which identified four tests for fair use: (1) the purpose and character of the use, (2) the nature of the copyrighted work, (3) the amount of the work that was copied, and (4) the economic impact of copying.[16] The criteria for the test still left a lot of room for interpretation.

Home taping was a particularly vexing problem for fair use since the character of its use and its economic impact were not publicly visible. Congress had briefly considered home taping in its debates about the 1976 law. An exchange occurred in 1971 where Rep. Robert Kastenmeier (D-Wisconsin), one of the leading congressional authorities on copyright, specified that home taping audio for private listening was fair use.[17] Universal explained to the court that his remarks were meant to be specific to audio and did not extend to movies and that visual material had received special consideration from Congress.

86   The plaintiffs then proceeded to make their economic impact argument about videotaping. Universal could not present figures on actual lost sales to the district court. The audience does not make actual payments for Universal shows in commercial broadcasting. It is the *value* that the audience itself creates that is bought by advertisers and sold by programmers. Constructions of this value are based on ratings that are indirect measures of the audience. The program suppliers, the television distributors (the networks), and the advertisers agree to accept these indirect measures as the basis on which to exchange billions of dollars that approximate the value of the audiences. Universal made a twofold argument that the VCRs were eroding the value of its shows: (1) The VCR might cause actual effective audience erosion if tapers shared their libraries and refused to see subsequent repeat broadcasts of the show. (2) Time shifting might cause the broadcasting and advertising communities to value the audience for Universal programs less than formerly. This is because advertisers would presume that VCR owners were using tape machines to avoid commercial breaks. In other words, the VCR would allow demographically targeted affluent audiences to "escape" advertisers.

Advertisers expressed concern about the effect of the VCR on the programming strategies that the networks had perfected through the 1970s. A spokesperson for the J. Walter Thompson ad agency noted that "[time shifting] in itself tends to undermine the elaborate network programming schedules (complete with lead-ins, cradling of 'soft' programs around popular ones and skedding [scheduling] of competing 'blockbusters') as viewers record shows (often while watching another) for subsequent viewing."[18]

Jack Valenti, the president of the MPAA and an indefatigable lobbyist for the major studios, trotted out a variant of this argument every chance he got. He testified that allowing night workers to tape an 8:00 P.M. show for a 2:00 A.M. viewing "would harm the producers and sponsors of those programs, who were 'directly targeting to people who are working at night.'"[19] He told Congress that Frito-Lay, TWA, Gillette, and Coca-Cola were just some of the more prominent advertisers concerned about the VCR.[20] It seemed a small point for multi-million-dollar corporations to complain that they were losing value because someone was viewing the sponsored program at 2 A.M. instead of at the scheduled 8 P.M. time slot. However, this nit-picking expressed both the abstractions on which commercial television was built and the fine gossamer out of which those abstractions were woven. The whole art of television advertising consisted of reaching the viewers desired by the advertiser. Surveys suggested that the viewers reached by time shifting were different from those viewers watching the same program at its scheduled time. It was the dedicated loyal fan who watched a show on playback. The more casual viewer was lost to the advertiser through time shifting. A husband and wife would watch the scheduled *L.A. Law* because there was nothing else to do at that moment. But if the wife taped *L.A. Law*, she would play it back when the husband was not watching television. The sponsors of *L.A. Law* had lost the husband's "eyeballs." In addition, if she was watching the tape, she was no longer available to watch *Dallas* or some other program during its scheduled time. The VCR was allowing the audience to become nomadic, upsetting the billion-dollar industry devoted to pinning it down.

Another source of audience erosion that Universal presented to the court came from the ability of the VCR owner to avoid commercial breaks in the programming. Universal described how the audience could avoid the advertising that had paid for the program by either zapping commercials (stopping the recording of commercial breaks) or more effectively by zipping commercials (fast forwarding through the advertisements while playing back the recorded program). The evidence that Universal presented of this effective erosion did not impress the district court or the majority of the Supreme Court. Judge Ferguson wrote as if zipping was an acceptable hazard of doing business. "Advertisers will have to make the same kinds of judgments they do now about whether persons viewing televised programs actually watch the advertisements which interrupt them."[21]

The questions of responsibilities and damages were elusive on both sides of the issue. The plaintiffs' damages argument was not a view shared by all television executives. In the late 1970s, *Television Digest's* editorial director David Lachenbruch interviewed the programming heads of the ABC, CBS, and NBC networks. They did not express apprehension about the effect of the VCR on the business of broadcast television, "considering the Betamax to be just another consumer appliance, 'like a toaster.'"[22] Sony lined up many program producers, notably Fred Rogers of *Mister Rogers' Neighborhood*, who welcomed the VCR as a machine that would expand his program's audience. When the Supreme Court finally reached a majority, it was because five justices decided to concur with the district court's impatience with the hypothetical nature of the damages the plaintiff presented. Judge Ferguson of the district court had summarized the plaintiffs' admission of the intangibility of time-shifting damages:

88   Plaintiffs' experts admitted at several points in the trial that the time-
            shifting without librarying would result in "not a great deal of harm."
            Plaintiffs' greatest concern about time-shifting is with "a point of im-
            portant philosophy that transcends even commercial judgment." They
            fear that with any Betamax usage, "invisible boundaries" are passed:
            "the copyright owner has lost control over his program."[23]

The phrase "invisible boundaries" was too vague for the district court and
the Supreme Court.

CONTRIBUTORY INFRINGEMENT

As far as the court was concerned, the plaintiffs were overly concerned about
the future. Meanwhile the buyers of the VCR were in the here and now and
growing by the moment. The popularity of the machine made Sony the sen-
timental favorite. The VCR lawsuit was constantly being ridiculed in the press
for the notion that every ordinary VCR owner was a time-shifting criminal.
For this reason, Universal sought redress only from the manufacturer. There
was a foreign precedent for this kind of compensation. In 1965, West German
copyright holders went to court to complain about audio recorders leading to
infringement by individual users. The court agreed to the complaint but did
not accept the proposed relief, that a society representing copyright holders
would collect fees from individual users. The court expressed concern that
this would violate privacy rights. The copyright holders sought and obtained
a legislative solution. A law was passed in that year that was the first in the
world to impose a royalty fee to be collected on the sale of recording equipment. The collected fees would be redistributed to copyright holders to
"compensate" them for the possible infringing (home taping) for which the
equipment would be used.[24] In the following decades several other countries
imposed similar fees.

   In order for Universal to win a similar solution in an American court, its
lawyers decided to argue that Sony had contributed to copyright infringement. This was perhaps the weakest part of its case. It forced Universal to argue only about the use of the VCR that Sony was promoting: time shifting.
The plaintiffs did not introduce issues of video piracy and public playing of
recorded tapes since they could not claim that Sony had promoted such activities and thus contributed to infringement.[25] Contributory infringement

therefore constricted Universal's ability to complain about the VCR. But it is hard to imagine that there was any alternative judicial argument that would have allowed a program supplier to seek redress against a manufacturer.

Contributory infringement was at the heart of one of those earlier copyright disputes that helped shape the growth of the film industry.[26] In 1911 the Supreme Court found that the Kalem Company, a film production company, had infringed the copyright of *Ben Hur*, a literary property, by making a film with the same title and plotline. One of Kalem's defenses was that it had not actually given a public performance of the property since the only activity it had engaged in was filming.[27] The implication was that if there had been an infringement, it had been committed by the exhibitor. Judge Oliver Wendell Holmes, writing the majority opinion, stated that the producers were liable since by their action of filming they had directly contributed to the infringement, which was the performance (screening the film).[28]

However, when the Supreme Court reviewed the history of contributory infringement, the justices found that it could apply only when the infringer supplied and controlled the work itself, not just the "means to accomplish an infringing activity."[29] Any other test would make every print and computer manufacturer liable for the infringements committed by their machines. Once this interpretation was reached, Sony had won its case. Both the district court and the majority of the Supreme Court justices had rejected Universal's two main points about economic damage and contributory infringement.

This decision was won by one vote, and legal scholars continue to question its consistency.[30] Many agree with Justice Blackmun's dissent, that copyright law does not require the proof of actual damages. One former register of copyrights, David Ladd, argued that proving actual harm is demeaning to the spirit of copyright and makes it a "means" test.[31] The strength of copyright is that it protects abstract property rights in principle so that actual markets will develop in the fairest way. Article 1, section 8 of the U.S. Constitution states the rationale for copyright, which is "to promote the progress of science and the useful arts."

As intellectual property becomes a central feature of postindustrial economy, media corporations have aggressively challenged perceived copyright infringement. Culture industries operate by creating a surplus of products in order to increase the probability that one of the products will become a breakout "hit" that will boost corporate profits. Because of this general principle, film distributors try to maximize their profits on every aspect of the sale

90   or licensing of their breakouts. Even a hypothetical loss of control is serious if it threatens the ability of a "hit" to earn maximum returns. It is for this reason that Justice Blackmun, in his dissent, was sympathetic to the copyright holders' aggressive need for control even when there are no actual damages.

Since the Universal case, the government has helped industry efforts to strengthen property rights in order to maximize earnings. The Universal case was the last high-profile decision limiting copyright. Congress has been continually examining the question of copyright protection since the extensions embodied in the 1976 Copyright Act. The latest extension became law when President Clinton signed the "Sonny Bono" amendment in October 1998. This added another twenty years (from fifty to seventy years after the author's death) to the effective length of most copyrights. There have only been a few voices arguing for a narrow application of copyright law, and for the protection of the public domain of cultural expression from the encroachment of expanded intellectual property.

The Universal case brought out excessive rhetoric on both sides of the issue. Many, not only in the film industry, but also in the music business, were claiming dire consequences if the case went against Universal.[32] In 1985, Madison Avenue executives panicked when the remote control became a common feature on the VCR. They had visions of viewers wielding the remote like a Buck Rogers space weapon, zipping past and otherwise zapping commercial breaks from the videotape.[33] Someone at the Ted Bates Agency even billed for network rebates in order to compensate the agency for all those time shifters using their VCRs to get rid of commercials.[34]

Researchers stepped into the breach to measure the exact extent of the VCR's damage on the "American" system of broadcasting. Was the public really using time shifting to escape the ubiquitous commercial breaks? Results were, of course, confusing.[35] Generally, most surveys found that VCR owners were fast forwarding through the commercial breaks on playback. Figures on the percentage of VCR owners engaged in this behavior ranged between 50 and 75 percent. This behavior became significant as VCR penetration of U.S. television households broke the 30 percent level. The advertisers were powerless except to try to renegotiate their contracts with television stations and networks. They could not pursue legal or legislative remedies since they did not have standing as victims of copyright infringement. In any case, the Universal case was closed. The courts had reiterated the simple principal that there were no constitutional guarantees that viewers had to watch commercials.

In the longer run, the VCR has proven to be a rich profit center for copyright holders and, in the greatest irony of the video age, a great friend of the co-plaintiff, Disney. This reversal of fortune had little to do with time shifting and everything to do with the sale of prerecorded tapes. Time shifting continues to be an important function for the home user, although more recent measurements show households devote about one-third the time to time shifting that they do to watching prerecorded cassettes.[36] The sale of prerecorded cassettes has had a far more important impact on the film entertainment industry than has time shifting. The Universal case took place in the transitional period when very few understood the VCR, and it serves as a coda on the issue of time shifting. The next section fills in the transitional moments and describes the rise of video rental.

VCR and Subversion

One industry commentator noted during the hoopla of 1980–1981 that the "VC" in VCR inspired the same panic as the Viet Cong (VC) had caused during the Vietnam War. This was a cute observation heavily tinged with technological romanticism. There was an aura of the subversive surrounding the VCR, a Japanese product that had drawn scorn and envy from American and European manufacturers and media suppliers. The use of the word "subversive" has to be heavily marked in quotes since those who could buy a thousand-dollar machine in the early days were obviously affluent and accepted the dominant consumerist ethos. By 1981, six years after the introduction of the Betamax, VCRs of all types had reached a global penetration, appearing in 3.2 percent of households owning televisions.[37] At this point, VCR owners were an "income elite." In many countries, the VCR "rebellion" was of the upper and upper middle class against their own media systems, an act of repudiation of local television fare.

However, in some developed countries, video use expanded swiftly from income elites to the working class, and this reshaped the video market. Great Britain quickly adopted the VCR and developed robust rental activity for both the machines and the videocassettes. This rental market was strongly associated with the blue-collar sector, and working-class taste dominated cas-

92   sette sales. "A large selection of home video buyers are workers who labor
during so called 'Unsociable Hours' (night work, etc.). Originally they time-
shifted but now want something prepackaged."[38] There was a bit of a "moral
panic" when this market favored movies known as "video nasties." Shows
such as I Spit on Your Grave (1978) depicted rape and vengeful violence and
inspired a strengthening of British censorship. Most industrialized countries
were experiencing the diffusion of videotapes into lower income groups by
1984.[39] The adoption patterns in nonindustrial or emerging countries remained more stratified.

The structure of various national media environments is an interesting
variable in the adoption of home video. Joseph Straubhaar has looked at VCR
penetration rates and found that they correlated negatively with "diversity in
television systems."[40] One typical example: "The sudden spread of new home
video technology throughout Scandinavia has come as a rude awakening for
most of the Nordic broadcasters. The obvious public appetite for the very sort
of programming state television has been 'protecting' its viewers against is
little short of a shock for those execs who have taken their public service du-
ties seriously."[41] In East Germany, government authorities started programming ten films per week to regain viewer interest.[42] VCR owners throughout
Europe purchased or rented American cassettes, and in a competitive move,
there was a rapid rise in the number of American films shown on European
television from the early 1980s. Several state television systems (such as
Denmark, Norway, et al.) were being deregulated and expanded to include
new networks. The background for such liberalization was the competition
for viewers that the new media technologies brought in. Yahia Mahamdi
specifically links home video with the deregulation of television.[43] The trade
press reported that in contrast to Europe, in Japan there was an initial soft
market in prerecorded cassettes despite strong VCR sales because VCR owners were satisfied with local network programming.[44] Japanese prerecorded
cassette sales did not surge until 1984.[45] Japan and U.S. adoption thus followed a two-step process, moving from time shifting to playback of prerecorded material.

X-rated Cassettes

Although consumers bought the VCR for time shifting and adjusting the television to their own schedule, there was a natural curiosity to see what else

they could do with this machine, now peacefully coexisting with their TV set. This coincided with a 1970s surge of interest in pornographic films. Short films depicting nudity and sexual activity as their sole raison d'être had become a constant enterprise soon after the invention of the movie camera. In the United States, these films were distributed out of the back of car trunks and through other small operations up through the 1960s. The films were short in length and had minimal story lines. Their intended audience was exclusively male. In 1967, Denmark announced its intentions to eliminate all obscenity laws (the law became effective in 1969). This came at a time when there had been a general loosening of sexual mores and increased depictions of sexuality in European feature films and subsequently in U.S. films. Swedish filmmakers released *I Am Curious, Yellow* in 1967. Its combination of explicit sex (explicit, at least, for those times) and politics attracted wide attention. These events, combined with indigenous relaxation of attitudes toward sex, heightened the ambitions of U.S. pornographic filmmakers and exhibitors. By 1972–1973, they had made and exhibited several sex features, such as *Deep Throat, The Devil in Miss Jones,* and *Behind the Green Door.* As a sign of the times, these films became cause célèbres and were well known in the mainstream media. They were also solid theatrical hits, making millions, although exact figures are notoriously uncertain in the adult film industry.[46] Unlike most concurrent nudies and sex films, these films were full length, had plotlines, and were well distributed to a growing number of adult movie theaters. Because of their relatively more sophisticated erotic fantasy plotlines, these films were thought to appeal to both men and women.

Pornographic films were entering the mainstream. In 1976, David Friedman, chair of the Adult Film Association, claimed that 2.5 million viewers watched theatrical adult films a week, approximately 13 percent of the audience that attended mainstream movies.[47] This is a year after the Betamax made it possible to view anything in the privacy of the home, and early VCR purchasers were inclined to view new and taboo products. By 1977, one pornography producer was already claiming to be the first to place his film on half-inch cassette.[48] Many followed quickly. As noted previously, some early purchasers bought the VCR rather than the videodisc systems because adult titles were unavailable on videodisc. Porno became a major propellant in the development of prerecorded cassettes.

The VCR easily captured the preexisting porno audience and added a larger public composed of viewers who would never think of stepping into an

94   adult movie theater. The concurrence of the Betamax and the new, more plot-driven erotica led to adult titles becoming the first big genre for prerecorded cassettes. Customers were willing to buy sex videos for $100 or more in order to view them at home. Many pornographers anticipated that the VCR made possible a new use of pornography for intimate viewing by married couples. Merrill Lynch reported that through the end of the 1970s "X-rated" cassettes accounted for half of all prerecorded sales.[49] As late as 1980, German and British video distributors reported that pornography accounted for 60 to 80 percent of their sales.[50] These same figures are reflected in various anecdotal reports about the U.S. market.

As the prerecorded market grew, erotic tapes held their own in absolute numbers but lost market share steadily. The Video Software Dealers Association surveyed video stores in 1984 and reported that adult material had fallen to only 13 percent of sale and rental activities, behind action/adventure (25.2 percent) and science fiction (19.6 percent).[51] By 1989, it was reported that adult constituted only 9 percent of video retail. The same report stated that the absolute value of adult video sitting on wholesalers' shelves had fallen from $430 million in 1986 to $380 million three years later.[52] However, it appears the 1990s were kinder to the industry. In 1997, one reporter estimated that adult video rental had risen to over $2.5 billion.[53]

Pornography was historically important to the emergence of home video. The distribution of X-rated tapes (in this context, *X-rated* is a generic term that does not necessarily mean the tape has been rated by the MPAA) inspired people in this genre to move into mainstream video distribution and retailing. Nonetheless, its presence as a motivating factor is hard to measure. Were the early users of adult videos just taking advantage of the possibilities, or were they driven to buy a VCR to seek adult viewing opportunities in the privacy of their own homes?

In turn, the VCR transformed the adult film industry. It is estimated that there were 1,500 theaters devoted to adult movies in 1980. By 1985 there were an estimated 700 such theaters, down to 250 in 1989.[54] Sexpo (sex exploitation) movie theaters become the first casualty of video. This became a broader trend when art houses and midnight showings of cult films also disappeared as video sliced off their audiences. Porno production was also transformed. Producers abandoned their 16mm film shoots with $60,000 budgets and moved to videotaping hour-long sex shows in two days for under $10,000.[55]

The Majors Start Video Distribution

By late 1977, the penetration rate of the Betamax and VHS in the U.S. was still under 2 percent. Most film suppliers were content to sit on their hands, although some had to be aware of the emerging market in X-rated and other material on tape. X-rated material had created the infrastructure for video distribution and, tentatively, from 1977 to 1981, each one of the MPAA film-distributing members entered the home video distribution of prerecorded cassette market. They chose several different methods of entering the market: on their own, with a partner, or by letting another company distribute their product. The last two options allowed the film companies to share the risks and the overhead costs. Twentieth Century Fox, Columbia, United Artists, MGM, and Orion preferred this entry strategy. Warner, Paramount, MCA/Universal, and Disney chose to immediately create their own video distribution arms. As the market matured, the other companies also started distributing on their own. Table 3.3 shows the various entry dates and stages of distribution.

Twentieth Century Fox was the first studio to release films to home video. It was convinced to do so after receiving a letter from Magnetic Video, a video duplicating company located in Michigan. Andre Blay, the head of Magnetic Video since 1969, had been thinking about prerecorded video marketing even before the introduction of Betamax. When Betamax was introduced in 1976, he sent letters to the various film studios offering to license their films for a video release. Fox responded and the two companies signed a deal toward the end of 1977. Magnetic Video guaranteed half a million dollars a year in exchange for the nonexclusive rights to fifty films. Fox was to receive a royalty of $7.50 for every tape unit sold.[56] The films had to be at least two years old and had already played on network television before they could be dubbed onto videotape.

Videotape Pricing

The most fateful problem Blay had to solve immediately was pricing. There was not much guidance for pricing the videocassettes. There were no other mainstream films in the market. Adult tape distributors charged upward of $100 for a tape. Another constraint was that the deal with Twentieth Century

TABLE 3.3 Origins of Major Home Video (HV) Distribution Divisions

Company	First Stage	Second Stage	Third Stage	Fourth Stage
Twentieth Century Fox	1977–1978, turns over HV rights to Magnetic Video	1979, buys out Magnetic Video and distributes on its own	1982–1991, forms 50/50 HV partnership with CBS	1991 on, has had its own HV division for feature films
United Artists (UA)	1981, acquired by MGM, leases domestic HV rights to CBS Fox for a limited time	1982, leases foreign HV rights to Warner	1982, forms its own HV distribution company	
Metro-Goldwyn-Mayer (MGM)	1980, forms HV partnership with CBS	1982, dissolves HV partnership with CBS and sets up MGM/UA HV distribution		
Columbia	1979, starts distributing HV on its own	1981, forms HV distributing partnership with RCA	1991, dissolves partnership with RCA and forms Columbia-TriStar Home Video division	
Orion	1982, leases various HV rights to Vestron and RCA/Columbia; in 1983, also leases HV rights to HBO	1988, forms its own HV distribution division	1990s, John Kluge starts acquiring Orion; eventually it merges with MGM/UA	
Warner	1978*, starts its HV division			
Paramount	1979, starts its HV division			
Disney	1980, starts its HV division			
MCA/Universal	1981, starts its HV division			

*No discernible commercial activity until 1980.

SOURCES: Various annual and 10-K reports.

Fox left Magnetic Video assuming all the risk. The company did not have deep pockets (in contrast to companies selling videodiscs, usually at a loss in order to boost hardware sales). Blay had to seek new loans from the bank in order to get his duplicating operations up to the scale needed for this new venture. Therefore, he was under pressure to earn a profit quickly by increasing the margin on each unit.

Blay looked around for an example of what the market would bear and decided to base his pricing on small-gauge films. Film companies had been in the practice of making 16mm prints of their films for both rental and sales to the educational, military, and other markets. They had also reduced their films to 8 mm for screenings on airplanes and to sell shorts and excerpts from feature films. The 16mm and 8mm market had revenues of $20 million a year. After considering these markets, Blay made the decision to price Magnetic Video's tapes at $50 to $70 per cassette.[57] This price range must have been already discussed when Fox and Magnetic Video agreed on a royalty of $7.50 or about 15 percent of retail. The company entered the video market with two movies that had first played the theaters in 1970, *Patton* and *M*A*S*H*, and the even older movie *The Sound of Music* (1965).

The price was set rather high in comparison to the cost of going out to the movies. An average ticket price in 1977 was $2.23.[58] Even a family of four would pay only $10 to $15 to see a movie if transportation and concession goods were added. Of course, it was not yet certain whether prerecorded videos would be bought instead of going to the movies or as a collector's item, more akin to the libraries of dedicated film buffs. One scholar, Douglas Gomery, speculated that the price reflected the Hollywood executives' experience of film buffs who paid hundreds of dollars to collect film prints. The executives thought that those who bought prerecorded tapes would view the tapes again and again and should pay accordingly.[59]

Blay's hunch was right. There were quite a few customers, even at Magnetic Video's high prices. The videocassettes were advertised in *TV Guide* and mail orders started pouring in. The cassette units were also placed in stores selling VCRs. Blay soon modeled his business on record distribution, which was based on two steps.[60] The first step was for Magnetic Video to sell tapes to wholesalers who could handle an $8,000 minimum order. The second step was for these wholesalers to resell the tapes individually and in small lots to various local retailers. Magnetic Video also sold directly to individual customers willing to join its mail-order club for a $10 fee. The mail-order club

98   had 60,000 members by 1980.[61] Magnetic Video was selling as fast as it could manufacture the tapes. Not even a year of operations had passed before Twentieth Century Fox bought the company outright in 1978 for $7.2 million and kept Andre Blay on to continue his home video operations within the new Fox division.

The other major film companies noticed the success of Magnetic Video and arranged for either self-distribution or subcontracted distribution of their titles on videocassettes over the next two years. The two companies that were suing Sony, MCA/Universal and Disney, hesitated the longest. Disney did not release titles to a wide market until September 1980.[62] MCA/Universal was the last to release cassettes, in 1981, and its tardiness stemmed both from its lawsuit against Sony and from its interest in Laservision. But the cassette market proved to be too much of a profit center for MCA/Universal to ignore.

Renting

The Twentieth Century Fox contract with Magnetic Video specified that the tapes were to be sold only for home use and not for rental purposes. The two-step process using wholesalers and subdistributors distanced Blay from another type of customer—the rental storeowner. Even before Twentieth Century Fox bought out Magnetic Video, there were several entrepreneurs buying cassettes for the purposes of renting them for one or two nights viewing. Future historians will undoubtedly debate who was the first to get the idea. Lardner chronicles the early rental business of George Atkinson in the Los Angeles area. Douglas Gomery cites Erol Oranan as an early rental pioneer in the Washington D.C./Arlington, Virginia area. Most of the early rental setups involved the creation of a club with membership fees. Some of these clubs did not use the word "rent" but rather charged their members for "exchanges" or "previews."[63]

The motivation for rental activities is not hard to find. The cost of buying a videotape was out of proportion with its use by a large audience. Only a small number of people had any need or desire to own a feature film, particularly in video form. Since the beginning, the popularity of moviegoing has been based on novelty—something new every week. In this manner, the narrative arts are utterly unlike music and painting since the pleasure in the latter two is repeated over and over again with the same item. Since most members of the audience are used to seeing a movie once, why should they pay twenty times the price of a movie ticket in order to watch the video? The consumer would naturally seek a way to share the initial cost of the tape through some sort of rental or exchange program. Somehow copyright holders and video manufacturers ignored this obvious fact. The popularity of renting videocassettes was unanticipated by all the major media corporations. Only the short-lived Cartrivision had set up a rental system as part of its rollout. Sony had abandoned similar efforts after failing to get cooperation from Hollywood on a rental plan for the U-matic.

The successful development of rental was a grassroots movement starting with video dealers and record shop owners that soon spread to other small business owners. They neither sought nor received guidance from Sony or Hollywood program suppliers. Rental shops started springing up all over the world, particularly in Great Britain, where the VCR machines were more often rented than purchased and it was a natural step to also rent the programming. Great Britain was one of the first countries to adopt the VCR, in rates surpassing even the U.S. The rental of prerecorded cassettes was a continuation of time-shifting habits. British time shifters used the VCR to record feature films more than any other type of programming.[64] They soon found it just as easy to rent as to record feature films. U.S. consumers followed this pattern. They were recording feature films from the TV set more than other types of programming.[65] However, they were just as happy to rent feature films as more titles became available at the rental store. It was not surprising that as rental of feature films became an option, such rentals became the dominant use of the VCR. Warner film executives were already claiming that rental usage had become the VCR's primary function by 1982.[66] At least one scholar places it two years later in 1984–1985.[67] The later date coincides with the emergence of America as the biggest market for video products, surpassing Japan and Northern Europe.

The spread of video through Europe was uneven. Northern Europe reached temporary saturation by 1983. In that same year, the French government instituted two policies that had the effect of derailing the VCR revolution. It only opened one port of entry for video machines, which slowed the imports to a trickle for several crucial months. The government also prosecuted video distributors who did not wait a full year until after the theatrical run of a movie before selling the cassettes. Although the one-year window did not help the dramatic decline in theatrical attendance at the time, it caused

100   a crisis in confidence in the video business. The VCR revolution was relatively slow in Benelux and Southern Europe in the early 1980s, because the
audience was either investing in subscription television or was satisfied by
the expansion of commercial television (in Italy this satisfaction precluded
widespread desire for time shifting or cassette rental). Therefore, the spurt in
foreign VCR sales of 1978–1981 soon gave way to the explosive rise in American markets in 1981–1984. This timing meant that the American film industry's perception of home video would be decisively shaped by domestic
developments.

American distributors had not anticipated the rise in American rentals
despite the European example. American culture favored outright purchase
through layaway plans and other expensive credit schemes. This common
view of American consumer behavior led film distributors to hope the rental
idea would prove to be a small niche market when it first appeared.[68] They
were surprised to learn that despite the inconvenience of the pickup and
return, the rental of videotapes grew exponentially everywhere. An ever-
expanding pool of new VCR owners seemed willing to rent titles in quantities
that have not been seen since. The stores found out that it was easy to rent
out even limited-appeal titles with turns (each rental was called a "turn") that
far exceeded the break-even point. It became popular in rural areas, in the
suburbs, and in urban areas. The only gap in its popularity was and continues to be in inner-city neighborhoods.

Table 3.4 shows the astronomical growth in rental stores. Column 2 is a
count of places where video is the primary business and does not include the
convenience store and other places that rent the occasional cassette. It does
include stand-alone rental centers located inside supermarkets.

Rental store growth was an explosion that reminded film historians of the
nickelodeon boom at the beginning of the twentieth century. Video stores
were the one growth industry during the general economic slump of the
first years of the Reagan administration. Noel Gimbel, owner of an early
large store called Sound Video, stated that the minimum a prospective store
owner needed for a start-up was $30,000.[69] This was one of the few low-
cost opportunities of the time. By 1986, the number of stores specializing
in the sale and rental of videocassettes surpassed the number of movie theater screens.[70] Video stores and theatrical screens continued at rough parity
through the mid-1990s.[71] Of course, the ownership patterns of the rental
stores has changed radically over the decade. In the early period, most stores

TABLE 3.4 Rental Stores and Rental Prices, 1979–1992

Year	Number of U.S. rental stores	Number of VCR households per store	Average rental price (dollars)
1979	700	1,600	n/a
1980	2,500	672.8	7.00
1981	5,500	553.2	5.00
1982	7,000	725.4	3.00
1983	10,000	916.9	2.80
1984	16,000	1,049.1	2.60
1985	23,000	1,222.7	2.38
1986	25,000	1,312	2.28
1987	27,000	1,585.19	2.15
1988	29,000	1,775.86	2.20
1989	30,000	1,943.33	2.26
1990	29,000	2,193.1	2.31
1991	28,000	2,446.43	2.30
1992	28,000	2,578.57	2.36

SOURCES: Column 2—*Video Store*, December 1990, p. 111. Column 3—*Video Marketing Newsletter*, 1980. Column 4—Veronis, Suhler, and Associates, *Communications Industry Forecast 1994–1998* (New York: Veronis, Suhler, and Associates, 1994), p. 142.

were independent of each other and were generally handling under 2,000 titles. Since that time there has been a rise in large chains such as Blockbuster and super stores handling 7,500 titles or more (see Chapter 5 for the Blockbuster story).

In the early years, shops were offering off-beat items such as shorts and features that had fallen into the public domain, films owned by companies other than the Hollywood majors, and, in particular, adult titles, in addition to the relatively few available Hollywood films. Despite the preponderance of adult titles, the rental market was demonstrating an enthusiasm for mainstream feature films. Consumers would rent half a dozen feature film cassettes at a time and choose just about every title on the shelf, with the mainstream films at the top of the pile. Obviously, the major film companies were self-defeating in their slow response to this unprecedented enthusiasm for a new market in film. The majors wanted to either sell directly to the customer or participate in each and every rental transaction—in other words, receive a cut of the rental fee. Both strategies worked against efficient exploitation of a red-hot market in rental tapes. The majors resented that the video business

102   was not developing toward direct consumer sales, and that there was nothing to stop entrepreneurs from buying cassettes outright and turning these cassettes over to rental shops. Contract provisions such as the one with Magnetic Video were powerless to stop this behavior.

Nonetheless, at first, representatives of Twentieth Century Fox and other studios asserted a naïve and incorrect notion that copyright holders could stop the rental of films. Several early renters became unsure of the status of their activity and used the exchange or club membership structure to avoid calling the transaction a rental. Such artifice was unnecessary. Renting videotapes without the permission of the copyright holder was perfectly legal. It was permitted by the "first sale" doctrine of the Copyright Act. First sale, like fair use, was developed in court cases struggling with the implications of intellectual ownership before it was finally written up as Section 109 of the 1976 Copyright Act. The logic of first sale comes from the idea that copyright gives the owner a "monopoly" over a particular expression of an idea. It does not allow that ownership to be extended to the physical embodiment of that expression. Therefore, people are perfectly free to do whatever they want with a particular copy of a book they have purchased: destroy it, use it to prop up a bed, resell it, or rent it. The only thing they cannot do is to copy the book, that is to say, transfer its expression to another physical embodiment. United States copyright case law had formalized this distinction in the notion that the first sale "exhausts" the copyright holder's rights in that particular item of sale.

Lawyers explained first sale doctrine to film executives as they monitored the growth of rental stores. A foreboding was growing on major studio lots. Film distributors could not fathom a future where they would not control the rental of their films, a future where instead some mom and pop store would control it. I discussed in Chapter 1 the importance of leasing prints for the development of centralized distribution, the ultimate source of power in the film industry. The film distributors figured that either they would lose a valuable source of income, since the rental store owners would take home all the rental profits, or they would lose control of the film, since ownership and distribution would become widespread. Illegal duplication of videocassettes was already becoming a major headache, and unauthorized rentals could only facilitate such behavior. Several majors decided that they had to reassert control of their inventory.

Rental is a variant of time shifting. Customers choose to rent for the same reasons they time shift, in order to pick the time and place for viewing. Rental was driven by the same stressed leisure that made the time shifting ad campaign such a success. In one aspect, the act of rental was vastly different from time shifting. It transformed the VCR from being an extension of the TV to being an alternate to the movie theater. This is why a major film distributor such as Warner Communications saw rental as much more of a threat than home taping. Warner and other major studios now improvised new strategies to meet the rental challenge. They stopped selling cassettes, offering leasing plans instead. They also pursued a legislative solution that would exempt the industry from the first sale doctrine. The majors failed in both strategies; the reasons for these failures will be explored in the next chapter.

The video revolution was part of the continuing quest to provide consumers with enhanced choices. However, the nature of "choice" was unclear. Was choice a quest for more programming or a quest for more control over the time in which the audience watches the show? During the period from 1975 through 1981, the answer was greatly obscured because events were taking place without much direction from the usual power centers of the culture industries. Social and cultural awareness of course lags behind actual history, and it is not surprising that hardly any media executives saw the connection between the increasing number of people working and the popularity of the VCR. Indeed, even if they had had such awareness, it would be hard to suggest how they should have responded. In hindsight, the Universal and Disney lawsuit was unnecessary. As the case slowly made its way to the Supreme Court, it was becoming clear that the VCR was about to return even higher revenues to the film industry than broadcast television ever did, despite industry hostility.

The Years of Independence: 1981–1986

The five years of 1981 to 1986 are the golden years of home video production and distribution. This period was one of new companies exploring new possibilities in film production and distribution, as well as developing a totally new approach to exhibition: the rental of videotapes. It is difficult to tell the story of these years in a linear sequence since it involves so many new and old players acting, reacting, and even ignoring each other. Our first task is to complete our survey of video distributors by looking at the new ones springing up alongside the major film studios (already discussed in the previous chapter). Although the majors scarcely admitted it, these new distributors represented new competition. The newcomers were not interested in legislative and contractual controls on the rental stores. They saw that more was to be gained by cooperating with than by controlling the stores. In turn, the rental business grew and matured due to new distributors enthusiastically selling tapes and spurring the reluctant major studios.

At the same time, cable TV was also growing into a major market for feature films and, for a while, the cable channels were more important financially than the video distributors. We need to look at the tandem growth of both media in order to properly evaluate the greater importance of home video. We want to look at the experiment distributors were making with non-feature film products and survey the ways independent producers were taking advantage of new video revenues to finance and increase their production schedules through such devices as "pre-selling." The chapter closes on this high point of independent production and distribution.

Independence on the Cusp of Video

Independence is an important and an elusive category. I have already mentioned that independent distribution is the best tangible evidence of allocative power. Still, within the visible category of independent distribution there are many shades of gray. There were relatively many independent distributors in the late 1970s. There were those that had been distributing exploitation films since the 1950s. There were newer ones that had formed in response to perceived opportunities such as favorable tax laws and the product famine of the 1960s and early 1970s. The product famine left many theaters willing to show films of limited appeal such as midnight cult movies and "art" films. The situation for independents was turning less favorable as 1981 approached. In 1976 the tax code was changed, giving less of a write-off to film investors.[1] The development of wide releasing in the aftermath of *Jaws* (1975) and *Star Wars* (1977) meant that many copies of major films were playing in hundreds if not thousands of theaters at the same time. In these circumstances, exhibitors lost interest in small cult and other off-beat movies. In addition, after *Jaws*, independents had to worry that the majors would steal away their audiences with more "bang for the buck" (more car crashes and beautiful girls per reel), with summer releasing, and with more efficient advertising. The majors were increasingly giving "A"-level budgets to "B"-level formula scripts. Analyzing independent film trends up through 1981, *Variety's* Todd McCarthy claimed that only the occasional horror movie could survive competition with the majors.[2]

Fewer distributors now had the complete freedom to distribute the products they wanted to make. In this transitional period in the late 1970s, many independents had to enter unequal power relationships with other media corporations in order to finance market access. On the other side of the coin, major studios sought to reduce their exposure to high union costs and other production risks. These studios were willing to fill out their release schedule with distribution partnerships and with "negative pickups." Negative pickups occur when an outside production company brings a completed film to a studio distributor and the studio agrees to distribute the film, typically paying the production company a guarantee immediately and a percentage of the profits from the revenues if the amount exceeds the guarantee. The production company has given up full participation in the profits but at least is secure that the film is now being handled by a major studio and will get the full

106   attention of the exhibitors and the public. The big studio gets a completed
film for less money than the studio itself could have made the film.[3] This deal
became popular and it was estimated that by the end of the 1970s, half of the
movies distributed by the majors were from such arrangements rather than
from their own internally financed productions.[4]

These partnerships and negative pickups were very important for the development of video distribution. Although such deals were often slanted in
favor of the major studios, independents such as Dino DeLaurentiis, Alexander Salkind, and many others typically only signed away the North American
theatrical rights. They retained all other ancillary rights, such as pay and
broadcast television and home video. In addition, independent film distributors such as Avco Embassy, Associated Film Distributors, Filmways/AIP, New
World, and others were producing several films each annually. Independent
and semi-independent producers were still prevalent despite the harsher atmosphere of the late 1970s and were making a wide range of products, from
the formulaic cheapies to the biggest budget event movies. There were many
movies around with their video rights available to the highest bidder, as the
rental market heated up. New or fledging distributors could build their inventories by snapping up the ancillary rights to big motion pictures from De-
Laurentiis, Orion (the successor company to Filmways/AIP), Time–Life,
Cannon, Goldcrest, and other producers.

New Companies Get into Video Business

The previous chapter described how the major studios formed their own
video distribution divisions. Other film companies jumped into the new market. Other media corporations also formed video distribution divisions, hoping to build upon their own operations in music, publishing, and so on. The
most interesting group from the point of view of the potential uses of video
were those companies that started on their own and dedicated the bulk of
their efforts toward video distribution.

Media Home Entertainment was formed as a video distribution company
in 1978, a few months after the Magnetic Video/Twentieth Century Fox deal.
Its principals were Joe Wolf, Ron Safnick, Murray Moss, Gunther Schiff, and
Irwin Yablans. Wolf stated the company's philosophy as "We fill the voids of
the majors."[5] Irwin Yablans had just produced one of those runaway hits for
which independents always hope. It was the horror film *Halloween* (1978),

directed by John Carpenter. Media built its video operations on this and other horror films. The company also distributed children's video when it had a chance. By 1981, Media was grossing $8 million in home video sales annually. It was sold to a British conglomerate, Heron Holdings, in 1983 and continued as a semi-autonomous division for the rest of the decade.

Family Home Entertainment (FHE) was another stand-alone video distributor. It was created in 1980 by Noel Bloom, the owner of Cabellero Control, a major adult production/distribution house. He had built the porno business up from a magazine his father had entitled *Swedish Erotica*. Through the sixties and seventies, Noel Bloom had progressed from nudie film loops to the sale and rental of ¾-inch U-matic tapes and ultimately VHS cassettes. Bloom decided to move into mainstream distribution. He had the idea of distributing children's video before anyone else had really started to do so—"before Disney had even thought about it."[6] Bloom, for obvious reasons, wanted to separate the "kidvid" from his adult business and created FHE as a separate company to acquire programming. He later formed another label, USA Home Video, to acquire and distribute independent films and "made-for-TV" shows. He formed a partnership with Charles Band to release *The Texas Chainsaw Massacre* (original theatrical release was in 1974) on video. The horror/slasher classic was very profitable and in 1984 Bloom reorganized FHE and USA under the International Video Entertainment (IVE) banner. All this time, he had kept Cabellero separate, finally giving up his participation in it in 1986.

The most influential stand-alone video distributor was founded in 1981. This was Vestron, whose first films were acquired from Time–Life, the publishing company. Time–Life had been interested in video distribution since the introduction of the U-matic system. It had also expanded into film production/distribution in the late 1970s. However, at the beginning of the video explosion, it decided to get out of the theatrical film business in order to concentrate on its successful cable operations, such as Home Box Office (HBO). A thirteen-year veteran of Time–Life, Austin Furst was brought over from a successful stint at the HBO division to handle the breakup of Time–Life Film. In 1981, he sold both the production and theatrical distribution divisions to Twentieth Century Fox, and the television division to Columbia films. Although these deals were successful, Furst was frustrated in his efforts to find a buyer for the home video division.

In his frustration, Furst came up with the idea of buying the home video rights by himself and forming his own company. Austin Furst had been in several divisions of Time–Life and could see that cable and other businesses were not providing many opportunities for entrepreneurs. On the other hand, home video distribution was a rare opportunity that could reward individual risk taking. The major studio executives were not developing the market properly. It was enterprising individuals such as Andre Blay and Noel Bloom who were showing the way. In 1981, Furst persuaded the other Time–Life executives to sell him the home video rights to the Time–Life films. He resigned to go into business for himself at the age of thirty-eight. His daughter suggested the Vestron name after the Roman goddess of the hearth, Vesta, and the Greek word for instrument, Tron.[7] Furst recruited another Time–Life executive, Jon Peisinger, to preside over the new company. Peisinger had spent a decade in various record companies but had only been at Time–Life for a year when he joined Vestron in the summer of 1981. Vestron Video began operations in February 1982, offering titles such as *Fort Apache, The Bronx* (1981), starring Paul Newman, and the Burt Reynolds hit *The Cannonball Run* (1981).

One small preexisting film company, Embassy, plunged into video distribution operations in 1981–1982. The prolific producer Joseph Levine created Embassy Pictures for the purpose of theatrical distribution in 1967, selling it to Avco Industries in 1974 (right after Avco's mishap with Cartrivision). Avco Embassy was a successful independent film producer/distributor with horror and action titles such as *The Fog* (1980), *Escape from New York* (1981) and *Time Bandits* (1981). Avco Industries decided to sell Embassy to Norman Lear and Jerry Perechino for $26 million at the end of 1981. The partners recruited Andre Blay, who had left the Magnetic Video division of Twentieth Century Fox in September 1981. Blay quickly built Embassy into a major independent, taking an average of 4 percent of the cassette market from 1983 to 1986.

These four companies, Media, FHE/IVE, Vestron, and Embassy, were aggressive in acquiring films and grabbing market share. The other video distributors tried to build cautiously on their existing expertise and product lines. Several media corporations without preexisting film interests moved into home video to see if they could extend their media markets. Western Publishing had published children's books since 1916. It started to produce and distribute videos based on its successful line of children books. However, its share of the prerecorded video market only rose to 1 percent in 1985, and it was a low-profile operation. Several other print publishers explored video production and distribution, especially after the success of the *Jane Fonda's Workout* video in 1982, which was inspired by her book of the same title. These publishers did not achieve high market share.

Video distribution attracted other record company executives in addition to Vestron's Peisinger. Many noticed the similarities between video and record distribution and thought that their record experience was a good background for the new medium. The same logic motivated record companies to add video distribution to their extant distribution operations. These companies were not very venturesome. For example, neither RCA Records nor CBS Records looked to acquire individual films. Instead, they looked for established film partners. CBS joined with MGM in 1980. Two years later it switched to the considerably stronger Twentieth Century Fox. CBS/Fox still exists and handles non-theatrical and other less popular videos. RCA allied with Columbia from 1981 to 1991. Foreign music companies with similar expertise, such as Thorn/EMI and Polygram, experimented with home video distribution as an extension of their record distributions. Thorn/EMI video division was created in 1982 and captured 6.2 percent of the American prerecorded cassette market in 1985 on the strength of such films as *Terminator* and *Amadeus*. It was now the eighth largest film supplier. Nonetheless, by 1986 Thorn/EMI had had enough of the headache of working in the film business and turned its home video division over to CBS/Fox.[8] Polygram was also a fickle participant. It nosed around the distribution business in the early 1980s, handling such titles as *An American Werewolf in London* (1981). It got out of the film business in 1983 during the great music record slump.

A few television distributors tried their hand at video distributing for a short period. Lorimar was an independent television supplier that moved aggressively into home video in 1984. It was acquired by Warner Communications on May 16, 1988. Taft Broadcasting formed Worldvision Home Video in 1981. It became part of Spelling, which is now part of Viacom. Other television distributors such as HBO and Turner have created their own video labels, but the former has been folded into Warner Home Video, and Turner is also now part of the Time Warner empire, although it continues to maintain a separate label.

Sony was the only electronic manufacturer (besides RCA) to try launching a video label division. This division grew out of its effort to distinguish its Betamax format from VHS by creating different content. In 1982, it began ex-

110   perimenting with its own production/distribution arm, creating and selling various music videos that were known for a while as Video 45s. However, sales were poor and certainly did nothing to stop the decline of Betamax.[9] Much later, both Sony and Matsushita made big splashes in home video distribution when they bought major film entertainment companies. Sony bought Columbia Entertainment in September 1989 and continues to own it. The leading VCR manufacturer, Matsushita, also got into home video distribution when it bought MCA/Universal in November 1990.

The video distributors that would make the biggest impression were the new autonomous independents, particularly IVE and Vestron. Their impact can be measured as a function of their market share, their explorations of different genres, their innovations in acquiring and financing film production, and, more subtly, the response of the major studios.

Hollywood Tries to Control Rentals

The video rental market had emerged as something thrust upon the major film distributors. The response of the major studios was to learn to coexist, albeit without enthusiasm, with the rental stores. Independent distributors, on the other hand, embraced the new market and became pioneers of selling film on video. The major Hollywood studios often seemed just to want the rental business to go away. Even as late as 1981, several home entertainment executives, such as Cy Leslie of MGM/CBS Home Video and Mel Harris of Paramount, hoped that the sale of cheaper videodiscs would eliminate video rentals.[10]

From 1979 to 1985, the major film distributors tried four types of strategies — contractual prohibition, partnerships and exclusive leasing, legislative exemption from first sale, and surcharges on purchase price of cassettes — to regain control of the rental market. These strategies overlapped, with some studios trying one and then the other, and others trying a combination. By 1985, the only strategy that endured was the one of placing a surcharge, which evolved into the two-tiered pricing system. Let us review the three failed strategies.

Twentieth Century Fox wrote an anti-rental provision into the initial 1977 contract with Magnetic Video. Other major companies copied this provision. These provisions were immediate failures for the major studios. Magnetic Video found that there were few enforcement possibilities when the cassette was sold to a third party. The few retailers who tried to abide by such clauses felt undercut as they turned away potential renters, who then went to other retailers to rent the tapes. By 1981 Cy Leslie of MGM/CBS bluntly stated that since a no rental clause "is not legally binding, it's nonsense." [11] In that year, most studios started to drop such clauses from their contracts.

At several points, film distributors tried various partnerships and leasing options for rental cassettes. The most obvious partnership candidates were national retailers, and the film studios sought them out. As early as 1979, Paramount entered into an arrangement with Fotomat, the one-day photo service chain. Fotomat used its 3,500 kiosk locations to distribute catalogs of the available videos. The customer would call Fotomat and order a cassette. The cassette would be available the next day at the kiosk. The customer would rent the cassette for $12 for five days. Paramount received from 20 to 50 percent of the rental fee. Thorn/EMI also signed with Fotomat, and Warner Communications announced plans to join this plan. It was the rise of neighborhood video stores that undermined Fotomat's business. Neighborhood stores had the significant advantage of allowing the customers to browse and to rent on the spot. By the beginning of 1982, Fotomat had suspended the video rental operation. [12]

Walt Disney Home Video was one distributor that actually put some energy into enforcing the no-rent contract. Disney was very hesitant about releasing its classic animated films on video. It placed the home video division under the guidance of James Jimirro, a man who had begun in the 16mm division of Disney when Walt Disney was still alive and who thus could be trusted with the company "jewels." Disney executives placed less popular cartoons and films from their library on tape, without much publicity. They were determined to keep a tight control over even these lesser titles. By November 1980, Disney accepted that tape rental was here to stay. However, Disney executives saw no reason why the distributor should not receive a part of the rental dollar just as it received part of the box office. In that month, the company instituted a dual inventory policy of placing certain cassettes for sales and other cassettes for rental. Both kinds of cassettes were shipped in boxes engraved with the proper use of those cassettes. Disney did not distribute through wholesalers but through sales representatives. The sales reps reported back on the suitability of the stores for Disney products and about the compliance with the dual inventory policy. Disney successfully settled out of court with several violating stores. It threatened other stores with the with-

112   drawal of the right to use Disney's trademark. However, the overall effectiveness of their enforcement was in doubt. Disney had set the leasing fee for a rental cassette at $52 for thirteen weeks. This fee assumed that a cassette would rent thirteen times during this period at $8 a turn. The store would make $104 and split it with Disney. However, cassettes rarely made all thirteen "turns" in thirteen weeks, and the mushrooming of competing rental stores drove the rental fees down. Clients, stuck with the Disney deal, expressed their anger and by April 1981 Disney retreated to a two-for-one deal.[13]

From the point of view of the Hollywood divisions, the offer to lease tapes to rental stores was actually a carrot, not a stick—a partnership, not a takeover. Morton Fink, the head of Warner's home video division, commissioned a study and concluded that direct studio participation in every rental transaction was not feasible because it would involve too much monitoring and paperwork. He proposed a system similar to Disney's but avoiding the thirteen-week commitment. The video store owner would lease cassettes from Warner for one-week periods at fees starting at $8.25.[14] The weekly periods were designed to help the stores maximize shelf space for the recent hits and to reduce their inventory investment since they no longer had to pay prices of $60 to $80 for a single cassette. Fink was able to convince various Warner executives that this could become an industry-wide plan and that the other studios would follow their example, at which point the rental stores would naturally accept. Warner Communications initiated Fink's leasing plan in the fall of 1981.

Fink seemed on target in his assessment that other studios would follow the plan. In November, Fox announced a similar plan with a license fee of $45 for six months.[15] MGM followed with a four-month plan. Warner's plan was a hit in Hollywood terms, since other distributors began imitating it. Out in the field it was not playing so well. The various renters and video retailers were upset. One immediate source of anger was that Warner withdrew titles that were already selling on the open market in order to convert to a lease-only policy. The renters were also aggravated by the increased need for paperwork. In addition, the switch from ownership of the cassettes to leasing deprived the rental stores of the tangible collateral of actually owning their inventory. This was an important consideration when the store owners sought bank loans and depreciation for tax purposes.

Fox and MGM deflected the anger by allowing their titles to be purchased.

Now Warner was stuck out on a limb. The company moved to make accommodations but not soon enough to forestall boycotts by some retailers. At a January 1982 industry convention in Las Vegas, Warner's booth was the site of a particularly vocal demonstration. Angry video dealers were motivated at this time to form two home video associations to look out for their interests: the Video Software Dealers Association (VSDA) and the Video Software Retailers of America (VSRA).[16]

The dealers' hostility toward the Warner plan was not strictly a matter of dollars and cents. Their anger was also triggered by the high-handedness of the major studios. These studios had ignored the videocassette business in the early high-risk stage. One dealer, Cheryl Benton, reminded everyone that "these are the same studios who told us four years ago rental wouldn't work."[17] The video dealers had built the business by themselves. They rarely made high profits and suffered a 66 percent bankruptcy rate. Even if the Warner plan would reduce the renter's exposure to risk, these dealers resented the implied loss of control of their own fate.

Disney, Warner, and the others had set fees to recapture 50 percent of the rental dollar. This figure was high even by the standards of theatrical exhibition and did not reflect the difficulties of an emerging video market. The dealers felt that they were being forced into unequal partnership. They could not detect any goodwill built into the various rental plans, but instead were afraid that the studios would always rewrite the rates just as the video store owners were starting to earn desirable profits. A Brooklyn dealer, Rocco LaCapria, voiced his mistrust of the movie industry loudly. He reminded his associates of the various anti-trust violations of the Hollywood studios. He also made the damaging point that Warner claimed that it had the dealers' interests at heart at the same time it was selling movies to cable in direct competition with rentals of those titles.[18]

The Warner leasing plan was phased out. Still, the majors did little more to placate the rental stores. For several years, the majors' association, MPAA, had been talking about legislative relief from the first sale doctrine. In the 98th U.S. Congress (1983 and 1984), bills were introduced to exempt the film industry from first sale. In these same sessions, bills were also introduced on behalf of the record companies for the same purpose of exemption from first sale doctrine. The two industries had the same complaint: that the combination of rental and the first sale doctrine allowed a damaging degree of home taping of copyrighted material (see Chapter 3 for a discussion of "first sale").

In other words, customers who rented an audiotape or videotape would copy the tape onto another tape and deprive the music or film company of a sale of that content. However, the two industries fared quite differently in the halls of Congress. Their presentations were quite divergent, and an understanding of the divergence illuminates the unique nature of home video.

The record companies were able to commission studies to put a dollar figure on the amount of sales they lost due to home taping. The only comparable figures the movie companies could offer were future projections from the next decade. Video sales were, after all, a new market and the preexisting market—the theaters—had not lost sales. The music industry had immediate, tangible wounds to show. The record companies had a slump from 1979 to 1984. There had been a dramatic downturn when sales of recordings dropped by almost 11 percent, from $4.1 billion in 1978 to $3.7 billion in 1979.[19] Total record sales did not again break the $4 billion barrier until after the phenomenal sales of Michael Jackson's *Thriller* album, released in 1983.

Therefore, during the 1983 and 1984 congressional hearings, the Record Industry Association of America (RIAA) and other music lobbyists convincingly portrayed themselves as being in dire straits. Alan Greenspan, the future Federal Reserve Board chair, testified as an economist for the RIAA, presenting numbers for lost sales due to home taping. These numbers were challenged. However, the RIAA was able to counter the challenge with another, more concrete, example of the dangers of record rentals. In June 1980 an enterprising student had opened up a record rental shop in a Tokyo suburb in Japan. The idea was very successful and thirty-four more rental shops were opened in that year.[20] Three years later there were 1,600 shops.[21] RIAA told Congress that as a result of record rentals, record sales in Japan plummeted by 30 percent.[22]

In these same hearings, legislators became increasingly skeptical about potential damage of rentals to the movie industry. They had a hard time envisioning videotaping cutting into existing markets since the representatives thought such taping was strictly for the purposes of time shifting. The box office was not declining and cassette sales were becoming a significant source of revenue because of rentals. The film industry realized that their case was weaker than the music industry's presentation. Alan Hirschfield, at that time the top executive at Twentieth Century Fox, tried to reassure the representatives that the movie industry was being reasonable. The movie companies did not want to prosecute the public for home taping; they did not even want to drive renters out of business; they only wished to participate in the rental transaction. The movie business is like all other cultural industries; it must maximize its earnings on a hit in order to offset the losses on the flops. It was only right that the movie companies should be able to participate in transactions of their own copyrighted material.

Hollywood's legislative friends were anxious about openly supporting first sale exemption, despite Hirschfield's plea, since that could only mean antagonizing the burgeoning ranks of video rental store owners, which were popping up in every congressional district. This consideration did not apply to audiotaping since there were only three or four record rental stores in the country at the time. This may have the decisive reason for Congress allowing the video bill to die even as it outlawed record rentals (exempting only libraries) by passing the Record Rental Amendment of 1984.

MGM/CBS started a partnership with Sears as a way to set up its own rental chains and hopefully circumvent the independent rental stores. By 1983, Sears terminated the agreement and declared the effort a failure. Mass merchandisers balked at the low penetration rate of home video, hovering at 9 percent in 1983, and did not want to invest in the overhead associated with renting out videocassettes. They also feared that renting would undercut their ongoing attempts to sell videos. Previously, when the music industry had faced the same mass merchandisers' reluctance, "rack jobbers" overcame the resistance. Rack jobbers were independent companies that took responsibility for buying and stocking the record sections of major department stores. It would have been natural for rack jobbers to move into video; however, in the early years, they were discouraged by the relatively high prices of cassettes. They could not afford to invest in all video titles and therefore could not build a profitable high-volume market.[23] As video penetration increased by the mid-eighties and high volume became normal, these music rack jobbers became important players in the video distribution business.

At this time, the film distributors had no alternative to working with the "mom and pop" video specialty stores. In addition to the lack of alternative retail sites, studios were afraid that refusal to provide product might leave a void for illegal duplicators. The Hollywood companies turned to the only remaining strategy. Since they could not lease their tapes, or force the rental stores to give them a percentage, they would simply charge more for the original sale. At the end of 1981, Paramount responded to the rental phenomenon by placing surcharges of up to $10 on titles where the company suspected

116   that most purchasers were renters.[24] This placed an upward pressure on cassette prices. The 1980–1982 list prices for popular feature films stayed up around $70 to $80 despite the decrease in per-unit manufacturing and handling costs.

Independent distributors saw an opportunity in the prolonged quest of the major studios to control the rental business. Video stores bought every and all prerecorded cassettes, not only to see what the new consumers were willing to rent but also to lessen their dependency on the few majors. The heavy-handedness of the majors gave further impetus to the effort to diversify the video inventory. The home video explosion gave a substantial second wind to those independent producers of filmed entertainment who retained the ancillary rights to their movies. The new "indies" had plenty of recent movies to feed to rental stores.

Video, Theater, and Cable

The film distributors were not operating in a void. As video rental grew into a $1 billion industry in the United States by 1983,[25] its operations were bound to draw reactions from other segments of the film industry. Theater owners had been worrying that cable and video would cut into their ticket buyers since the mid-1970s.[26] They could do little to stop the new markets, but they could improve their own situation. Theater counterstrategy involved safeguarding the period of an exclusive theatrical run and improving choice and convenience at the theater. They experienced only minor fluctuations in admittance between 1979 and 1986, with four years of growth and four years of decline and an overall average of a 1 percent decline per year. In the very same period, box office revenue went up 33 percent due to ticket price increases.[27] Video was not substantially hurting their business. Their counterparts in Europe suffered a more substantial decline in this period, undoubtedly partially due to video.[28] The steady American box office is even more remarkable when we consider that both video and cable were expanding tremendously in these years.

For the film industry, the coincident rise of cable and home video looked like a series of leapfrog jumps. From 1978 to 1984, the cable industry was the most important new source for film production funds. By 1984, home video overtook cable as a larger source of film financing. Early home video distri-

bution successes often worked in partnership with cable financing. This symbiotic relationship is ironic since the two modes of distribution became competitive as the number of households owning VCRs reached parity with the
number of basic cable subscribers by 1986–1987.[29] Competition is evident in
the way home video rentals severely undercut the pay-per-view market for
feature films and dampened subscription rates for premium cable services.[30]

There was cooperation between the two industries for production financing, and there was competition for advantageous release windows and for audiences. Cable financing for filmmaking emerged in 1981, just slightly ahead
of video financing, when domestic theater revenues were stagnating and foreign theatrical revenues were declining.[31] HBO and other cable distributors'
license fees therefore provided the difference between life and death for
the perennially hungry independent producers. Films like *On Golden Pond*
(1981), *Tootsie* (1982), and *Sophie's Choice* (1982) were made with the active
pre-production support of HBO. Typically HBO provided 25 percent of the
negative costs of making the movie, for the exclusive right of showing a movie
on cable one year after its theatrical release. It is estimated that from 1977 to
1983, HBO participated in more than 100 movies on this basis.[32]

While indies found HBO to be a savior, major film distributors resented
HBO's refusal to tie its licensing fees to the number of viewers for individual
films or to give in on other film studio demands. They set up cable competi-
tors. Viacom, a television distributor, started Showtime in 1976. Warner
Communications collaborated with American Express to form The Movie
Channel in 1979. In 1980 Twentieth Century Fox, Universal, Paramount, and
Columbia, along with Getty Oil, created Premiere, a pay cable TV service that
would show the participants' films in an exclusive nine-month window. The
Justice Department sued the Premiere participants for anti-trust activity and
the New York Federal District Court ruled against the defendants. An appeal
looked hopeless and Premiere was dissolved. The movie studios started to
formulate other strategies.

The major suppliers had played with the exclusive window for each market release. Twentieth Century Fox initially did not allow a video release of
any movie less than two years old. In 1981, the company announced plans to
release *Nine to Five* just ten weeks after its theatrical release. Steve Roberts,
president of the telecommunications division, argued that the demographics
for the video audience were so different from those for the theatrical audi-

118   ence that this release would not hurt ticket sales and would take maximum
advantage of the theatrical advertising. It was rumored that this early release
was a strategy to upset HBO by favoring the video over the cable market.
Roberts had to back down when the theater owners complained that the
video release would cannibalize ticket sales (since potential ticket buyers
would wait for the video release). Afterward a six-month waiting period became the standard as a balance between adequate theatrical exclusivity and
the time when the film marketing campaign would still be fresh in the consumer's mind as the video appeared.

In 1982, American film companies received over $300 million from all pay
television programmers—HBO, The Movie Channel, Showtime, and others.[33]
This led to some new initiatives. For instance, former United Artists executives took over Filmways in February 1982 in order to acquire a film distributor. They could do this because they had the promise of HBO money that
would enable financing of the $26 million purchase. They renamed their
integrated production/distribution company Orion Pictures. In 1983, American film companies received over $500 million from pay television. A bench-
mark of sorts was reached in that year. The British producing company Goldcrest sold the American television rights for *Gandhi* for $20 million, to a
subdistributor. The success of its cable sale led the company to launch other
big-budget movies. This sum was roughly equivalent to its North American
box office returns. The gamble paid off when HBO paid $23 million for the
biopic in the subsequent bidding. This probably was an overpayment made
in the heat of fierce competition between HBO and Showtime.

It is surprising that despite 1983's frenetic pace of cable financing, within
a year home video soon surpassed it as the best new source of financing. But
the transition is understandable if we consider the difference between the
two industry cultures. Independent video distributors were entrepreneurs
without the corporate resources of the cable channels. They had to be aggressive and spend money freely in order to fill their pipelines. The VCR population was expanding, tempting these companies to bid for films, not on the
basis of what films had already earned in the video market, but in anticipation of breaking new sales records. Their aggression was due not only to an
expanding universe of rental stores but also to wide-open competition, without recent precedent in the filmed entertainment world. Andre Blay observed
that in 1983 pay TV effectively had only two buyers, and that the six majors
dominated theatrical distribution, but that for home video the six majors

were joined by three equally strong independents (Thorn/EMI, Vestron, and Embassy) and others for a total of twenty or so buyers.[34]

Goldman Sachs, the Wall Street research firm, stated that home video contributions matched pay TV contributions as early as 1982. By 1984, the research firm estimated that home video was giving film suppliers a total of $1.4 billion, while pay TV's contribution stagnated at $600 million.[35] Proportionately more of the video money was going to independent companies. However, even majors were surprised to find that video was returning more than cable for their films. Four companies boasted of this phenomenon to stockholders by breaking out the actual figures in their 1984 annual reports. Of the four, only MGM/UA reported slightly higher earnings from pay TV. Disney, Orion, and the even the litigious MCA/Universal were drawing more from home video than from pay TV.[36] The trend only deepened the next year. Merrill Lynch, another Wall Street investment firm, stated that video contributed 23 percent of the film industry's total revenues in 1985, significantly ahead of pay TV, with its 17.9 percent contribution.[37]

Cable and Pay Per View (PPV) kept losing ground to home video in terms of exclusivity and release dates. As the VCR population surged, cable subscribers fell behind. In 1986, there were 32.5 million VCR households, with an equal number of cable subscriptions. In 1988, there were only 48.6 million basic cable households, of which 37.2 million had premium subscriptions, compared to 56.2 million VCR households.[38] Since that time there has consistently been 10 million or more VCR households than basic cable households. In addition, the prerecorded video market returns an even greater amount of money per consumer to the film supplier than either cable or PPV.

From 1980 through 1983, major studios expressed fondness for PPV as the potentially best new distribution technology. The split of PPV revenue was just like the theatrical split since the studio received 50 percent of the money each viewer paid to watch the movie. But the mass audience did not materialize. In September 1982, *Star Wars* became the most popular PPV film of the early 1980s, with 300,000 subscribers. If we estimate that Twentieth Century Fox got $4 per viewer, the resulting $1.2 million still pales against the $8.3 million the studio received from the 1983 home video release.[39] The situation for PPV has never really improved, although related schemes such as Video On Demand (VOD) and others have occasionally been promoted as having the potential to undermine the prerecorded video market. It is of enduring importance that by 1983, the studios had learned that video was their best new market. At this point, it was standard practice to release a title on video at least three months before cable was allowed to show the film and a year before a network broadcast.

In more than one case, cable money served as the seed money for projects that eventually attracted even more money and attention from video distributors. For example, Orion, the company created by HBO financing, became an important source of independent films for the video market. This occurred when it signed a deal for Vestron to handle its domestic video distribution.

Vestron's president, Jon Peisinger, had made a point of opposing the various Hollywood leasing plans and the effort of studios to rescind first sale doctrine. Vestron wanted to cooperate with video rental stores on marketing and other resources.[40] Furst and Peisinger had decided that the key to success was to treat video as a unique market. Vestron moved forward quickly to become the biggest independent distributor. By the end of its first year, it had released fifty-one videocassette titles. Within another year, it had reached parity with the majors in the number of releases and revenue share. The company was taking its revenue and putting it right back into buying more films.

Vestron's Furst relished the resulting fierce competition. He had left HBO in order to get involved in a risky and rewarding market. He told *Variety* that "home video is the most 'democratic' video business around right now, . . . All a company has to do to enter is to get a product that will sell to the wholesalers, and through them to the retailers."[41] David Whitten, a sales veteran of those days, reports that Vestron would send five buyers to film markets such as the American Film Market. They would enter on the first day and put in preemptive bids on every film that still had open video rights. Other distributors were forced to increase their own bids or stay out of the game. Vestron's biggest coups were getting the rights to the *Benji* series, two films from ABC, and the international rights to Merchant Ivory productions. Vestron also managed to lock up the entire 1983 and 1984 output of Orion Pictures, the producers of Woody Allen's films, and other high-profile titles. The aggressive acquisition of product gave Vestron and its wholesalers the ability to quickly stock the shelves of the new and/or expanding video stores. More film producers wanted to jump on the Vestron bandwagon and take advantage of Vestron's newly won power with retailers.

All the major film libraries had been licensed to home video distributors by the end of 1983. Now the bidding for video rights to unattached films went up another notch. Embassy raised eyebrows when it broke the million-dollar barrier by paying $1.6 million for the North American home video rights to *Silkwood* as it began its theatrical run.[42] Nonetheless, it was reported that Embassy turned a profit on the deal.[43] Several companies were now over-reaching. Noel Bloom acquired the North American video rights to *Supergirl* from Alexander Salkind for a rumored $3.25 million.[44] He completed the deal in May 1984, before the movie flopped in its theatrical release and subsequently suffered a loss in the video release. An all-time record for buying a completed film may have been set when CBS/Fox paid somewhere between $10 and $15 million for the rights to *The Empire Strikes Back* in 1984. Outsiders speculated that the video release did not return a profit for at least several years.[45]

Pre-Selling/Pre-Buying

One way to reduce the very high prices film producers were demanding was for video distributors to pre-buy the film before it had been completed. It is at this stage of negotiations that a video distributor has an advantage. The producers need to raise cash and the competing distributors are much less willing to take a risk on an unknown product. Dino DeLaurentiis had pioneered pre-selling in 1972 with the help of the Dutch banker Frans Afman. DeLaurentiis solicited commitments from distributors around the world to buy a film that had yet to be made, for their territories. Afman used the commitments as collateral and advanced the money to DeLaurentiis to make the film. It was an excellent way to maintain autonomy. DeLaurentiis treated Paramount (his U.S. distributor) as a co-equal in power sharing as he produced a string of hits—including *Serpico* (1973) and *Death Wish* (1974)—from this novel form of financing.[46] The same techniques and even the same people were now engaged in pre-selling to video distributors. Frans Afman was now working with the French bank Crédit Lyonnais. Because of his success and influence, Crédit Lyonnais became a major lender to the independent producers and distributors, underwriting the pre-selling.

Video pre-buying was first initiated for low-budget films (under $5 million in negative costs). It is impossible to chart the amount of home video money financing low-budget films. A few reports indicate the trend. One low-budget outfit, Manson Productions, reported getting one-third of its money from home video as early as 1981.[47] By 1984, video distributors had enough money and confidence to pre-buy high-budget films ($10 million or more). Media

122   Home Entertainment, armed with the backing of a billion-dollar-plus con-
glomerate (the Heron Group), was the first when it paid $2.6 million for North
American video rights to *Santa Claus—The Movie*, another Alexander
Salkind production, in March 1984.

The hot action in buying was highly visible at the new and expanding film
markets of the 1980s. Film markets had come to be important soon after
World War II. The most famous was the Cannes Film Festival, which first
opened in September 1946. In addition to its famous competition and the debut of films to the public, Cannes had also become the site where distributors
from all parts of the film world could pick up unsold rights from film producers. Several new filmed entertainment markets were formed in response
to the expansion of ancillary markets and of global television syndication.
MiFed was started in Milan in 1980, and the American Film Marketing Association (AFMA) was formed in 1981 with its own annual market in Los Angeles. International buyers and sellers of independent films traveled to all three
markets, and video buyers made quite a splash at these places. Foreign television was still dominated by single-channel state monopolies, and European
video dealers sought average or below-average American films in order to fill
the pent-up demand for an alternative to TV.

By 1984, AFMA was reporting that home video accounted for one-third of
the foreign sales or $120 million out of a total of $375 million.[48] The following year AFMA reported that 60 percent of the total market activity (domestic and foreign) came from home video.[49] MiFed reported similar results.
Orion and a production consortium, Producer Service Organization (PSO),
both reported getting 50 percent of their sales for home video rights. Cannon
got 40 percent from home video.[50] The presence of companies such as Cannon and PSO showed that pre-buying was not just helping established producers but also creating opportunity for new ones. Pre-buying was the
primary activity that reinforced diversity in video distribution and film production.

Cannon Films represented a new breed of production companies, one
whose business plan was a direct response to the new home video money. It
had first drawn attention as the producer/distributor of the cult film *Joe*,
which earned $9.5 million after its 1970 release. It settled into a routine pack-
age of soft porn and horror films for the rest of the decade. In 1979, Men-
achem Golan and Yoram Globus, two Israeli cousins, borrowed money from
Slavenburg Bank of The Netherlands and bought Cannon Films. Both they

and their loan officer, Frans Afman, had decided that quantity was the key to success as home video and other markets expanded for film products. Golan, in his usual colorful manner, said to the press in 1986, "Theatrical is not the only mouth to feed. If Hollywood produced five times as many films as it does now, it would still not meet the demand. There is space for the mediocre!"[51] Afman reiterated that view when he said in an interview: "We're told that only eight titles a year will succeed. When I heard that figure, I told my clients to get a lot of B movies ready because in a situation like that there will be an enormous product shortage."[52] Afman anticipated that the few big films from the major studios would not be enough to feed the ancillary markets. His lending activities became a big part of independent production expansion from 1984 to 1987.

Cannon needed little encouragement from its banker to be off and running. They had a preexisting library of sixty Cannon titles, to which they added their own Israeli films. Golan and Globus expanded their production schedule every year without slowing down to add up their returns from the previous year's releases. They adopted the strategy of seeking every possible line of credit, with a particular emphasis on foreign and home video pre-sales, to build up their library. In 1983 they got $12 million from video distributors.[53] In 1985 they sold the video rights for thirty-two films for $50 million to Media Home Entertainment. The next year they got a pre-buy of $50 million for twenty-three future pictures.[54] The company experimented with a variety of budgets. They generally averaged $5 million in negative costs per title in 1985, about one-third of the costs on an MPAA film at that time.[55] Golan and Globus produced an eclectic mixture of action (e.g., *Missing in Action* [1984]), dance fads (e.g., *Breakin'* [1984]), and even films by such art cinema "auteurs" as Jean-Luc Godard and John Cassavetes. Among the many movies they were making they hoped that one would become a hit. Nonetheless, Golan/Globus insisted that their primary goal was to make many movies to fill the perceived void, not to create a breakaway hit.

By 1986, Cannon had many more films in production than any other film company. It announced that it had started forty-one new film productions. The second most prolific production company was New World, which announced eighteen. The independent Hemdale announced fifteen. In contrast, each of the major film companies had, at most, nine or ten new films in production.

Afman had expanded Crédit Lyonnais' portfolio beyond DeLaurentiis and

124   Cannon to include independent producers at all budget levels. Video was a
key component of the collateral for Afman. Eventually Crédit Lyonnais lent
a total of $2.5 billion.[56] Crédit Lyonnais' client list included production com-
panies such as Cannon, DeLaurentiis, Carolco, Cinergi, Largo, Sovereign,
Castle Rock, Morgan Creek, Nelson Entertainment, Hemdale, New World,
and Empire. Some of the more interesting films that Afman lent money for
include *Superman* (1978), *Superman II* (1980), and a string of films released
in 1986, including *Crimes of the Heart, Blue Velvet, Salvador, Platoon, Hoos-
iers,* and *A Room with a View.*

Carolco was another company that built itself up by pre-selling to home
video and foreign markets. This company was also owned by men who had
started their careers outside the U.S.—Mario Kassar and Andrew Vajna. They
had been selling films to foreign distributors since 1975. As the foreign theatrical market eroded, they decided to upgrade their product by going into
production themselves. They cleverly picked a project that combined enough
action to attract a global audience with a plotline "that is . . . meaningful
enough for the American market."[57] They produced *First Blood*, starring
Sylvester Stallone, in 1982. Its international market was not bothered by the
noticeable lack of dialogue. It did well in its theatrical release and became a
very big video hit after it was released by Thorn/EMI. Kassar and Vajna had
discovered the hybrid blockbuster formula and moved on to the higher
budget sequel. *Rambo: First Blood Part II* was released in 1985 and earned
$78 million in rentals for its distributor. In the aftermath of the success of
Rambo, the partners created Carolco Pictures in Los Angeles to produce and
exploit "event" films that would hopefully do as well as *Rambo*. Carolco concentrated its money on only two to four releases every year. This strategy was
opposed to that employed by Cannon Films because it emphasized "quality"
over quantity. Kassar and Vajna had no interest in the mediocre. An "event"
film costs in excess of $20 million and represents the top end of budgets. Car-
olco offset the risk of such high-budget movies by pre-selling, and it also
avoided the hazards of domestic theatrical distribution by entering into an
ongoing agreement with Tri-Star to handle that market for it.

Carolco also displayed interest in video distribution. In 1986, Noel Bloom's
International Video Enterprises (IVE) had run into trouble. It had an operating profit of $6.5 million in the fiscal year ending August 31, 1985, and then
lost $14 million in 1986. Bloom held on by selling stock in his company to Ca-

rolco in stages through the second half of 1986. By December 31, Carolco held 100 percent of IVE. The purchase price was $4,775,000.[58]

Video money had permeated independent financing and was responsible for a new international presence in Hollywood. The international players—DeLaurentiis, Carolco, Cannon, Hemdale, et al., together with comparable American film companies such as Orion, Samuel Goldwyn, et al.—were known as mini-majors. They had enough money from pre-sales and other sources to release a full schedule of films (a dozen or so per year). However, compared to the majors, they were underfinanced and did not possess fixed assets such as physical studios or large libraries. Even those producers who had been quite successful before video needed the added cash flow at this point. The definitive statement about how much U.S. home video was contributing to the financing of films comes in a 1986 DeLaurentiis prospectus. It indicates that domestic home video contributed about 10 percent more than foreign pre-sales—50 to 60 percent of negative costs versus 40 to 50 percent from foreign distribution rights.[59] If we remember that part of the foreign pre-sale money comes from foreign home video, we can safely say that in total, home video accounted for 65 to 72 percent of the money DeLaurentiis needed to make films.

Video and New Genres

Independent distributors experimented with several new cassette genres besides theatrical feature films. The first and biggest excitement over a non-feature videotape was due to the breakout sales of *Jane Fonda's Workout*. This "how-to" tape was produced and distributed by the entrepreneur Stuart Karl and released in the spring of 1982. Three years later, it had earned $34.2 million for the supplier on sales of 950,000 units.[60] The tape had several unique aspects. It was sold at the relatively high price of $59.95, and yet most of its sales were to individual customers rather than rental stores. It had a relatively long shelf life, developing strong steady sales for a sustained period. Many other companies engaged in the sincerest form of flattery by putting out their own "how-to" cassettes featuring celebrities. Lorimar bought Karl Video in October 1984 for a rumored $3 million.[61] Yet, the "how-to" category did not live up to its initial promise. In 1983, this category was estimated to be 10 percent of the business. No one could match the success of Jane Fonda's first

126   tape. Her own sequel, released by Lorimar-Karl at the end of 1984, had
barely one-fifth the sales volume of the original. In that year, "how-to" tapes
dropped to 5 percent of the cassette sale business and remained at that percentage for the rest of the decade.[62]

A further experiment with forms of the videocassette involved music.
MTV had been a popular innovation in pay TV since its inception in 1981.
Video companies naturally searched for a way to translate the MTV phenomenon into videocassette sales. MTV music clips were too short to be sold,
and various companies tried ways of lengthening them with interviews, other
concert footage, and so on. In this pursuit, Vestron scored the breakout hit.
Peisinger actively courted Michael Jackson and finally signed a deal with the
singer/dancer in conjunction with the cable outlet Showtime to pay $1.1 mil-
lion for a show that not only showed Michael Jackson's music video *Thriller*
but also included other behind-the-scenes material to fill out the show to an
hour's length. It was directed by John Landis, still under indictment for his
conduct during the filming of *The Twilight Zone—The Movie* in 1982. The
video was entitled *The Making of Michael Jackson's Thriller* and was released
at the end of 1983 for the low price of $29.95. The low price was designed to
attract purchases from individual viewers as well as rental stores. It sold
550,000 units in North America and 750,000 worldwide. Vestron had the first
major musical hit, receiving revenues in excess of $10 million.[63]

In hindsight, Peisinger has concluded that the runaway success of *Thriller*
had more to do with Michael Jackson's celebrity power than with a repeat-
able popular music format. Part of his reasoning was that other attempts to
build music into a major part of the pre-recorded cassette business fell short.
By 1984, RCA/Columbia was expressing disappointment in its music titles.[64]
Sony Video had debuted Video 45s in 1983 but had trouble finding buyers.
The 45s suffered from being too short at ten to fifteen minutes in length. Producers of music videos moved from illustrating the song in the video to using
a creative separation between song lyrics and visual imagery to encourage repeat video viewings. However, the customers seemed satisfied with repeat
viewings on cable and neither bought nor rented the cassettes in large enough
numbers. Videocassette proved to be a less than ideal format for music video.

There was also a structural reason for the music customer's reluctance.
The video store owners were relying heavily on rental as the source of their
income. Music videos were much more viable as a sell-through rather than as
a rental. Therefore these store owners hesitated in giving shelf space to mu-

sic videos. They also did not understand the music business and were not likely to satisfy customer inquiries about the availability of particular music bands. The store owners' lack of interest was further amplified by the whole-salers.[65] The wholesalers would not stock items that could not be quickly re-sold to the store owners. These wholesalers had fewer connections with record stores that would stock the music videos. Of course, if there had been customer demand, alternative supply routes would have been developed, but structurally music videos suffered by being between two different divisions in the suppliers' organizations and by not being satisfactorily distributed by ei-ther the home video or the record distribution system.

Music videos were a higher share of the European and Japanese markets. Even Americans supported music on video if presented as a feature film. *Purple Rain*, written by and starring the Minneapolis pop star Prince, was the fifth historic best-selling videocassette in 1985. In genre classification it could just as easily be regarded as an extended music video as it could a feature-length narrative film. *Flashdance*, another music-driven feature, was ninth, and *Footloose* was twenty-second.[66] Vestron's *Thriller* was the only best-seller that set the music in a format different from the theatrical film.

Vestron's Video Publishing

Vestron forcefully developed and marketed *Thriller* because its philosophy was that home video was a new business. Film people only knew the film busi-ness; Vestron was going to provide a different mix of product and marketing for the video business. Jon Peisinger, the president of Vestron, used lessons and language drawn from his record industry background. The video had to be sold while it was new and "hot." He had that in mind as Vestron was pio-neering the concept of "instant" publishing. This involved buying ABC footage of the Pope's visit to the Statue of Liberty and hitting the street with videocassette while the news was still fresh. The moviegoer made a decision on which movie to see before embarking for the theater. The video pur-chaser/renter was much more impulsive and did not make a choice of video until he or she was already in the video store. The "hot" stuff would grab the customer's attention.

Vestron publicized its difference from the major film distributors over the issue of first sale doctrine and its refusal to institute rental policies in order to emphasize its concern for video rental stores. It was the first big distribu-

128   tor to offer the video store owner cooperative advertising and to emphasize point of purchase displays.[67] One film company, Artists Releasing, assigned video rights to Vestron because it appreciated Vestron's supplying
chopsticks as a promotional device for the comic karate film *They Call Me
Bruce?* (1982).[68]

Vestron wanted strength from diversity. Furst stated that his model for
the company was a book publisher.[69] The company even tried magazine-
formatted videos with *Penthouse* and *National Geographic* along with a
mixed slate of adult sex titles and children's video, low-budget horror and
big-budget drama. The point was to distinguish Vestron from Hollywood
"hit"-driven philosophy. Vestron even claimed a virtue in placing its corporate headquarters in Stamford, Connecticut, near Furst's residence, far from
the hype and "interference" of the Los Angeles film industry and psycholog-
ically distant even from the nearby media center of New York. Vestron was
perpetuating the regional separation from New York and Los Angeles that
had become popular in the 1970s when film activities increased in San Francisco, Salt Lake City, Oregon, and the southeastern states. Unlike these earlier activities, Vestron did not seek any aesthetic difference from Los Angeles. Furst and Peisinger did not denounce Hollywood decadence. Their point
was merely to escape the community pressures of the film industry, where
everyone was looking over everyone's shoulder and developed blockbuster
strategies almost in common. In this way, they distinguished themselves not
only from the majors but also from the other independent video distributors.

Vestron was gathering momentum, with earnings of $12 million in 1982
and $45 million in 1983 and a net income of $2 million and $6.6 million, re-
spectively, in those two years. It was clearly outpacing its independent rivals
and closing in on the major film suppliers. Annual market share ratings from
Video Week show that Vestron was number seven out of ten in 1983 with
6 percent of the total prerecorded videocassette sales. Vestron's acquisitions
from independents and mini-majors were proving advantageous.

The company was accused of starting bidding wars for films, but never
went to the lengths Embassy and Noel Bloom did, because it was assured of
mainstream films from its ongoing contract with Orion. However, contracts
with Orion and others had expiration dates, and Vestron started exploring in-
house production and theatrical distribution divisions in order to position itself for the future when Orion and other product would not be available. Already Vestron realized that a supply of theatrical films was critical even for a

video "publisher." Still it was surprised by how decisively the market turned toward mainstream theatricals in 1986.

Conclusion

In the period up through 1986, the market for prerecorded cassettes passed several milestones. I have deliberately separated the narrative of the major studios from that of the independents because in this time these two groups can be usefully contrasted. The studios had formed home video divisions and were making a great deal of money from the expanding market, but they seemed oddly hostile to its emergence. It may be too convenient to conclude that they left a void for the independents to fill, but it is true that the smaller companies were innovating and pushing new approaches. The majors did not move aggressively in the late 1970s to secure video rights for the various co-productions and other movies for which they had theatrical distribution rights. This left a pool of films, including many popular ones, available for in-dependent distributors. The big Hollywood studios continued to be distracted by efforts to control rental through contracts or through legislation. These ef-forts proved futile and worse since relationships with video retailers were damaged.

On the other hand, the independents and the newcomers were quick to develop and exploit the new market. They made use of existing techniques such as pre-selling in order to drive production and to expand their catalogs quickly. They cultivated the video retailer and they helped promote the new video market through advertising and other publicity mechanisms. They ex-plored the new possibilities of the medium by investing in "how-to" tapes, "instant" publishing, and music videos. Through pre-selling and global sales of video rights, these distributors reinvigorated marginal film genres such as horror (e.g., *Halloween*) and military action (e.g., *Rambo, Missing in Action*). Oliver Stone told the Academy of Motion Pictures that his Oscar-winning film *Platoon* (1986) was possible only because Vestron pre-bought it.[70] Indepen-dents had gone where majors did not dare.

Some of the new video distributors had worked with pornographic films and understood that viewers might be more willing to take salacious or sleazy titles home to watch than they would be to go to see these movies in the the-ater. Noel Bloom and others used a successful reverse logic and decided that if adults were taking home movies that they would not share with their fam-

130   ily, they would also want cassettes that were appropriate for children. This turned out to be a permanent innovation of home video: that it directly contributed to the renaissance of children's programming. We will deal with this in detail in the next chapter, where I discuss the transformations at Disney when the new executives decided to embrace home video. The irony is that Noel Bloom, not a Disney executive, can plausibly claim to have started children's home video.

This period was a time when the structures of the American film industry were loosening. It was a preliminary stage. The video machine offered the audience two types of choices: access to more product and control over the time and place of viewing movies. In the growth stage the structures of distribution experimented with facilitating both types of choices. As the market matured, the open question was whether economies of scale would harden the distribution channels and restrict the range of movies being produced with the new video money. As 1986 drew to an end, it was clear that the video distribution market would mature by shaking out some of the experimental business practices. If we understand the precise nature of this shakeout, we will be able to understand the way in which the video market turned against independence and diversity and toward the big blockbuster strategy that is the hallmark of New Hollywood.

The cumbersome mechanics of video recording in the mid-1950s. This machine probably holds only ten minutes or less of programming. Ampex was able to demonstrate a more workable model in 1956. Nonetheless, it would be another decade before the recognizable cassette was introduced. SOURCE: NEW YORK PUBLIC LIBRARY.

A display ad created by Doyle, Dane, and Bernbach for the original Sony release of the Betamax. Its emphasis on time-shifting irked Universal City Studios and Disney Productions into initiating a major lawsuit that went all the way to the Supreme Court in 1984. The case was one of the last instances in which the U.S. government refused to extend copyright protection. SOURCE: NEW YORK PUBLIC LIBRARY.

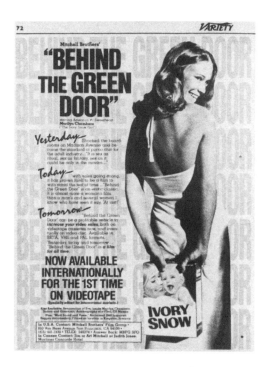

Adult films were key to developing the mechanics of video marketing and rental. An ad for the famous *Behind the Green Door* from the First Variety Home Video Annual in 1980. SOURCE: COLLECTION OF THE AUTHOR.

As Laserdisc failed to gain market share against the vastly more popular video cassette recorders, it concentrated on niche markets such as opera buffs in the United States and Europe and karaoke singers in Asia. SOURCE: NEW YORK PUBLIC LIBRARY.

Twentieth Century Fox must have felt as bold as General Patton when it authorized magnetic video release of *Patton* in 1978, eight years after the film had been released in theaters. It was one of the first "recent" Hollywood films to go to video and was a great success in this fast-developing new market. SOURCE: PHOTOFEST.

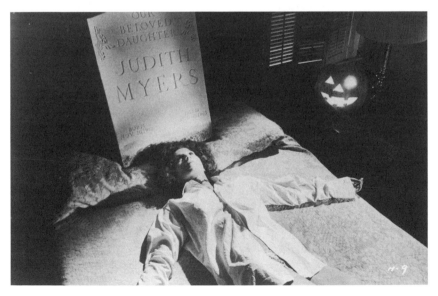

Halloween (1978) was a major video release for Media Home Entertainment, one of the first important independent video distributors. SOURCE: PHOTOFEST.

Noel Bloom moved quickly into independent video distribution. In 1980 he pioneered the video-for-children market ("kidvid") with the creation of Family Home Entertainment. These and other Bloom companies eventually formed the basis for LIVE Entertainment. Although Bloom has long since departed, LIVE is the only independent that continues to be a significant player under its new name, Artisan Releasing. The irony is that Mr. Bloom started in adult film distribution. SOURCE: NOEL BLOOM.

Jon Peisinger was president of Vestron Video as the independent company moved into theatrical film production. SOURCE: JON PEISINGER.

Jane Fonda and Stuart Karl accepted the Billboard award for their breakthrough video *Jane Fonda's Workout* in 1982. Their achievement has not been surpassed in the field of "how-to" videos. SOURCE: PHOTOFEST.

Pre-selling and the video market sparked a boom in independent production. Cannon, an independent production and distribution company, practically bragged about the vast quantity of its productions in this display ad from the 1983 *Variety* annual. SOURCE: PERSONAL COLLECTION.

The Michael Jackson phenomenon crossed media lines when Vestron Video released *Making Michael Jackson's "Thriller"* in late 1983. The video sold well enough to earn the Golden Videocassette Award in 1984. Left to right: Vestron president Jon Peisinger, Michael Jackson, Vestron CEO Austin Furst. SOURCE: JON PEISINGER.

Dirty Dancing, Vestron's first feature production, was a hit both in the theater and on video. Its 1987 release gave Vestron another three years of life, then Vestron sold its assets to LIVE in 1990. SOURCE: PHOTOFEST.

Star Trek I, a high-concept film, was released on video at the end of 1980, priced at $79.95, and became a major seller for Paramount Home Video. SOURCE: PHOTOFEST.

Paramount had one of video's big sellers in the 1980s with *Top Gun*. The 1986 release also featured a cross-promotional tie-in with Pepsi-Cola. A Pepsi ad was placed at the beginning of the original video release, and Pepsi mentioned *Top Gun* in its own advertising. Although video advertising has not become widespread, the promotional tie-ins between Hollywood and consumer marketing have become closer because of the video market. SOURCE: PERSONAL COLLECTION.

Star Trek II was the first "sell-through" video, released at the end of 1982 by Paramount at a price of $39.95. Its sales surpassed those of the first *Star Trek* by a third and equaled its earnings. SOURCE: PERSONAL COLLECTION.

Disney executives were worried about their own images as they debated whether to release the 1940 classic *Pinocchio* on video in 1985. They finally took the risk and successfully exploited the video earnings from their animated films to finance their increased operations. Video is a key to Disney's current position as the third-largest global media corporation.
SOURCE: PHOTOFEST.

Disney perfected its manipulation of theatrical and video releasing when it launched *Aladdin* into the theaters in 1992. It went on to sell *Aladdin* as a sell-through title on video and then to release the sequels to *Aladdin* such as *Aladdin's Arabian Adventures* directly to video without theatrical play. SOURCE: PHOTOFEST.

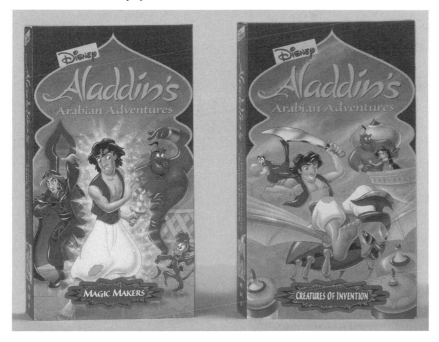

CHAPTER FIVE

Video Becomes Big Business

By 1986, the sale of prerecorded cassettes had matured. There were shake-outs and consolidations in the American and international film industries in the following years. The shakeouts were predictable, although their scope and shape were not natural occurrences. Indeed, many important results were counterintuitive. Despite video's popularity, theatrical attendance remained steady and the theatrical release continued to draw the overwhelming share of attention and promotional budgets. The vastly expanded market of home video did not result in a permanent escalation of production. Production actually dropped below levels of the 1970s. This was despite the ever-escalating home video revenue flow, which exceeded box office returns by 1987–1988.

Chapters 5 and 6 will describe the circumstances of the maturing of the video market. These descriptions will support the argument that the shakeouts were determined by the distribution practices of New Hollywood responding to changing audience desires as video stabilized. The two chapters divide along industrial lines. In this chapter, we consider the mechanics of getting the film to the consumer during this development. In the next chapter, we return to the struggle of the distributors and producers.

The studios' continuing hostility to renting led to two-tiered pricing. "Two-tiered" refers to the situation that continues to this day—pricing certain titles under $25 in order to stimulate high-volume sales to consumers and pricing other titles three times as much for maximum profit despite lower sale volume. The two-tiered pricing system, once in place, effectively doubled the home video revenue streams for the few mainstream studios that owned easily marketed films. Two-tiered pricing becomes an important albeit indirect component in the overall decline of independents and weaker film dis-

132   tributors. Because of the studios' ability to pool video earnings, it is better to look at the aggregate effects of new video money rather than its impact on individual film productions or specific marketing strategies. On the other side of the equation, both video retailing and the wholesale distribution of cassettes were consolidating and introducing higher entry barriers. This can be fully understood when we look at the pricing system of video in its context. These industrial changes became the enabling conditions of the cultural opportunities and limitations for New Hollywood.

The Development of Two-Tiered Pricing

The development of the rental market had maintained the upward pressure on the list price of videocassettes. The $80 price was introduced in 1982 because Mel Harris and Robert Klingensmith, the two leading executives at Paramount Home Video, got tired of the leasing struggles. They decided simply to charge more for the first sale. The rest of the industry followed suit.

Some distributors attempted price competition, hoping to sell more units if they charged less. Generally, many believed that the value of price competition would be limited as long as the market was limited to 25,000 video rental stores. Price competition made sense only if the intended market was millions of individual customers. By 1982, five million households owned VCRs (see Table 2.1). Before this time, videocassette distributors had been distributing non-feature film titles for a wide range of prices. The question was whether five million was enough of a critical mass to support a low price for a high-profile feature movie. Paramount decided to experiment by releasing *Star Trek II: The Wrath of Khan* at the end of the year, at $39.95. This was still a relatively high price, but consumers responded and the show became the biggest seller of the year, eventually shipping 290,000 units. In contrast, the first *Star Trek* movie, released at $79.95 in November 1980, had been selling at half that rate. After subsequent price reductions, the first movie eventually shipped 187,000 units.[1] Of course, the Paramount price reduction increased its risk exposure since the fixed costs of duplicating and packaging were still the same per unit. In this case, Paramount probably earned $2.2 to $2.8 million after deducting such costs. This roughly matched the earnings on the first *Star Trek*.[2]

The other studios took an interest in this experiment and dissected the numbers. One nameless rival publicly estimated the breakdown on the $39.95 price as follows: The dealer paid Paramount $25. Paramount paid $9–$10 for manufacturing and marketing, and $5 for royalties. The studio therefore cleared $9–$10 on each unit sold.[3] These were rough ballpark figures that varied depending on the royalty deal. In the *Star Trek* case, Paramount also retained a large share of the royalties, boosting its earnings by perhaps another $3 per unit. Paramount continued to issue films at the $39.95 list price, breaking unit/sales records with titles such as *Flashdance* and *Raiders of the Lost Ark* (both in 1983). *Raiders* ultimately surpassed *Jane Fonda's Workout* in units sold and was the first videocassette to break the 1 million unit mark by 1985 (when VCR households had reached 23 million).

Other video distributors debated whether Paramount had increased its actual profits by reducing prices and hesitated to follow its lead. Some did. Embassy had success with a $39.95 release of *Blade Runner* in February of 1983. A year later it suffered a disappointment with *The Day After* at that same price and retreated back to $79.95 for *The Golden Seal* and *Eddie and the Cruisers*. Warner tried a price slash to $39.95 in March 1983 and reverted to a higher price three months later.[4] In November, David Geffen, a partner in *Risky Business*, urged Warner Home Video to release the film at $39.95. Warner agreed.

CBS/Fox, in particular, was lobbying heavily for the repeal of the first sale doctrine. Alan Hirschfield of Twentieth Century Fox had told Congress in 1984 that once the repeal went through, the studios would be able to reduce video prices. CBS/Fox Video, of which Twentieth Century Fox owned half, could not very well undercut Hirschfield's argument by participating in the lower price experiment. On the other hand, Paramount had made the decision not to pursue repeal but to move the market away from rental stores to direct consumer purchases. Klingensmith was pleased to report that 75 percent of *Raiders* units were being sold to consumers compared to only 10 percent of the higher priced *Tootsie* cassettes.[5] Although earnings were roughly equivalent for both high and low prices, Klingensmith felt that lower prices built a customer base. The number of these customers would expand as the video population expanded. Paramount continued the low price experiment in order to shift the video business to direct purchases.

It was Walt Disney Productions that finally validated the experiment. Disney's aborted leasing program and its decision not to transfer the more popular animated classics to video gave the company the lowest market share of

134   the major video distributors in 1980–1981. This was the void for children's titles that provided opportunity for Noel Bloom, Western Publishing, and others. In 1984, the lackluster performance of Walt Disney Productions in all its divisions (film, theme parks, merchandising, and real estate) attracted the attention of Wall Street raiders. Even Jim Jimirro of the Disney old guard urged the CEO Ron Miller to become more aggressive about releasing the great classics in order to generate income quickly to revalue the stock. The theatrical division continued to argue successfully that this would ruin future theatrical re-releases of the classics.[6] That summer, a frustrated Jimirro ordered Disney's home video division to try an even lower price than Paramount for its new releases. This home video promotion was called "Limited Gold Edition," and it featured seven non-feature animation titles for the list price of $29.95 for a limited time. The promotion drew attention when it resulted in $9 million for Disney from sales of 500,000 units.

Paramount executives pondered Disney's success. They realized that a new price level had been made possible by a reduction in manufacturing costs. Paramount Home Video expanded its own low-price campaign. The company dropped prices to $24.95 for 25 "A" titles (recent big-budget films) for the 1984 Christmas season.[7] The Paramount campaign was a success, with shipments of 675,000 units (which returned almost $10 million in revenue to the film supplier). This coincided with huge sales (450,000 units) for Warner's *Purple Rain*, also priced at $24.95. The "$25 and under" tapes were here to stay.

This success led to the "two-tiered" pricing system. Videocassettes are either list priced at the high $90-plus or at low prices ranging from the break-even price of $8 through the $30 range, most typically between $15 and $25. The rental stores are free to buy low-priced tapes and consumers are free to buy high-priced ones. However, it is generally the case that only rental stores will invest so much money in the high-priced tapes and will have less interest in the low-priced tapes, since part of the audience for such tapes will have already purchased them and will not be renting those titles. The high-priced tapes are therefore known as rental tapes and the low priced ones are "sell-throughs" since they have been sold directly to the ultimate user of the tape. Sell-through tapes are routed to mass merchandisers and rack jobbers. Rental tapes are advertised in wholesaling trade journals for the video retailer purchases. Many analysts think that the sell-through price is justified if it generates sales four or five times the anticipated sales volume of the rental-priced tape.[8] In addition to the arithmetic of higher volume sales, sell-through tapes need a more expensive marketing campaign since they are sold to the general public rather than video specialty stores.

The double-digit growth of the rental market ended by 1988. Since that point, there have been predictions that sell-through will dominate the prerecorded cassette business. The market continues to be two tiered. Through 1993–1994 (the end point for this study), rental-priced tapes still supplied 55 percent of the total video revenues that studios received. Consumer spending on rentals was twice the amount spent on purchasing prerecorded cassettes for most of the 1990s.[9] Sell-through pricing dominates the children's video market and most of the non-feature film market. Meanwhile, "B" titles are invariably priced as rentals.

A contentious question for video executives is which big hit movie should have a sell-through release. It is not the popularity of the film, but the nature of that popularity. Is it the kind of show that people want to own or give as gifts to their friends?

The development of low-priced tapes in 1984 was an early manifestation of the budding relationship between the home video market and the acceleration of concentration in the film industry. Although the film industry had failed to get government help to control the emerging video rental market, in several instances the video phenomenon helped deregulation and thereby facilitated media conglomerates. I have already mentioned the mutually reinforcing coincidence of home video and the deregulation of broadcasting in Northern Europe. An analogous event in the U.S. was the effective reentry of Hollywood studios into theater ownership.

The New Movie Theater

The new media of home video and cable contributed to an atmospheric change at the Justice Department. The Reagan appointees were looking to scale back the anti-trust activities of previous administrations. In the world of filmed entertainment the Attorney General's office undermined the spirit of the 1948 *Paramount et al.* consent decree in a press release dated February 4, 1985. "The Department announced that they would no longer enforce the Paramount decree because of changed circumstances in the industry."[10] Assistant Attorney General William Baxter and his advisers had accepted the

136   argument that home video and cable made film distribution diverse enough to re-allow vertical integration of theatrical exhibition and distribution. The film industry responded. Major U.S. distributors negotiated theater purchases worth over $1.5 billion in 1986 and acquired significant ownership positions in one-fifth of the North American movie screens.

By the mid-1980s, the movie theaters needed further construction and revamping to attract an audience that now had a choice in where and when to consume movies. The most dynamic part of this reinvestment has been the expansion of "multiplexing." To some degree, multiplexing is the real estate version of time shifting, since the additional screens within a theater give the viewer additional choices over which movie to see and/or when to see a particular movie. The history of multiplexing began slowly, thirty years before the video revolution.

In 1948, Nathan Taylor put together several movie theaters in one location in Toronto, offering customers flexibility in choosing a movie to see once they arrived at the location. Thirty-one years later Garth Drabinsky convinced Taylor to build a movie theater complex under one roof. The patron enters the building and has a choice of theater and movie to attend. The two men dubbed this a "cineplex." Cineplexing becomes the exhibitor's way of matching the new range of choices that videocassette stores are offering. The choice was relatively modest at first, with only at most a half-dozen movies to choose from, but the concept was popular. In 1982, Taylor and Drabinsky moved into the U.S. by building a cineplex in the Beverly Center in West Los Angeles, the heart of the movie colony. Three years later they bought another theater chain called the Odeon, and renamed their company Cineplex Odeon.[11]

The development of the home video and other ancillary revenue streams gave the major studios money to buy and to improve the movie theaters. They wanted to develop multiplexing (a more generic term for Taylor and Drabinsky's cineplex concept) as part of the new emphasis on audience convenience. After the Reagan administration had signaled that it would no longer prevent distributors from buying movie theaters, MCA/Universal took a 49 percent equity position in Cineplex Odeon in 1986. Columbia/Tri-Star and Paramount also bought domestic theaters. Warner and other movie companies were already involved in upgrading foreign theater chains.

The conversion to multiplexes proceeded first by breaking the power of the projectionist union, whose work rules mandated one projectionist per showing. Projection rooms were built with movies mounted on horizontal platters, which eliminated the need for reel changeovers, and one projectionist could show several movies at a time. The customer drove to the theater and could postpone choosing among various current movies until arrival. The customer now found that no matter how late or early she or he was in arriving, there was often a movie about to start. The cineplex offered both a choice of content and a choice of starting times. The most popular movie played on several screens at staggered showing times, which yielded benefits to both the theater owner and the customer. The theater owner was now able to move different shows in and out of various screening rooms from week to week as the lead movie declined or gained in popularity and other movies become available.[12] The customer enjoyed a wider selection of starting times. Multiplexes became the contemporary approach to movie exhibition, getting bigger and bigger through the nineties.

Under the competitive pressure of Cineplex Odeon and other multiplexes, theaters in North America have been reconditioned for maximum profits. Improvements have included enhanced viewer comforts such as better chairs with individual cup holders, and multichannel sound. Older cineastes quibbled that these improvements were scant compensation for smaller average screen size and overtaxed projectionists working on three or four shows simultaneously. The wave of rebuilding and refurbishing has spread to European theaters and has helped stem the decline in movie attendance. The U.S. film distributors—Paramount, MCA, MGM, and Warner—own many of these theaters, particularly in Great Britain, and are financing the improvements.[13]

Two-tiered video pricing and studio participation in global multiplexing were outwardly separate events. However, they were unified by an emerging market logic that propels New Hollywood's relentless pursuit of the audience across media. The movie industry has always sought the mass audience, and now it had quantitatively more opportunities to do so. This intensification of the quantitative effort started to result in a qualitative shift in the mid-1980s. Video sales were routinely exceeding 100,000 copies for each new feature film by 1985. When executives and outside investors did the arithmetic on the videocassette sales, they realized that the additional earning of $3 to $4 million per title was an opportunity to restructure the film industry. An examination of the microeconomics of cassette sales at this point allows us to reimagine the macro-opportunities various distributors and retailers saw.

Microeconomics 1: Overview

The video business has four distinct levels:

1. Film producer/copyright holder
2. Video distributor/film supplier/manufacturer
3. Wholesaler
4. Retailer/video specialty store

A quick observation is in order before discussing each level in detail. Level 3, the wholesaler, is somewhat autonomous in function. In contrast, the other levels are characterized by fluid boundaries and a complicated mix of cooperation and competition.

COPYRIGHT HOLDER

Someone always owns a film. This simple statement hides a baffling array of various rights holders who can do various things with the film. In the beginning, the film producer is the copyright holder. The producer is generally the company that made the film and that has purchased or otherwise controls all the various copyrights that are part of the film, such as the story and the music. Therefore, the right to lease or sell the film in any media and any territory belongs to this company. A company rarely loses control of the copyright of a film willingly. There is a statute of limitation on the length of time a company may own a copyright. The period of copyright control was lengthened again in 1998, and hardly any sound film is in danger of falling into the public domain (losing copyright protection). We have already distinguished between physical ownership and copyright ownership in the section on "first sale" doctrine. A company that sells a videocassette loses control of that physical embodiment of the film it has sold.

VIDEO DISTRIBUTOR

The video distributor or film supplier is the company that has the right to distribute the film to the home video market in a specific territory (the United States and Canada together are generally known as the "domestic" territory). I use the terms "distributors" and "suppliers" interchangeably. As the video market became more lucrative in the mid-1980s, theatrical distributors demanded and received the rights to video distribution as part of the theatrical distribution deal. Currently most films are distributed in the video market by the same outfit that distributes the film in the theatrical market for that territory. There are still small, specialized video distributors handling non-feature videos. Very few video distributors who handle recent feature-length movies are without theatrical releasing capability. Artisan, MPI, and Trimark are surviving video specialists catering to video rental stores. Their theatrical distribution capabilities are weak in comparison to the majors.

It is standard that the video distributor takes financial responsibility for the manufacturing of the prerecorded cassettes of the film. The actual work of producing the cassettes goes on at a factory run by a "duplicator" company. At first, many video distributors had in-house duplicators. Columbia and Paramount formed a large duplicating company with Bell and Howell. FHE and several other companies had their own smaller in-house operations. Tapes were at first copied in real time (a one-hour master tape took one hour to make one copy). Sony introduced high-speed duplicating (which takes a mere fraction of one hour to copy a one-hour master) as part of its failing effort to keep the Beta format profitable by reducing manufacturing costs. High-speed duplicating machines were very expensive, but their adoption in the late 1980s drastically lowered the per/unit costs. At that time, most distributors sold their in-house duplicating units, since only the highest production volumes justified the expense. The two largest duplicating divisions are now owned by The Rank Organisation and Carlton Communications (both are British conglomerates).

WHOLESALER

The film suppliers sell the tapes to independent wholesalers, who in turn resell the tapes to retailers and rental stores. Some trade journals refer to the wholesaler as the "distributor," but this is confusing. I have only used the term "wholesaler" for this level of activity. The suggested list price is set by the film supplier. The wholesale price is discounted from the list. The supplier can also directly distribute to retailers, bypassing the wholesaler. This has occurred occasionally in the video rental business, and is the trend for the future, especially with large retailers such as Blockbuster. Direct distribution has not yet become common.

140   Wholesalers are under pressure to maximize profits. They do not have exclusive relations with either the outlets or the suppliers. The major distributors (suppliers) often demand packaged purchases (forcing the wholesaler to buy several shows in order to obtain a desired show). They also pressure wholesalers to meet sales goals and force them to administer promotional campaigns. Wholesalers and distributors/suppliers often dispute the issue of returns. Wholesalers have generally not been able to return unsold cassettes to distributors for full value. Powerful distributors allow only a percentage value of the return tapes as credit for future tapes. Wholesalers would prefer full credit for future tapes and often force weaker (i.e., low-volume) distributors to give them full credit. In general, returns are more restrictive in the video business than in the music record business. This obviously works against unknown movie titles that have yet to demonstrate their popularity.

The pressures of wholesaling reduced the markups to 1 percent profit margins by 1988.[14] This low margin continues to this day. In 1984 there were 30 big wholesalers, servicing an average of 5,000 outlets. In 1995, there were only 13 in North America.[15] Wholesalers are most typically owned by bigger groups that can supply the large amounts of cash needed to maintain an inventory. Ingram Entertainment has been the largest since its 1992 acquisition of Commtron. Just like its rival, Baker and Taylor, Ingram got into video distributing from its book and print distributing operations. Other wholesalers began as warehouses for video store chains.

RETAILER

Retailing ranges from stores that specialize in renting videocassettes to stores dedicated to selling videotapes. There are also large retailers such as mass merchandisers (K-Mart, et al.), supermarkets, and others that sell and/or rent tapes directly or rent space and split the profits with independent "rack jobbers" who sell/rent cassettes inside the large store. Video specialty stores still account for most rentals; however, they have less than half of the video sales business. Mass merchandisers, rack jobbers, and even fast food stores and other promotional partners sell videocassettes on a mass scale. Video specialty stores are now dominated by large chains such as Blockbuster, although single ownership or two-store chains still survive.

Video rental stores are prevalent throughout the U.S. with the exception of low-income, inner-city neighborhoods. However, low-income rural areas can generally support a rental store or two. There are many pitfalls to running these stores. Rental stores have to invest a great deal of money in the inventory (often 25 percent of their revenues) and therefore face challenges in building their libraries. Should the rental store buy several copies of the current big movie, or invest the money in several different titles? This is known as the breadth (of different titles) versus depth (many copies of a popular title) issue. Most customers ask for the latest movies, but if the store buys too many of a single title, the owner might not recoup the investment before the audience moves on to the next batch of recent releases. Older and less popular titles often prove profitable but over a longer period, a duration that poorly capitalized stores cannot endure. There are two prominent trade journals targeted at video store owners—*Video Business* and *Video Store*. Store owners also receive a great deal of information about upcoming releases from wholesalers.

Microeconomics 2: Rental

The following is a breakdown of the various payments between supplier, wholesaler, and retailer. There are many variations, but the percentages have remained consistent since the mid-1980s.

Video distributors obtain rights by paying royalties to the actual copyright owners of the film. The industry's rule of thumb is that royalty payments equal 20 percent of the video distributors' adjusted receipts.[16] In other words, the royalty percentage of the gross video receipts is calculated after a 25–35 percent distribution fee is subtracted. A major studio that owns both the copyrights on the film and the video distribution division will still transfer the producer royalty in its books. This separates the money the studio made as a producer from the money it made as a distributor. The studio calculates co-partnership deals, net profit sharing plans, and residual payments, not from the gross video revenue, but according to the producer royalty payments.

Talent guilds are constantly monitoring royalty payments. Since the advent of television, the Screen Actors Guild (SAG) has taken the lead in arranging for producers to pay residual fees to their members whenever products entered new markets created by new technologies. When home video and pay TV took off, the old 1971 contract seemed inadequate. This led to new demands and to strikes by SAG and the Writers Guild of America (WGA)

142   in the early 1980s. The 1983 SAG settlement stipulated that the actors would collect an increased share — 4.5 to 6 percent — of the distributors' gross in residual payments from all ancillary markets (home video and pay TV). The definition of "distributor's gross" continues to be a sore point since it need not include the distributor's fee. The definition of "profit participation" has also been an object of contention in negotiations. Only the biggest stars and directors, such as Steven Spielberg, George Lucas, and Arnold Schwarzenegger, are able to participate in the distributing fees studios earn from video. The others are limited to profit participation based on the royalty fees.[17]

The distribution fee is a standard procedure in theatrical distribution and is now standard in video distribution. It is considered just compensation for the distributor's overhead. However, it is not standard in other cultural industries such as book publishing and has often been criticized. A fundamental purpose of a distribution fee is to help the distributor "cross-collateralize" revenue across a whole schedule of winning and losing movies. It vastly improves the earnings of the most powerful companies. For instance, independent distributors often contract with larger distributors. In such contracts, the larger company always takes the distribution fee off the top. Despite the dilution of potential profits, small independent distributors have been forced into such arrangements because they needed the power of a major supplier in order to get wholesalers to stock their products.

Once the distributor has obtained a film by paying an advance against future royalty payments, the next step is manufacturing. Although the cost of magnetic tape fell rapidly through the 1970s, the real-time method of duplication (see above) kept the cost of manufacturing a feature-length cassette in the $7.50 to $10 range through the mid-eighties. Once the cost of the box and cover art and shipping was added in, the accepted figure increased to $10 to $15. There was a substantial saving in manufacturing costs per unit after 1984, enabling the delivery of large volumes for the "sell-through" market. Currently the cost of duplicating a tape can fall below a dollar a unit, albeit on the lowest quality tape. Acceptable quality can be obtained for approximately $4 a unit.[18] We should remember that manufacturing costs vary according of the length of the show.

The suppliers have such a high markup on tapes destined for the rental market that royalties and manufacturing costs have exerted only minimal pressures on the price. Suppliers are free to set a list price according to what they think the market will bear. Since the market is not directly for consumers

TABLE 5.1 **Price Breakdown of Prerecorded Cassette (PRC)**

List price	$79.95
Wholesaler buys PRC at list times 0.65	$52.00
Supplier receives	$52.00
Retailer buys PRC at list times 0.75	$60.00
Wholesaler receives	$8.00

Rental break-even point is 20 turns (20 times @ $3.00 per rental equals $60.00)

Retailer is in profits on 21st rental turn

but for wholesalers and video specialty stores, tapes rarely compete on an individual price basis. There are many occasions when suppliers try to interest wholesalers by offering separate discounts. Therefore, packages of titles can be subject to separate negotiations. However, judging from the available numbers, the supplier usually charges the wholesaler 65 percent of the list price.

The wholesaler, in turn, minimizes risk by soliciting pre-orders from retailers before actually buying the tape from the supplier. These pre-orders usually account for 95 to 100 percent of the total sales of a rental video. The various sales charts that are published in the trades are compiled from these pre-orders and often underestimate sales that occur after the first month. The wholesaler marks up the price on the cassette another few percentage points and therefore is paid about 70 to 75 percent of the list price.

The video retailer may either sell or rent. The optimum situation is to do both with the same unit. In the early years, many retailers made money selling a "previously viewed" tape to specialists who resold the tapes to a new store just starting up. In a mature market, most inventories have been built up, so the public is the primary purchaser of used tapes. Reselling continues to be "hit or miss" at best. Generally, retailers would prefer to make their profit solely on rental activity. At the list price of $80, the tape needs to be rented 20 times at $3/rental in order to break even. Tape wear and tear is a negligible factor at this level of usage. The price breakdown for prerecorded videocassettes is shown in Table 5.1, and a breakdown of the supplier's fee is shown in Table 5.2.

The figures in the tables are taken from the maturing period of 1983 to 1987. After 1987, many distributors increased their list prices by $10. In 1991, there was another $3 increase for a total of $92.95. Some titles have gone as

TABLE 5.2 Breakdown of Supplier's Fee

Supplier receives	$52.00
Supplier deducts 25% distribution fee (-$13.00)	39.00
Copyright holder receives 20% royalty (-$7.80)	31.20
Manufacturing and packaging costs (-$15.00)	
Supplier's income	16.20
*Add distribution fee (+$13.00)	
Total supplier's earning	$29.20

high as $99.95. Since neither the wholesaler nor the retailer pays list price, such increases are not fully reflective of added costs. Retailers may even get a price break for buying in volume as low as three cassettes of the same title. List prices have changed but the percentages and even the cost figures in Table 5.1 are still roughly accurate for the rental industry to this day.

In sum, video microeconomics involves the confluence of several previous business models. The two-step distribution system was borrowed from record and book distribution. The division of the supplier's dollar between the copyright holder and the distributor/supplier appropriated the concept of distribution fees from the movie business. The high markup that has been sustained even after manufacturing costs have gone down closely parallels the development in the sale of compact discs and may become a feature of future technologies of mass entertainment.

Nicholas Garnham observed that new leisure technologies tend to result in higher costs to the consumer per unit of time since leisure time cannot be expanded. Therefore, distributors of leisure products cannot spread their costs over increasing amounts of aggregate leisure time in the general population. Instead, they will increase the price for the more affluent members of the audience.[19] This observation is perfectly suited to home video. The home video consumer buys the hardware (similar to the radio and television owner), pays for the content (similar to the moviegoer), and even watches advertising placed on the videotape (similar to the radio and television viewer). This triple expenditure was modified by the development of the rental market, since consumers generally shunned the full purchase price of the cassette. A further modification came when product ads decreased on videotapes in the 1990s.

After 1986, lower priced tapes (see above section on two-tiered pricing) finally brought the mass merchandisers into the video business. The national merchandisers had hesitated, first over the format wars and the initially small number of VCR owners. Then they refused to get involved with the paperwork and risk of renting videotapes. Now, low-priced sell-through tapes encouraged Sears, K-Mart, Wal-Mart, et al. to start videocassette sections. Those merchandisers who still wanted to avoid risk contracted with the big rack jobbers, Lieberman and Handleman. These companies rent space in the store in order to set up a videotape rack. They take on the responsibility of stocking the rack with popular and discounted titles and pay the stores a percentage of the tape sales.

Video and Other Commodities

The next step was a closer marriage between video and other movable commodities through promotional tie-ins. Again, Paramount took the pioneering lead when it placed a Pepsi commercial on its 1986 video release of *Top Gun*. In return, Pepsi mentioned the *Top Gun* video in its own network and local television commercials. The tape was sold at $26.95, a new low price for a recent hit. It sold 3 million units, a record that lasted for a year.[20] Other companies emulated the cross-advertising. In 1987, Vestron placed a 30-second spot for Nestlé's white chocolate on its *Dirty Dancing* tape. Video retailers were urged to stock Nestlé candy bars and Nestlé promoted *Dirty Dancing* in its own advertising as part of the campaign.

The theme park and merchandising divisions of Disney had often cooperated with other corporations in tie-ins and partnerships. Bill Mechanic, Disney's home video executive, applied the same idea to video when he engineered a four-year relationship for the home video division with McDonald's, from 1987 to 1991. The deal allowed the food company to offer Disney cassettes for a reduced price as an incentive to buy McDonald's meals. The fast food chain compensated Disney by promoting the films as part of its own advertising. In the second half of the 1990s, Disney played off McDonald's by working with Burger King on such films as *The Lion King* (1994) and *Pocahontas* (1995). Other studios also sought opportunities to work with McDonald's, and as of this writing, Disney has switched again to McDonald's. These mutual promotional campaigns start with the theatrical release of the movie, but the video release is always an important element since the cassette is a physical item that can be sold as part of the meal plan. There is some controversy about incentive pricing. Video specialty stores resent that the public

146   can obtain cassettes from food chains for as little as $5.99, when the video stores can sell tapes at prices only slightly discounted from the $24.95 or $19.95 list price.

M&M/Mars' Snickers, Chrysler, and Hershey have all made straightforward (without cross-promotion) ad buys on video releases, paying between $1 to $2 per cassette in order to place their ads. The results have been mixed. A survey of the literature by Lee and Katz shows that the advertising community is still debating the value of such a buy.[21] There is a consensus that the prices are too high considering how many viewers fast forward through the commercial messages. In general, advertising for products on videotape, except for advertising other videos, has not become a significant part of its commodification.

Retailing Consolidation

There was an inevitable consolidation of video retailing after 1986. This consolidation led to stabilization and even a slight pullback in the number of video stores by 1989 (see Table 3.4), and a decrease in the number of companies engaged in video retailing. The most dramatic consolidation was the expansion of Blockbuster Entertainment from 1986 to a point in 1993 (the year before its merger with Viacom) when it controlled over 3,593 domestic video specialty stores and 775 more in Great Britain. It has become, by far, the biggest chain in the world. Its expansion occurred by building and purchasing previously existing video stores and chains. At times in its buildup, Blockbuster sold franchises, although more recently it has been buying them back.

David Cook started Blockbuster in Dallas, Texas in 1985. His background was in computer software, and he approached rental inventory with some of the tricks he had already learned. He decided the answer to successful rentals was the "super" store, with ample floor space for a wider selection of titles, more copies of recent films, and longer hours than the competition. He started with 6,500 titles among 8,000 units.[22] By 1990, the typical Blockbuster outlet had 8,000 titles among 10,000 units.[23] In contrast, the number of units at the average video specialty store was about 3,600.[24] The super store concept spread beyond Blockbuster, with the number of super stores rising to 27 percent of all video specialty outlets by 1992.[25] Cook did not get to enjoy the full fruits of his innovation. He sought outside investors, and in 1987 one of these investors, Wayne Huizenga, took over and forced him out.

Huizenga started out in the garbage business and cashed out after building Waste Management Incorporated into a national chain. His ambition in video rentals was focused strictly on the cash and stock value. He had very limited interest in the entertainment business or in films per se. In fact, Huizenga confided that he could not remember watching an entire film.[26] His executives did not have a background, or much interest, in entertainment. Blockbuster's upper management had two basic objectives in regard to the content of the movies in their stores: to eliminate controversy and to emphasize wide selection. Blockbuster did little else to influence either the content or the nature of the video business. (Huizenga continues to display the "it's only the money" attitude from time to time in his current activity as a baseball team owner.)

Blockbuster emphasized that it provided a desirable space for the entire family, in a manner reminiscent of the early movie exhibitors courting a "respectable" audience at the beginning of the twentieth century. If home video still had an unsavory reputation because of its early emphasis on porno, Blockbuster would lean over backward to ensure its own clean image. Huizenga brought in a marketer from McDonald's food chain, Tom Gruber, who instituted a chainwide ban on X-rated films and other controversial titles. This policy drew some negative attention when Blockbuster refused to stock *The Last Temptation of Christ* (1988), Martin Scorsese's controversial adaptation of the Kazantzakis novel about Christ's human dimension. The possibilities of sophisticated cinematic expression and creativity would not get in the way of Blockbuster's squeaky clean campaign to dominate video retailing and drive up stock prices. Most large rental chains have adopted Blockbuster's strategy of avoiding sexually explicit tapes. Smaller chains and "mom and pop" operations have discovered the counterstrategy of filling the void. Adult rentals now often provide the margin for survival for small stores.

Blockbuster marched across the country, setting up stores and/or buying out the competition, reminiscent of Adolph Zukor's 1916 theater-buying spree. It was a case of the big fish swallowing anything even slightly smaller. In January 1989 it acquired Major Video Corporation; in August it obtained Video Superstore; and two years later it bought Erol's, the biggest survivor from the pioneer days of video, which had been operating since 1981. In 1991

148   Huizenga recruited Joseph Baczko from Toys R Us to become president and chief operating officer. Baczko had more interest in the shape of the business and actively tried to promote selling directly to the customer in addition to renting. He also used volume buying to get better deals with film suppliers. Both Orion and Disney Home Video executives started complaining to the boss. Huizenga feared that if there was a perception of conflict between the video chain and the suppliers, Wall Street would get nervous and share prices would plunge.[27] Baczko was out of the company by January 1993, and Blockbuster made no further attempt to innovate better deals with suppliers.

In 1993, Blockbuster finally decided to move into programming. It acquired the program distributor Republic Pictures and an allied production house, Spelling Entertainment, headed by the legendary TV producer Aaron Spelling. Spelling convinced Blockbuster to produce a TV movie called *Texas* that was released to home video in 1994 and then to network television without the benefit of a theatrical run. The show received revenues of $5.2 million from video sales, a modest but respectable sum.

Huizenga's activities in building an integrated video company were short-lived. He became involved with Sumner Redstone, the owner of National Amusements and Viacom. Redstone acknowledges a fascination with the movie business that goes back to running his father's movie theater chain in New England. As part of his fascination, Redstone was making a bid for Paramount and was in a desperate bidding war against Barry Diller and his associates. Redstone needed cash and Huizenga saw an opportunity for a profitable stock swap. He merged Blockbuster with Viacom as part of a complex deal to finance Viacom's purchase of Paramount Communications. Huizenga then left the video rental business, after dominating it for just over six years.

As Blockbuster demonstrates, video retailers have historically not sought control over distribution, although there was one attempt. Several retailers formed First Video Feature (FVF) in August 1988 to pool retailers to obtain exclusive territories for films on video. Each retailer would deposit $800 and agree to buy seven copies of each FVF release. FVF anticipated that obtaining the rights to films would cost $3 million plus $2 million for advertising.[28] Eventually FVF wanted to move into financing productions. This idea recalls the history of First National pooling exhibitors' money to move into film production in 1917. However, too many video retailers were skeptical of the feasibility of such a pooled effort and the proposal was withdrawn. When video retailers were asked in a 1990 informal survey what they would do if they ran a movie studio, they did not mention the type or amount of movies that were being released. They talked only of marketing matters such as point of purchase advertising and so on.[29]

Large chains like Blockbuster now dominate video retailing among stores specializing in video. West Coast Video and Hollywood Entertainment are other major rental chains. The top 100 retailers generate 39 percent of specialty revenues while they own only 15 percent of the outlets.[30] However, the chains neither seek nor have influence over suppliers and distributors regarding film production. Blockbuster was typical in refusing to link its ability to buy in bulk with any demands or favors. Daniel Moret, in his evocatively titled study of video retailing, *The New Nickelodeons*, discusses the political and economic effects of the consolidation of video retailing.[31] He notes the threat of censorship and higher consumer costs, but does not detect a strong relationship between the consolidation of retailing and the increasing domination of hit titles in the video business.

Breadth versus Depth

Nonetheless, retailing has had an influence on film production. It is indirect and has more to do with consolidation at the wholesale level than at the retail. The influence can be summed up in the debate that emerged during the maturing stage of video retail: "breadth versus depth." This was a three-way debate between retailers, wholesalers, and distributors, perhaps beginning with the latter. As the video market matured and the number of stores peaked, major distributors increased their sales to stores seeking to own more copies of individual titles. This was referred to as "depth of copy."

It was intuitive that the most popular rental titles closely corresponded to the most popular theatrical titles. There was some deviation between theatrical and rental popularity if only because the video store presents a wide selection in thousands of "backshelf" titles, while the most fragmented multiplex theater can still only offer a dozen choices. Newly released titles received the greatest consumer interest. On the other hand, a few titles continued to command interest after the first six weeks. Several market surveys have indicated that customers often leave the video rental store without their first choice under their arm.[32] While customers reported that they were disappointed, retailers still rang up rental fees when they persuaded these renters to take an older show home. As retailers made their purchasing decisions, they began to perform a balancing act between the breadth of having many titles on the store shelves and the depth they had in the number of copies of a few titles.

Copies per title per store climbed throughout 1985. At the end of that year, *Ghostbusters* broke the 400,000 units-sold barrier for rental-priced cassettes (fourteen copies per North American video store), and several other titles quickly followed in the early months of 1986.[33] "Depth of copy" continued to hover around this figure for the top titles. Two years later, Paramount tried to push the depth-of-copy strategy further. Klingensmith, now the president of the home video division, decided to spend $10 million to market high-priced rental films in 1988. Disney's *Three Men and a Baby* pushed through the 450,000 barrier in 1988 with 460,000 units, returning $26.4 million to the supplier. The upper ceiling on high-priced tapes was 500,000 units until Paramount's *Ghost* sold almost 600,000 in the beginning of 1991.

Retailers have been ambivalent about buying multiple copies of "A" titles. *Video Store* has featured many owners who like to buy "B" titles instead and steer their customers toward alternatives to the hits. One video retailer identified as Salzer claimed that ". . . pretty much the 'B' titles are what bring the traffic in. You can't have all the 'A' titles you need. It's the 'B' titles that differentiate us from the competition."[34] Sam Goldstein, president of a ten-store chain, told *Video Store*, "People always want what's new, so the idea is to keep them interested in older titles."[35] Retailers such as Kims in New York City and Vidiots in Santa Monica, California have made a virtue of having very off-beat titles in stock for their sophisticated video fans. The debate goes on.

It is the wholesaler who unambiguously favors depth, since that provides economy of scale. Every new title and every additional supplier adds to the overhead costs for the wholesaler, who wishes for as few titles and few suppliers as possible. Of course, suppliers who provide high-volume, popular titles have the most power in their dealings with wholesalers. Suppliers are not shy about punishing wholesalers that do not move their product. By early 1989 HBO, IVE, MCA/Universal, RCA/Columbia, and Vestron had all shortened the list of wholesalers with whom they would do business.[36] Due to such pressures, wholesalers consolidated and lost interest in product that does not move quickly. They reserve their warehouse space for product that does.

Wholesalers will not handle marginal products unless the distributors are willing to provide some discount or support. They pressure weaker film suppliers to take out advertisements in the wholesalers' monthly mailers.[37] They demand better return policies than they get from major distributors/suppliers. Independents also have to try to encourage wholesalers to give them support and shelf space by discounting their prices 5 to 10 percent below the majors. Wholesalers often pocket the discount, selling the low-budget films at the same price as the popular blockbusters.

One way retailers can have greater depth of current hits without spending the entire budget is to lease tapes. Initially store owners resented and rejected the high-handedness of the early studio leasing schemes. However, they have been more amenable to non-studio leasing. In 1982, store owner Ron Berger formulated a more favorable leasing system. He convinced the participating rental stores that leasing would allow them to have more copies without raising inventory costs. He also convinced studios to participate, giving up the tight control these studios had demanded in 1981, such as exclusive relations and strict paperwork.

Berger built the leasing scheme out of his own chain of video rental stores until he had enough critical mass to form a separate company called Rentrak in 1986. Rentrak has been quietly adding customers since then. Stores participate on a title-per-title basis. Super Comm is a rival leasing outfit (purchased by The Walt Disney Company in 1995), and as of 1998, together the two leasing outfits had contracts with 75 of the top 100 high-revenue video rental stores.[38] Leasing is also attractive as a future hedge as inventories switch to DVD and other formats. Stores that participate in leasing also continue to purchase tapes. It is becoming common for video stores to both purchase and lease in order to fill their shelves.

Video Advertising

Direct video advertising was an afterthought. As noted, Twentieth Century Fox threw the entire risk of developing a market for videotapes on the shoulders of Andre Blay's Magnetic Video. The studios used the format wars between Betamax and VHS to justify their aversion to video advertising. The format wars were confusing the public and were forcing the studios to double their inventory costs in order to have product available in either for-

152 mat. Why not hold off on advertising until the dust was clear and a clear winner emerged? When a clear winner did emerge, the Hollywood majors still refused to advertise video since they did not want to encourage renting and thought such advertising would only help the retailer. Only the new independents committed money to video promotions.

It was only as the two-tiered price structure developed that major studios started to promote the video releases to the public. The Disney Company placed the first major television commercial for home videocassettes on the television show *Little House on the Prairie* during the fall season of 1983.[39] It promoted Disney prerecorded cassettes as a gift-giving item during the Christmas season. The relationship between sell-through and mass advertising was obvious. However, advertising in order to support films that were bought primarily by video rental stores was thought to be less effective, since the only financial interest the studio had was in the first sale, not in the subsequent rentals. Following this logic, studios committed some of their money to advertising video releases through wholesaler catalogs. Wholesalers also committed some money to advertising to retailers. In order to arouse store owners' interest, video campaigns started a month or more before the street date of the video release (the date when stores can place the tapes on the shelves).

Independents have historically had more interest in advertising rental titles. The budgets are set as a percentage of anticipated gross sales of cassettes. At Orion, the formula as of 1993 was that 15–20 percent of the anticipated gross should be spent on marketing.[40] This is still relatively cheap since in this period the theatrical advertising for a movie reached 31–35 percent of the average North American gross box office. In terms of absolute numbers, film suppliers committed $50 million to video advertising in 1988, up from $16.9 million in 1987.[41] The $50 million (mostly devoted to sell-throughs) spent on video was of course a pale fraction of the $1.4 billion the movie industry spent on domestic advertising in that year. There have been sporadic calls for Hollywood to promote the activity of renting videos. The responses of the studios have always been extremely tepid.

Video and Revenue Streams

It is important to understand that the market for videocassettes matured without weakening other revenue sources for the film industries. In the previous chapter, we looked at the strained relationship between the Hollywood studios and pay television, particularly with HBO. However, cable continued to improve as a revenue source for the film industry, although it could not keep up with cassette sales. Its own rate decelerated through the late 1980s, but one should not conclude that home video was undermining cable revenues. Sales of feature films to network television did weaken in response to home video. One triggering event was the disappointing share of only 25 percent of TV viewers that *Star Wars* received when CBS broadcast it on February 26, 1984. Its 1982 pay TV airing and 1983 video release had eroded its audience. In 1986, Lawrence Tisch took control of CBS, and he started to complain about the average $3 million the networks were paying for feature film rights.[42] However, the resulting decline in network fees was modest and short-lived. In other venues, the domestic box office remained stable throughout the period, reporting a dip only in 1985. The situation was murkier overseas, where European box offices weakened in the 1980s and video, television deregulation, and subscription TV were all blamed. However, Western European theaters started to upgrade along American lines after 1985 and a full-scale recovery was evident by 1987.

Table 5.3 shows how Wall Street analysts documented the lack of cannibalization between video and other revenue sources.

TABLE 5.3 Goldman Sachs Estimates of Worldwide Sources of U.S. Theatrical Film Revenues (in billions of dollars), 1980–1992

Year	Box Office	Home Video	Pay TV	Television	Total
1980	1.9	0.03	0.1	0.4	2.5
1981	2.0	0.15	0.2	0.5	2.9
1982	2.3	0.35	0.4	0.5	3.6
1983	2.6	0.75	0.6	0.5	4.6
1984	2.7	1.4	0.6	0.5	5.3
1985	2.4	2.0	0.6	0.6	5.7
1986	2.5	2.5	0.6	0.7	6.4
1987	2.8	3.1	0.6	0.7	7.2
1988	3.0	3.9	0.7	1.0	8.8
1989	3.4	4.5	0.9	1.1	10.0
1990	3.7	5.2	1.0	1.3	11.5
1991	3.8	5.9	1.1	1.4	12.5
1992	4.0	6.6	1.1	1.5	13.6

Production Increase

Home video had become an important part of the dazzling array of American consumer products. Consumer products tend to proliferate; did home video? What were its gross effects on filmmaking, as measured by as simple an index as production levels? For a brief moment, the number of feature films in production increased because of video. It seemed appropriate that as more money came in, more product went out. Table 5.4 demonstrates that this *was* the response of the independent distributors during the years 1984 through 1988.

The actual count in Table 5.4 reflects the judgment of the writers for the trade journal *Variety* and statisticians at the Motion Picture Association of America. I have combined their figures for the table.

The major studios did not respond to new revenues in the same manner as the non-MPAA distributors. Independent and MPAA distribution had a negative correlation (see Figure 5.1). The number of independent releases went up as MPAA releases declined in the 1971 to 1974 and the 1984 to 1987 periods. When independent releases permanently declined in 1989, the MPAA companies made a very limited effort to fill the slack. Periods of declining independent releases have been periods of overall decline in the number of films available to the American audience. The major studios have felt that ten to fifteen major films are needed a year to justify their distribution and administrative overhead, and they resist further expansion. Since there are seven full-fledged majors (Warner, Paramount, Twentieth Century Fox, Columbia, Universal MGM/UA, and Disney [particularly after Eisner and Katzenberg decided to increase production in 1984]), this provides a base of 70 to 100 films per year. During this period there have been two other MPAA members besides the seven: Tri-Star (until it was absorbed into Sony, along with Columbia) and Orion (until it started to falter in the late 1980s). These account for the additional MPAA releases.

More Money, Same Product

The influx of new money was overwhelmingly due to the sale of videocassettes (see Table 5.3). At least 70 percent of the overall increase in theatrical film revenues from 1983 to 1988 was due to cassette sales. The reticence to increase production despite the expansion of the market and the influx of

TABLE 5.4 Number of Independent Films Distributed in U.S., 1970–1992

Year	Independent releases	MPAA releases	Total releases	Total film revenues (billions of dollars)
1970	133	185	318	
1971	246	183	429	
1972	239	193	432	
1973	294	163	457	
1974	357	155	512	
1975	292	138	430	
1976	312	133	445	
1977	299	110	409	
1978	225	114	339	
1979	189	138	327	Goldman Sachs
1980	205	161	366	2.5
1981	171	173	344	2.9
1982	192	173	365	3.6
1983	154	190	344	4.6
1984	144	167	311	5.3
1985	156	153	309	5.7
1986	176	139	315	6.4
1987	200	129	329	7.2
1988	179	160	339	8.8
1989	142	169	311	10.0
1990	142	169	311	11.5
1991	143	164	307	12.5
1992	126	150	276	13.6

SOURCES: Todd McCarthy, "Indie Share of Mkt. Hits 6-Year High," *Variety,* June 18, 1986, p. 5; Lawrence Cohn, "WB Biggest Pic Supplier—Again," *Variety,* December 21, 1992; MPAA, "U.S. Economic Review," various years.

new video money demands an explanation. It is a vital clue to the struggle of the new video distributors and their allies, the independent film producers. If home video was not eating into other markets and if the revenue increase was significant, why were production increases so ephemeral? Was there something about the video money that was discouraging increased production?

This chapter has outlined the various business practices surrounding the home video market. Video retailing consolidation was largely a neutral factor in film industry production, but other aspects of the video business had a greater impact. Two-tiered pricing obviously favored the few, big, high-profile

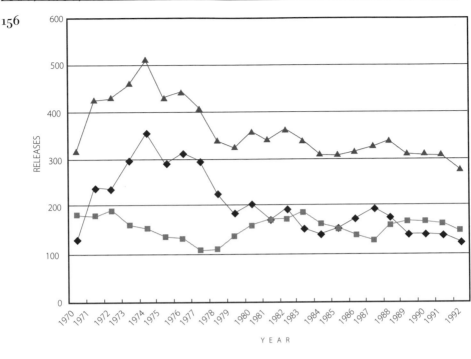

FIGURE 5.1 Number of independent and MPAA film releases, 1970–1992

films over the many medium-sized films financed by independent video pre-selling. It also gave a large amount of money to established studios with which to enhance their other marketing operations and increase their competitive edge. The profit pressure on wholesalers also worked against titles with only moderate popularity and distributors with limited power. The distribution fee system and methods of calculating royalties favored the major studios and gave them higher returns proportionately on hit movies than independent producers and distributors could command. The mature video industry was no longer friendly territory for those who had pioneered the business.

New Hollywood, which consisted of new distribution practices as well as new ways of making films, was putting the money into bigger movies and expensive theatrical campaigns. It is on this basis that there would be a shake-out. Exhibitors responded to the home video challenge by refurbishing their theaters. It is more significant that the major studios were helping them, with

their new video revenue, to enhance the movie theatrical experience. Those   157
who could not make big theatrical movies or finance expensive advertisements would be left by the side of the road. Wholesalers did not want to stock
their tapes, and retailers hesitated between breadth and depth. In the next
chapter, the inferences that have been drawn from this detailed look at business practices will be confirmed by the actual history of distribution after
1986. It is now time to look at the actual players—independent and major—
and learn their fates.

CHAPTER SIX

Consolidation and Shakeouts

On the first page of Vestron's 1986 annual report, Austin Furst explained "dramatically lower earnings" by stating that "home video rental demand for movies reflected a narrowing focus on titles, which had achieved strong consumer awareness through significant theatrical exposure and promotional support. . . . Many of the movies that Vestron released into the home video market had very limited theatrical exposure and did not sell as well as we might have expected based on the performance of similar films released by the company in the past." [1]

These few words pinpointed the challenge for the new independent video distributors—"significant theatrical exposure." Since the new distributors generally could not meet the challenge, these words mark the crest of the independent wave. The phrase also helps to explain the relatively stable level of production. Significant exposure had to be paid for, through larger production budgets and bigger advertising campaigns. The preceding chapter covered the enhancement of multiplexed movie theaters and the development of sell-through pricing. These schemes gave greater market share to the majors. The multiplexed theater had a higher overhead per seat and therefore a lower tolerance for non-performing movies. A good opening weekend became all important in guaranteeing that a movie could have a profitable run while exhibitors responded to disappointing openings by quickly seeking rival products. The rewards of a good opening went beyond the actual box office, since hit films led directly to high video sales either as sell-throughs or as rentals. Then the new video money was invested into the next round of expensive wide releases and marketing.

The independents were rarely able to take advantage of the sell-through

market. In this chapter, we will see that independents lost video market share   159
as the cost of theatrical releasing grew higher. Eroding profit margins are
even a more powerful explanation of the independent bankruptcy than lost
market share. The independents did make hit movies, sometimes in the same
ratio as the majors. They just did not make enough of them to accumulate
power and long-term relationships with wholesalers and exhibitors. While
almost every non-major video and theatrical distributor declared bankruptcy
or sought a protective merger, the majors gained unprecedented power within
New Hollywood and the world. The two most successful independents to be
still standing at the end of the era were New Line and Miramax, and they
were bought by old-line Hollywood conglomerates in 1993.

This thesis is not just an abstract economic model, but is the actual historical truth of the relative fortunes of Paramount, Disney, Vestron, and Carolco et al. during the 1980s. It is in following the individual narratives of
these companies that we finally synthesize cultural analysis with the eco-
nomic/technological/industrial structures that have been described and an-
alyzed in the foregoing chapters. The wholesaling pressures on retailers to
stock hits in depth coincides with and reinforces Paramount's "high concept"
approach to filmmaking and marketing. The sell-through market reanimates
the Walt Disney Company. Multi-market opportunities led to global media
mergers and a strengthening of global audiences for Hollywood blockbusters.

I wish to make clear that the strengthening of the global audience does not
mean that these events are the result of the autonomous will of the audience.
The actual intentions of consumers in 1986 were hard to measure. The first
video owners were willing to rent anything and everything. Their omnivorous
appetites naturally diminished as the novelty of rentals wore off. Nonetheless,
we must acknowledge that moderately popular films continued to rent. Perhaps consumer intentions had not changed that drastically. It was from the
distributor's point of view that medium-sized films were unprofitable. This is
because the *costs* of acquiring these films from producers became excessive.
The bidding wars had forced video distributors to exhaust their assets and
their credit lines as they tried to sign deals with producers asking for larger
and larger advances. In this tightening situation, market share became more
important than actual dollar figures because it meant that the successful distributor had power both with the producers eager to reach the video market
and with the video wholesalers. The 1986 Vestron report was as much about

160   market share falling away from films with "limited theatrical exposure" as it
was about an actual shift in consumer preference. Theatrical exposure was
becoming the only way to convince wholesalers and retailers to put the prerecorded shows on the shelf. It was now evident that the structure of multiple
markets increasingly favored a "winner take all" situation for Hollywood
films.

By 1984, independent distributors realized that the supplies of current
films were drying up. Some companies, such as Orion, that were once willing
to sell the video rights to these independents now wanted to exploit those
rights themselves. In addition, theatrical distributors were demanding that
all the rights, including video, be sold together. Independent producers had
been used to splitting theatrical distribution from video distribution and
seeking the best bid for each. These new demands meant that producers
could no longer cut separate deals with video distributors. Independent video
distributors now had to produce their own theatrical films, just to keep their
video inventory up. Some tried the direct-to-video route. Only a very few
built a substantial distribution business on such a basis. David Whitten, an
independent distributor who helps and consults other independents, told his
clients that even the lowest budget films needed to have a theatrical run. This
became accepted wisdom in the industry and was true even if the distributor
anticipated that such a release would only lose more money. The reason for
such a release was to gain some attention and therefore get a reasonable
(hopefully a profitable) video sale.

Both the positive (the increase in overall filmed entertainment earnings)
and the negative (the demise of smaller companies) outcomes in 1986 are a
result of the connections between the changing nature of the theatrical release and concentration in video distribution. I will tease out the larger issues
involved by following the differing fates of Vestron, Carolco, and Disney. Disney and Vestron form a complementary pair in this narrative, one rising like
a helium balloon as the other deflates. Vestron and Carolco also form an instructive contrast. Vestron moved from the "publishing" model of video distributing back into the traditional integrated production/distribution studio
model. Carolco was a production company that sought a close alliance with a
video distributor. It ultimately collapsed, while its video distributor partner
still survives. The three models illuminate all the issues of integrated video
distribution from 1986 to 1994. Both for the choices they did not make as
well as for the choices they did make, they are emblematic of an era.

High Concept

The story of video and Disney begins at ABC, where Michael Eisner began his career, and at Paramount, where he subsequently moved and met Jeffrey Katzenberg, William Mechanic, and other future key members of the Disney "team." ABC and Paramount were the nurturing incubators of a more refined approach to marketing big-budget movies called "high concept." A short definition of high-concept films is that they are designed for maximum market success. This definition is, of course, broad enough to include any film. As the term became more popular in 1980s Hollywood, Steven Spielberg gave it a more operative definition. "If a person can tell me the idea in twenty-five words or less, it's going to make a pretty good [high-concept] movie. I like ideas, especially movie ideas, that you can hold in your hand."[2] Justin Wyatt is a film scholar who has tackled the problem of differentiating high-concept moviemaking from other periods and other styles. Wyatt summarizes his own view of high concept as "the look, the hook, and the book," by which he means that the look of the images, the marketing hooks, and the reduced narratives are distinguishable aspects of a high-concept film.[3] Each one of these elements was geared toward quick recognition in order to facilitate not only movie attendance but also sales of all commodities associated with the film, from record albums to toys to home videos. The elements can be comic book heroes, as in *Batman* (1989), dinosaurs, as in *Jurassic Park* (1993), or universally known shipwrecks, as in *Titanic* (1997). A high-concept film tends to fulfill the "instant recognition" requirement more efficiently than a "low-concept" film, even though both exist within the continuum of selling entertainment products.

My argument rests on the chronological development of high concept that finally flourishes in the marketing bonanza of Disney's home video division starting in late 1985. High concept's pre-formative development began at ABC in 1973–1974, when Barry Diller was chief programming executive. It was articulated after Diller and Eisner moved to Paramount in 1974. High concept became the enabling "ideology" for Paramount's sell-through strategy, which was perfected by the Walt Disney Company once Eisner and Mechanic moved there from Paramount in 1984. In a way, high concept originated in television, moved to theatricals, and reached fulfillment in three media when low-priced video caught on.

When Barry Diller was at ABC, he demanded film projects that could be

162   easily summarized in both the abbreviated 30-second TV commercial and in the sentence synopsis of *TV Guide* and other published TV schedules. In 1974, Diller and his team moved into theatrical film by taking key positions at Paramount studios. They started applying their hard-nosed marketing ideology to theatrical movies. Diller's inner circle at Paramount included Michael Eisner and Jeffrey Katzenberg. Their demand for an easy-to-recognize film concept was different enough from the prevailing approaches to film marketing such as "star power" that Paramount's approach earned the appreciation of its rivals. Other film executives started using the Paramount formula to assess how closely the design of the film fit its marketing strategy. As video matured, Paramount's Klingensmith realized that films made according to the high-concept formula could attract high-volume video sales. *Star Trek II: The Wrath of Khan* (1982) (the first low-priced tape) was one such film, relying on instantly recognizable elements of the popular TV show.

Rapid recognition becomes important in a society that is readjusting leisure patterns to fit new time demands. High concept directs film producers and distributors to focus on the commodity nature of the film and to stress recognizable, sellable elements. This commodity can be sold quickly to a public who easily recognizes it because of the considerations of high concept—"the look, the hook, and the book." It fits an audience that increasingly watches the film on the television set with the attention span associated with a distracted glance rather than an intent gaze.[4] The biggest part of the sell-through market is the young audience, the very audience members who demand repetition and immediately rewarding images. The parallels between sell-through and high concept suggest that both are responses to an audience dealing with new stresses on leisure by seeking known media products.

Disney Comes Back On-line

Disney was the most publicized "Cinderella" company of the 1980s. The changeover was thorough enough that the company changed the name from Walt Disney Productions to The Walt Disney Company in 1986. Since the opening of Disneyland in 1954, Disney has been a successful company, but it lost its aggressive edge after the death of Walt Disney in 1966. By 1980, it was a decidedly lackluster feature film distributor, placing seventh, with its share of box office, in a field of eight. The crisis deepened over the next four years. In late September 1984, the company dumped its top executives and hired

Michael Eisner to become the CEO. The success of Paramount was the de-
ciding factor in his selection.

Eisner promised Disney's board that he would hit the ground running. His
team was under pressure to make money quickly. One of the first items on the
agenda was to review the home video question again. Disney had succeeded
in the sell-through market in the summer of 1984. However, the outgoing
team still refused to place any classic animated feature on tape. As Eisner took
over, the 1940 feature animation *Pinocchio* was playing in the theaters. The
new team debated the opportunity. Richard Frank and other executives argued for *Pinocchio*'s subsequent release to video. Surprisingly Jeffrey Katzenberg, the new studio head, took up the old argument that a home video release would erode the future value of the film by undermining its theatrical
re-release. Eisner finally decided to go ahead with the video release. He did
listen to Katzenberg's plea that the tape should be priced high to maximize
profits and to limit the number of copies in circulation at the time of the next
theatrical release.[5]

Eisner and Katzenberg had brought over many other recruits from Paramount to help re-energize Disney. One of the executives was William Mechanic. Mechanic had earned a Ph.D. in film at USC and started his career in
cable by working as a programmer for SelecTV. In 1985 Disney reorganized
the home video division and placed Mechanic in charge. The initial sale figures for *Pinocchio* had stalled at a disappointing $5 million. Mechanic re-
membered the lesson of sell-through. He knew he had a highly recognizable
film that could practically market itself. He cut the price to $29.95. This in-
curred the anger of retailers and purchasers who had already bought the
tape. But he was vindicated when the title sold its entire inventory of 300,000
units, earning in excess of $8 million for Disney. A new triumphant attitude
was now in place at Walt Disney Home Video (soon to be renamed Buena
Vista Home Video as the umbrella distributor for the three Disney production units: Disney, Touchstone, and Hollywood).

The next spring Mechanic announced twenty-one more titles available
at $29.95. Most of these were non-feature films, but the package included a
re-release of the feature animation *Alice in Wonderland*. He also committed
$1.5 million to the advertising for this package. By October, Mechanic had
put together a package of six films headed by the 1959 *Sleeping Beauty*. He
spent $6 million on advertising and the package sold 5 million units. *Sleep-
ing Beauty* broke the million-unit barrier to become the fifth largest video re-

164   lease up to that time, behind *Beverly Hills Cop* (1985), *Indiana Jones and the Temple of Doom* (1985), *Raiders of the Lost Ark* (1983), and *Jane Fonda's Workout* (1982). Three of the top five were Paramount releases.

Disney had successfully moved forward. In 1984 Disney was only the eighth largest U.S. home video distributor with revenues of $78.1 million. By 1987, it had become one of the largest distributors, with sales of $175 million.[6] The next year it was the undisputed number one home video distributor.

The pre-Eisner Disney was producing only three films per year. When Eisner took over Walt Disney, he had already decided to match the other major studios by offering a full production schedule of between twelve and fifteen films. The new markets of cable and video were just begging for new releases and there was not a moment to spare. Despite the best efforts of Eisner's executive team, and in particular the new studio chief, Jeffrey Katzenberg, it was taking time to increase production. The team needed stars and other production talent and, most of all, money. They were not playing in a vacuum. While the other majors were barely increasing their production schedule, the independents were ramping up going from 144 releases in 1984 to 200 in 1987, a 40 percent increase (see Table 5.4).

Disney had an advantage over the independents. Despite the filmmaking frenzy, Disney executives could locate and develop more marketable scripts than the indies. It had power because it had a top line studio, an experienced animation staff, strong distribution channels, and a formidable library of children's films and cartoons. It quickly accumulated a large war chest. The relatively short time it took to increase Disney production was due largely to innovations in finding capital. Video sales from the library provided Disney with $109.5 million in 1985. In addition, the company pioneered a collaboration with Silver Screen II, an investment partnership specializing in movie deals. The partnership invested $170 million in Disney films from its 1985 offering. In turn, the partnership received 50 percent of the box office and 25 percent of the video sales and other revenues earned by the shows in which it was invested. By 1986, the company had doubled its film production budget to $230.1 million, from $102.5 million in 1984.[7] By 1988, the Walt Disney Company was issuing twelve films annually.

Katzenberg and Eisner launched a two-pronged attack to return to full production. They were very interested in competing head to head with other major studios by releasing films of general appeal and not limiting themselves

to only "children" or "family" titles. The previous regime at Disney had tried $\qquad$ 165
to expand its repertoire but had done poorly with its 1982 attempt, *Tron*. The
older team lacked enthusiasm for the vulgarities that seemed to be de rigueur
for contemporary general interest films. Eisner's and Katzenberg's experience
at ABC and Paramount allowed them to move easily between the crudities of
the New Hollywood and the saccharine atmosphere of a typical Disney film.
At the studio screening, Eisner may have squirmed as he sat together with
Roy Disney (Walt Disney's brother) through the explicit language of *Down
and Out in Beverly Hills* (1986), but the studio had to send a signal to the rest
of Hollywood.[8] Disney released *Down and Out* and *Ruthless People* (1986)
and were soon capturing the same grown-up audiences as Paramount.

The second prong was to expand the original Disney franchise by giving
the go-ahead to produce the first full-length animations that the company
had done in a decade. Although the classic movies were designed and produced long before video, the sell-through versions of these old animations
had become critical in pushing Disney to the top rank of the video market.
The executives decided to maximize the shelf life of the classics by offering
the videotapes for sale for limited periods, maximizing sales without flooding
the market with tapes that would circulate indefinitely. The challenge was to
avoid exhausting the old library of classic animation and to build further.
Katzenberg decided to make new Disney classics to replenish the old ones.
Oliver & Company was the first new one in 1988. A more successful attempt
to recapture the timeless magic of Disney animation was achieved the next
year with the release of *The Little Mermaid*.

The Majors Hold the Line on Production Expansion

Disney was using the new money to "rebound." How were the other majors using their video money? A look at releases by members of the MPAA in
Table 6.1 shows production fluctuations during the 1980s, without a discernible trend until 1987. In 1988, Disney's increases in production leveled
out at twelve to fifteen annually. After 1987, the major studios averaged 163
releases per year through 1994. Unlike the independents, the major studios
did not use the ancillary revenues to increase the number of films. Instead,
these companies decided to use the new revenue to increase dramatically the
budget and advertising (for the domestic theatrical release) on each one of
their mainstream films.

TABLE 6.1 MPAA Expenditures on Advertising and Negative Costs, 1980–1994

Year	Advertising per film (millions of dollars)	Percentage annual change	Percentage change compared to 1994	Av. neg. cost (millions of dollars)	Percentage annual change	Advertising plus neg. (millions of dollars)	Percentage change compared to 1994	Number MPAA releases
1980	3.54		291.8	9.40		12.94	272.2	161
1981	3.54	−0.1	291.8	11.30	20.8	14.84	224.5	173
1982	4.06	14.7	241.6	11.80	4.5	15.86	203.7	173
1983	4.18	3.0	231.8	11.90	0.3	16.08	199.5	190
1984	5.63	28.2	146.4	14.40	21.3	20.03	140.4	167
1985	5.24	−2.3	164.7	16.80	16.4	22.04	118.5	153
1986	5.44	3.7	155.0	17.50	4.0	22.94	109.9	139
1987	6.87	26.3	101.9	20.00	14.9	26.87	79.2	129
1988	7.12	3.7	94.8	18.10	−9.9	25.22	91.0	160
1989	7.81	9.7	77.6	23.50	29.9	31.31	53.8	169
1990	10.24	31.1	35.4	26.80	14.2	37.04	30.0	169
1991	10.41	1.7	33.2	26.10	−2.4	36.51	31.9	164
1992	11.49	10.3	20.7	28.90	10.4	40.39	19.2	150
1993	12.13	5.6	14.3	29.90	3.6	42.03	14.6	161
1994	13.87	14.3		34.29	14.7	48.16		167

SOURCE: MPAA, "U.S. Economic Review," various years.

The exact linkage between video earnings and increased production and advertising expenses is not a matter of direct proof. Money is fungible and allocative decisions are rarely fully articulated. That is to say, studio heads did not announce increases in production and advertising budgets as part of a long-range rational plan to reinvest video dollars.[9] However, they knew they had the new money as they increased spending to beat the competition and to grab market share. Successful theatrical releases leading to successful video releases were the only justification they needed for the increasing the promotion budgets for the theatrical release.

At this time, U.S. spending on all advertising was also increasing significantly. However, Table 6.2 demonstrates that movie advertising was increasing at nearly twice the general advertising rate. The new media markets for films motivated the increased spending.

Figures for movie advertising come strictly from the theatrical release campaign and do not include the added cost of promoting films for sell-through or other ancillary markets. The big increases of the late 1980s were the culmination of a decade-long trend of buying more and more television

TABLE 6.2 Movie Advertising versus General Advertising, 1980–1994

Year	Advertising per film (millions of dollars)	Percentage annual change	Percentage change compared to 1994	Total U.S. advertising (millions of dollars)	Percentage annual change	Percentage change compared to 1994
1980	3.54		291.8	54,590		174.8
1981	3.54	−0.10	291.8	60,430	10.70	148.2
1982	4.06	14.70	241.6	66,580	10.18	125.3
1983	4.18	3.00	231.8	75,850	13.92	97.8
1984	5.63	28.20	146.4	87,820	15.78	70.8
1985	5.24	−2.30	164.7	94,750	7.89	58.3
1986	5.44	3.70	155.0	102,140	7.80	46.9
1987	6.87	26.30	101.9	109,650	7.35	36.8
1988	7.12	3.70	94.8	118,050	7.66	27.1
1989	7.81	9.70	77.6	123,930	4.98	21.0
1990	10.24	31.10	35.4	128,640	3.80	16.6
1991	10.41	1.70	33.2	126,400	−1.74	18.7
1992	11.49	10.30	20.7	132,130	4.53	13.5
1993	12.13	5.60	14.3	138,100	8.6	8.6
1994	13.87	14.3		150,000		

SOURCES: Figures for movie advertising from MPAA, *U.S. Economic Review*, 1993. Figures for advertising from various issues of U.S. Bureau of the Census, *Statistical Abstract of the United States* (Washington, D.C.: U.S. Government Printing Office).

time in order to attract the audience for the first weekend. Peter Hoffman, a prominent movie attorney and former president of Carolco, told industry mavens at the 1992 Cannes Film Festival that marketing strategies for major films now try to buy spots on television shows whose combined gross rating points are in the 600–800 range.[10] He reported that this was more than double the previous industry consensus on television buying. National network advertising became an efficient strategy in an era when films were opening wide on a thousand or more screens across the country. The switch to TV was also more effective than the newspaper display ad in reaching the potential home video renter.

The promotion and support that the theatrical release received goes beyond the actual paid advertising. The film industry has always been blessed by an ability to attract a lot of attention from the media. However, its ability to promote "event" films has been unparalleled in recent years. The term "event film" is like "high concept" in that it is not a precise category but a relative definition. It signifies films that are able to attract so much attention that the audience for the film expands beyond the devotees of a particular genre—or even beyond movie fans in general. *Birth of a Nation* (1915), *Gone With the Wind* (1939), and a few others in the historic past were the "event" films of their day. By the late 1980s/early 1990s, there seems to have been an event film every year. There was *Three Men and a Baby* in 1987, *Who Framed Roger Rabbit* in 1988, the phenomenon of *Batman* in 1989, *Home Alone* and *Ghost* in 1990, *Terminator 2: Judgment Day* in 1991, *Aladdin* in 1992, and the unprecedented global success of *Jurassic Park* in 1993. The phenomenon of event films has continued since with titles such as *The Lion King* (1994) and *Titanic* (1997). One is isolated from the popular culture discourse if one knows nothing about these films.

The attention that these films attract goes beyond what is just in the movie. A large part of this added attention is focused on the production budget and the subsequent box office earning of event films. Newspapers, magazines, and pundits in other media have paid increasing attention to the details of production, and in particular to the size of the budget. That is, the budget not only buys things that command attention, such as famous stars—it has become an object of attention itself.

When the movie opens, attention turns to the size of the theatrical opening. Before the age of video and high concept, only specialty trade papers reported opening weekend earnings. The new wider public attention was helped by changes in the computerization of news gathering. In 1976, Marcy Polier started a small company called Entertainment Data, Inc. (EDI). The company contracted with the studios to provide overnight box office results from the participating theaters. By the early 1980s, EDI's information was coming from as much as an estimated 80 percent of the nation's theaters. Its computers generated overnight figures that became industry standards. The quick, accurate reporting fed the growing trend in mainstream newspapers to report box office figures as a news item.

As EDI gained attention, mainstream newspapers such as *The New York Times* et al. have dutifully reported the weekend grosses of blockbuster movies as a weekly feature. In 1990, Time Warner started the magazine *Entertainment Weekly*. It broke new ground for a general audience magazine by concentrating on the business of culture, such as reporting on movie budgets. This was done alongside more traditional reviews and short features. General interest in the business aspects of mass culture was increasing. This interest resulted in a "horse race" model of reporting about films. Who is winning, who is losing? Reporters keep score by comparing production budgets to box office grosses. In this kind of coverage, even big money makers, such as *Hook* (1991), directed by Steven Spielberg, or *Last Action Hero* (1993), starring Arnold Schwarzenegger, were labeled disappointments. Both these films returned a profit after all the markets—theatrical, home video, foreign, and domestic—were tallied. However, these movies were very expensive to make and did not return the same proportion on investment as other big-budget movies.

Can we conclude that home video revenue was supporting the increase in these budgets? I would argue that this revenue has not received its due as the driving force behind event movies. The argument against the importance of home video revenue comes from skeptics who hold to a "Las Vegas" model of film box office. They argue that the theatrical rewards on one movie are so great that they justify a producer risking a higher budget, and thus that box office alone is sufficient to explain the production budget rise. This is a weak model that overly romanticizes what is going on, since it concentrates on individual budget choices. It ignores that studios use their distribution fees and income to finance an entire schedule of movies.

Studio money should be looked at in aggregate sums and compared to aggregate production budgets. Total budget financing is not a crapshoot but is carefully pegged to market performance. Historically the American box office provided at least enough money for studios to recover their negative costs, with television and foreign markets providing the profit. This formula remained in place even as cable money added more revenue. By 1986, however, box office receipts were declining dramatically as a percentage of market performance. Studios no longer pegged their anticipated negative costs to either the U.S. or global box office. Home video's increasing importance gave studios the courage to increase production budgets beyond the capacity of the U.S. theatrical rentals. Lawrence Cohn noted this transition in 1987 when he published industry-wide figures on film rentals as a percentage of negative costs (see Table 6.3).

Variety compiled similar statistics to Cohn's 1987 analysis for 1994. With some additional arithmetic we can confirm that the trend continues, with the domestic box office rentals now accounting for only 67 percent of negative costs.[11] The trend proves that allocative decisions by distributors carefully correlated the amount of production money available with market returns.

TABLE 6.3 North American Film Rentals as
Percentage of Negative Costs, 1981–1986

Year	North American Film Rentals as Percentage of Negative Costs
1981	94
1982	99
1983	90
1984	95
1985	79
1986	76

SOURCE: Lawrence Cohn, "Pics Pay-Back Keeps on Perking,"
Variety, March 4, 1987, p. 1.

This trend would fluctuate violently from year to year if there was a "crap-shoot" mentality at work, since in some years there would be runaway successes and in other years the audience would stay away from the theaters. However, Cohn's analysis shows a linear predictable decline in box office as percentage of aggregate negative costs. Cohn used conservative numbers because he thought that the MPAA reports on average negative costs were skewed toward higher budget films. A more dramatic result can be obtained by combining MPAA numbers with Goldman Sachs' estimates of earnings (see Table 6.4).

The home video figures lump together sell-through and rental tapes. These figures support the statement that negative costs were as much tied to home video as to theatrical earnings. The analysts who estimate the figures do not have access to actual studio numbers. However, the numbers are based on careful compilations from various public sources such as *Variety* and *Video Week* and are certainly accurate enough for determining trends.

The value of the theatrical market had remained constant in absolute terms and had declined in relative terms. It, therefore, was counterintuitive that executives were spending so much on marketing the theatrical release. The theatrical release was taking on a new function as home video became an essential revenue source. Without much forethought, the major distributors muscled each other for better and better theatrical exposure throughout the rise of the video market. Their bidding wars proved serendipitous, since

TABLE 6.4 Film/Home Video (HV) Rentals as a Percentage of Negative Costs,
1980–1993

Year	MPAA total negative costs (millions of dollars)	Box office rentals (North America) (millions of dollars)	Studios' returns from North American HV (millions of dollars)	Box office rental as percentage of negative costs	HV returns as percentage of negative costs
1980	1,260	1,235	10	98.05	0.79
1981	1,639	1,335	50	81.48	3.05
1982	1,770	1,555	150	87.85	8.47
1983	1,975	1,700	400	86.06	20.25
1984	2,189	1,800	950	82.24	43.40
1985	2,318	1,635	1,335	70.52	57.58
1986	2,328	1,650	1,630	70.89	70.03
1987	2,440	1,830	1,915	75.00	78.48
1988	2,769	1,920	2,460	69.33	88.83
1989	3,690	2,165	2,760	58.68	74.81
1990	4,234	2,260	3,220	53.37	76.04
1991	3,915	2,160	3,760	55.17	96.04
1992	4,075	2,100	4,150	51.54	101.84
1993	4,664	2,163	4,360	46.37	93.47

SOURCES: MPAA, *U.S. Economic Review*, 1994; Goldman Sachs, *Movie Industry Update*, 1994.

the theatrical promotion was the legs for the video market. The theatrical release provided the advertising that pushed the product through its many subsequent markets. It also established, in the long run, effective entry barriers against the video newcomers.

Vestron Responds

By the mid-eighties, the concentration of resources on a few high-profile titles was putting added pressure on middle-range titles, which were primarily handled by the newcomers. Did the new distributors have a chance as the market matured? The answer is revealed in the fate of Vestron. It had distinguished itself in the new media market. The Vestron team treated video as a publishing business. They had distanced video distributions from the usual glamorous albeit fatal distractions of handling film. This approach had worked through 1985. They hoped, once more, to find a niche that the ma-

172   jors had ignored even as they faced the challenges in their 1986 annual report. Vestron was the one new independent video distributor with the best chance at survival.

However, the company had a problem to solve with its program supply. In 1985, Furst wanted to take the company public. He had begun talks with Wall Street financiers who were impressed by the substantial growth in company revenues and profits but were concerned about the long-term inventory. Vestron's most important contract was with Orion, and it was running out. Other sources of mainstream popular movies were disappearing. The advisers urged Furst to produce his own movies to guarantee a future supply and maximum profits. Vestron announced such an operation in the beginning of 1986.[12] In March 1986, it sold $115 million in 9 percent convertible debentures to capitalize these operations. For the rest of the year, Vestron struggled with the changing marketplace. It was challenged by wholesalers, retailers, and audience demands for the same hit-driven structure that was prevalent in theatrical distribution.

As the production division started looking at scripts and putting together actors and directors, Vestron Video was on the market snapping up video rights for the remaining "quality" feature films. In January 1986, it paid an advance of $4.5 million for *Prizzi's Honor*. In May, it struck deals with Taft-Barish, the DeLaurentiis Entertainment Group, and the Samuel Goldwyn Company to get the home video rights for existing and future movies. Despite the recapitalization and the multiple film purchases, Vestron was losing ground to tough competition. It had captured 10 percent of the cassette sales market in 1984 and 1985 but had slipped to 8 percent in 1986.[13] Revenues had increased by 7 percent but gross profit had declined by 14 percent. Table 6.5, which shows the number of Vestron releases by year, gives an idea of the problem Vestron was facing.

The 1986 release program was overburdened with too many low-quality titles. By 1987, Vestron had painfully repositioned itself by restricting the number of releases to higher quality titles and by finally placing on the market its own productions, films that would earn money in every medium for the company. The first leg of the repositioning worked to a limited extent. Several titles sold well in home video. Vestron Video received sixteen RIAA gold certificates and five platinum ones. However, its market share slipped to 6.4 percent, and the cost of acquiring and producing led to an operating loss of $57 million for the year. It needed a winning slate.

TABLE 6.5 Vestron Release Pattern, 1982–1988

Year	Number of video releases (features and non-features)	Percentage Change
1982	51	
1983	104	104
1984	131	26
1985	234	79
1986	324	38
1987	149	−54
1988	90	−40

SOURCES: Various Vestron annual reports.

As Vestron was forced into production, it tried to maintain a low-key approach and to not "go Hollywood." Vestron's Stamford, Connecticut location helped keep a distance from the usual Hollywood cliques. The company would be releasing its films during a frenzy of new filmmaking that it was partly responsible for because of its liberal pre-buying strategies of the previous years. At least Vestron had not weakened itself with pre-selling. When the company started releasing its own movies in 1987, it stood to earn the full amount the movie received. Vestron also distanced itself from other independents by the type of movies it was releasing. Cannon, DeLaurentiis, Hemdale, and other independents favored action films that played well on the global market. That genre became fiercely competitive. Vestron chose more offbeat, harder-to-define scripts.

Dirty Dancing (1987) was Vestron's first project. It had a very American setting and sensibility and the producers specifically targeted a female audience. Linda Gottlieb had developed the script at MGM when Frank Yablans was in charge. When Alan Ladd Jr. took over MGM/UA, he passed on the project and Gottlieb took it to Ruth Vitale at Vestron.[14] She put the film into production and it became Vestron's impressive debut hit. *Dirty Dancing* was shot for $6 million. This was a decidedly small-budget effort starring the relative newcomers Patrick Swayze and Jennifer Grey (previously paired in *Red Dawn* [1984]) in a low-key script about a girl's romance with a dancer in a 1960s-era Catskill resort. Despite its modest pretenses, it returned $25 million to the company from its domestic theatrical and $40 million in 1988

174   from its U.S. video release.[15] The theatrical release was well handled, despite a month-long delay as Vestron waited for the kind of theaters it wanted. Furst and Peisinger were now some $59 million ahead of the game. Vestron also had a succès d'estime: *The Dead* (1987) was directed by John Huston from a James Joyce short story. Its box office gross was less than $4 million, and it returned $3 million to the company through video sales.[16] The company returned to profitability in the first quarter of 1988 on the combined power of its various video and theatrical releases.

In 1988, the number of independent film releases declined dramatically throughout the American film industry. Vestron might now survive in this less frenzied atmosphere. However, the company still did not have the resources to properly launch a full schedule of theatrical releases. It could not get hold of the high-concept projects because the recognizable elements— a popular music score or elaborate action—cost too much money. A more hopeful strategy was to produce modest-budget movies that would get adequate theatrical exposure to ensure a profitable video run.

There are those home video releases that do relatively better in the home video market than in the initial theatrical release. This discrepancy undoubtedly has to do with the flexibility of video. Customers are tempted to rent an intriguing title with the knowledge that they are not obliged to sit through the showing, as they would be at the theater. Some of the titles that have become famous because of good video sales despite a disappointing theatrical release are *Missing in Action 2—The Beginning* (1985 Cannon theatrical release, 1985 MGM/UA video release) and *The Cotton Club* (1984 Orion theatrical release, 1985 Embassy video release). This was an ongoing occurrence. Another movie that attracted attention because it was disproportionately successful in video was *Everybody's All-American* (1988 Warner theatrical release, 1989 Warner video release). Most video "sleepers" have had theatrical exposure.

Not enough work has been done to pinpoint the reasons for this discrepancy. One suggestion is that this phenomenon is tied to a certain kind of celebrity star such as Chuck Norris, Richard Gere, or Dennis Quaid. In any case, such successful video releases gave hope to Vestron. The company sought out medium- or small-budget movies that had stars such as Jack Nicholson, Meryl Streep, and James Woods. In the words of Jon Peisinger, these films were "well-programmed."[17] With this philosophy, Vestron proceeded to produce or coproduce shows such as *Ironweed* (1987; Nicholson, Streep), *Best*

Seller (1987; Woods), and so on. With the well-programmed strategy, Vestron hoped to avoid the punishing costs of full theatrical releases while earning profits in the video store. The stars were interested in working on such films for less than their usual fees because the films were different and offbeat. Of course, the reason the films were different was that they were not tailored to the formula of high concept.

Offbeat films probably needed even more publicity than the easily recognizable high-concept films. However, Vestron just could not compete with the major studios, which were increasing their advertising budgets to $7 to $8 million. Peisinger stated that he had to pick his shots on which films he could give an adequate release. Vestron handled theatrical distribution on forty films between 1986 and 1989. He remembers that only three got a wide release. *Dirty Dancing* was the only hit of the three. Profits were elusive. The other two—*Earth Girls Are Easy*, with Jeff Goldblum and Geena Davis, and *Dream a Little Dream* (both 1989)—were disappointments.[18]

Vestron was being squeezed as it tried to operate in the middle range in terms of its advertising, budgets, and audience appeal. Well-programmed films may make money in the video release, but they rarely make enough to justify the expenses of a theatrical release. Furst realized that Vestron's earnings were fragile because of the "catch-22" of theatrical releasing. He needed better films even if they did cost more. Since Vestron was still healthy, it was a relatively easy task for Furst to seek out and obtain a promise of a $100 million loan from Security Pacific to finance future acquisitions. After making the agreement, Security Pacific reneged in the middle of 1989 and refused to lend the money. Furst started selling off divisions of Vestron and closed down production.[19] In that year, Vestron suffered a 26 percent decline in revenue and lost $113.6 million after having made $25.7 million the previous year. In 1990 the company declared bankruptcy and sold its name and its core operation, video distribution, to LIVE. Furst places the blame for the failure of Vestron on the reneged loan.[20]

There were post mortems on the demise of Vestron. It was, after all, the one new company that had taken full advantage of the video revolution and was well on its way to becoming a part of the filmed entertainment industry. Its travails were more significant than the usual rise and fall of undercapitalized independent producers/distributors. Its fate proved that modest-budget films have their own problems in the new era that video itself had helped create. "Well-programmed" was not going to make it against "high concept."

176   Sam Kitt, the acquisitions executive at Universal, made a revealing observation about Vestron movies:

> Except in budget terms, they lacked a vision of the kinds of movie they wanted to make. Their films were off-center and review dependent. A promising movie like *Parents* didn't get the reviews.[21]

In the shorthand of the industry, Kitt's comments suggested that since Vestron did not have the expensive marketing machine to push through "off-center" movies, it needed reviews to give the films some free publicity. It did not get the reviews. Although small-budget films sometimes get good reviews and enough media attention to benefit earnings, this did not occur often enough to save Vestron.

The Fate of Pre-Selling and the Mini-Majors

The other independent strategy, in addition to releasing medium-budget, well-programmed films, was to produce a global version of high-concept films. These were big action films starring international stars such as Sylvester Stallone, Arnold Schwarzenegger, Chuck Norris, and Charles Bronson. DeLaurentiis, Cannon, and Carolco had pursued this strategy avidly. They had built up their production through pre-selling in order to enhance their own weak distribution divisions. However, pre-selling had a fatal weakness in a maturing market. It split the revenue among too many subdistributors. The primary distributor/producer did not receive enough money from even the biggest hits to cover losses on the inevitable flops and disappointments. The entire client list of Crédit Lyonnais, which included the three mentioned above and many others, such as Empire and Hemdale, suffered from this problem. We should remember that pre-selling was premised on the belief that video and the new markets would demand more films. It was also an advanced wedge in the internationalization of the film industry.

There were other pernicious aspects of pre-selling. Sometimes these companies pre-sold several films at the same time. In these multi-picture deals, the outside distributor often demanded the right to cross-collateralize. In other words, the outsider wrote off earnings from a hit against losses from a flop. The producer ended up not getting any money from the hit movie. In addition, it was often written into the contract that the independent had to finance the print manufacturing and advertising (P&A) for the North American theatrical release. Many pre-sale contracts specified how much money the independent was obligated to spend on promoting the film theatrically. This proved to be the straw that broke several international companies.

Cannon, the most prolific of the mini-major production companies, was the first to falter. Cannon and the others (New World, Atlantic Releasing, and Empire) used extensive pre-selling to cover 90 percent and more of their negative costs, with little risk to themselves since the film was already paid for. At first Cannon had MGM/UA handle its domestic distribution in order to avoid the expense of a North American theatrical release. The deal soured after a few releases because of MGM/UA's disappointment in the quality of Cannon's film offerings.

Golan/Globus went into domestic distribution themselves. They arguably upgraded their product. *Runaway Train* (1985; from a story idea by Akira Kurosawa) and *52 Pick-Up* (1986) received critical acclaim but did not earn commensurate box office returns. Self-distribution only increased the company's risk exposure and did not improve its profitability. Andrew Yule's figures show that Cannon's P&A was on average only 36 percent of the negative costs and nonetheless was 27 percent greater than its domestic theatrical rentals for 1986.[22] Substantial P&A expenditures weakened the mini-majors increasingly as they continued to release additional films into an unforgiving market. Cannon's accounting procedures and stock market offerings got it into further trouble.[23] The company started selling off assets in various attempts to avoid bankruptcy. By 1988 it was acquired by Giancarlo Parretti, and it dwindled in market presence as Parretti pyramided his way to a short-lived (and fraudulent) purchase of MGM/UA. In summation, Cannon used home video money to build a large library, but the long-term value of the library was not adequate to offset operating expenses.

The structure of pre-selling had also weakened other mini-majors and independents. New World turned toward television production, and away from filmmaking, in the wake of such disappointments. Empire Pictures faced a similar decline on a much smaller scale and defaulted on a loan from Crédit Lyonnais in 1988. An important erosion occurred with DeLaurentiis. He had not pursued the Cannon strategy of producing as many films as possible with the new home video revenue, but had continued to make a few big-budget movies underwritten by pre-sales. He wanted a bigger library and his own domestic distribution division. In 1985, he purchased Embassy's film library

178   with various rights to 244 films for $18.4 million. Soon afterward, he issued stocks and bonds in order to raise cash to create his own domestic distribution company. The cash was not enough to buy his way out of the same pre-selling troubles that Cannon had. From 1986 through 1988, DeLaurentiis films did not do well in the domestic box office, and although pre-sales covered production costs, advertising costs were a loss.[24] The DeLaurentiis Entertainment Group went into Chapter XI in 1988 and never emerged.

The company that took the global market most to heart, while staking a major position in domestic video distribution, was Carolco. I described their early years briefly in Chapter 4. Vajna and Kassar had cleverly parlayed their earnings from the *Rambo* franchise into an integrated company making very big-budget movies for the global action adventure audience. They lowered their exposure to the risks of the American theatrical release by distributing their films through Tri-Star, a subsidiary of Columbia Pictures Entertainment. They pre-sold their films to Tri-Star and other foreign distributors for large sums of money. They maximized their video profits with a series of stock swaps starting in 1986 with Lieberman, a rack jobbing company, and with IVE, the umbrella group for Noel Bloom's various video operations, including Family Home Entertainment.

Lieberman Enterprises started as a music distributor in 1937. Since the 1960s it had become a primary rack jobber, contracting with mass merchandisers such as Wal-Mart to stock racks with prerecorded music (LPs, cassettes, CDs) and/or videocassettes, discs. The company either paid a flat rental for the store space or a percentage of the sales from the rack. In either case, the rack jobber provided the expertise and volume discounting that the merchandiser did not have access to. Lieberman began handling video in June 1984, when the video population had reached over 16 million households. Lieberman generated $1.5 million in video sales in 1985, $10.1 million the next year, and $32.6 million in 1987.[25] Video was the future of the company, and this would be accomplished through full integration with a video distributor.

Lieberman and IVE were finally integrated in 1988. The resulting video distribution company was renamed LIVE. Jose Menendez, a former music executive for RCA and an associate of Kassar and Vajna, became the CEO. He did not have much time to put the company on a solid footing. Menendez and his wife were murdered in 1989, by their two sons, in a case that grabbed national attention. LIVE struggled on, failing to earn profits from 1991 through

1994, but was always able to raise capital because of its access to Carolco's big-budget action films.

Carolco had a partnership deal with IVE that allowed it to collect 50 percent of the receipts on the video sale of Carolco movies. This was much higher than the usual payment of royalties to a copyright holder. Carolco's close relationship persisted as LIVE emerged from the union of Lieberman and IVE. In 1988 Carolco and LIVE shared $18 million from the U.S. video sales of *Rambo III*. The following year they handled Carolco's *Red Heat* and shared almost $16 million. The next two years the relationship hit some jackpots. In 1990, Carolco's *Total Recall* returned $46 million to the distributor from video sales, and a year later Carolco's *Terminator 2: Judgment Day* earned another $42 million for LIVE.[26]

Carolco and LIVE were benefiting from Carolco's ability to produce a successful big-budget movie every year. Its "A" budget level of production distinguished Carolco from Cannon, which had adopted the strategy of producing many "B" budget films. Both companies favored the global action market and relied heavily on international stars and directors. Carolco can also be distinguished from the medium-budget efforts of Vestron and other such independents as the Samuel Goldwyn Company, or the increasingly eclectic output of Orion Pictures. Nonetheless, Carolco ultimately faltered for the same reason as DeLaurentiis. Carolco was financing its films through pre-sales. This deprived it of full participation in overseas earnings and in the domestic box office rentals collected by Tri-Star. In fact, home video was the one market in which Carolco could collect its full earnings. In the high-stakes game that Carolco was playing, there would always be flops, such as *Mountains of the Moon* (1990), *Johnny Handsome* (1989), and so on. The inability to realize full earnings from the hits such as *Terminator 2: Judgment Day* increased the downside of the disappointments.

Vajna and Kassar seemed to live in full knowledge that Carolco's long-term prospects were limited because they refused to economize. Hollywood executives accused Carolco of spending too much money on stars and other talent and thus forcing up the price levels for actors. Of course, this is a hoary accusation, first leveled against the salary Adolph Zukor started paying Mary Pickford in 1915. In many ways Vajna and Kassar were throwbacks to a more flamboyant era, and they stuck out from the corporate ethos of the contemporary film industry. When people did business with Vajna or Kassar, they got the regal touch. Carolco would provide corporate jets, expensive hotels, and the other accoutrements of global filmmaking. Carolco had no use for the prudent caution of the Disney team. Their claim to fame was extravagance and aggressiveness. Unfortunately, the party could not go on forever.

The irony was that the aggressive techniques of Carolco were putting just as much money in the pocket of its rival Tri-Star as in its own pocket. Tri-Star, safely nestled in the Columbia (subsequently Sony) Entertainment group conglomerate since 1985, survived and prospered, while Carolco sank. Vajna and Kassar had an admirable track record at picking popular films, perhaps even better than DeLaurentiis or other pre-sellers. Nonetheless, Carolco was on thin ice despite their successes of 1990–1991.

When Vestron went out of business in 1990, the independent scene was fading rapidly. Media Home Entertainment had maintained a steady low profile, handling horror and other formulaic low-budget films through the 1980s with dwindling revenues. The parent company, Heron, finally had enough and sold off the two video distribution arms of Media to Handleman and CBS/Fox in 1990 and 1991, respectively.[27] Orion obtained bankruptcy protection in 1991. It continued to distribute videos, the only profitable segment of the company as it tried to reorganize. Embassy passed through several hands during its slide toward bankruptcy. In 1986 Columbia bought Embassy and spun off its home video division to Nelson Entertainment. Nelson was a subdivision of the Canadian holding company Nelson Holdings. It was not able to make a profit out of film and home video distribution and sold its assets to New Line in 1991. To sum up: By the end of 1991 Vestron, Embassy/Nelson, and Media, the largest of the independent video distributors, were gone. Among the mini-majors, Cannon, DeLaurentiis, Hemdale, and Empire were either gone or on the way out. Carolco, Orion, and Samuel Goldwyn were in long-term trouble that would turn out to be fatal.

LIVE, Miramax, and New Line

In 1991, three large independent companies were still healthy. One was the video distributor LIVE. The other two were mini-majors without video distribution divisions: Miramax, New Line, and LIVE. LIVE was surviving because as the competition folded, it was becoming the default video distributor for independent productions. For example, a big boost came in 1990 when LIVE earned $102 million for the video distribution of *Teenage Mutant Ninja*

Turtles (*TMNT*), which was produced by New Line. It had managed to challenge Disney's domination in the sell-through market by selling *TMNT* cassettes directly to consumers at prices below $25.

Miramax and New Line both trace their company origins to the 1970s, although neither became prominent until the late 1980s. Their late blooming occurred in part because of the opportunities created by the collapse of other independent distributors. New Line was founded by Robert Shaye in 1971, while he was distributing Jean-Luc Godard's film portrait of the Rolling Stones, *Sympathy for the Devil* (1970). Shaye carefully harbored his resources from one cult movie to another. A new plateau was reached in 1984 when New Line produced and released Wes Craven's *Nightmare on Elm Street*. The film cost $1.8 million and grossed $25.5 million. The company went on to make seven sequels and New Line became a prominent independent production/distribution studio.

Miramax was founded by two brothers, Harvey and Robert Weinstein, in 1979. The company had not really participated in the independent buildup in the mid-eighties. It did not handle video distribution. It remained a small boutique operation until the troubles of Vestron, Orion, Goldwyn, and other independents lowered the asking price for small films. The brothers sought bargain films with some potential to get good reviews and to reach a wide audience. Miramax started to gain attention when it released Errol Morris' documentary *The Thin Blue Line* in 1988. Then, it gained not only attention but also sizable profits with Steven Soderbergh's *sex, lies, and videotape* (1989). The big breakthrough came in 1993 when Miramax released Neil Jordan's *The Crying Game*. The sophisticated tale of political and sexual ambiguity caught the critics' and "art house" audience's fancy and the film received $26.6 million in North American rentals. The Hollywood majors took notice.

The events of 1990 might have just indicated that a cycle of independent distribution had reached its low point, although the number of bankruptcies had been proportionately higher than the previous downturn of independents in the late 1970s. However, LIVE, Miramax, and New Line were still standing. One academic study concluded that video independent distribution was still alive and healthy in 1990.[28] This conclusion, though, was largely premised on LIVE's viability, which quickly became an illusion. Its sales fell by 22 percent the next year and continued to fall at that rate for the next four years.[29] The health of Miramax and New Line was more enduring, but their independence was not. The bankruptcy of Vestron in 1990 was a prelude to

182   the mergers of New Line and Miramax into the Hollywood establishment in 1993.

As the 1990s took shape, the Walt Disney Company feature film division was losing steam. The bulk of Katzenberg's studio earnings came from children's shows, and the bulk of their earnings came from sell-through home video. Touchstone and Hollywood, the two distribution arms that the Disney people had set up to produce and release general interest films, had stumbled with such disappointments as *The Rocketeer, The Marrying Man, V. I. Warshawski,* and *Billy Bathgate* (all in 1991). These were not cheap disappointments. The successful Disney studio chief was chagrined to find that the cost of producing both animation and live action had eroded profit margins. Katzenberg started to research other companies for clues to their success. He noticed the string of breakout hits the independent distributor Miramax was having at this time. He decided not to imitate Miramax. Instead, he wanted to buy it.

By the spring of 1993, the Weinstein brothers and Disney agreed to bring Miramax within the Disney camp. The number of successful independent distributors dwindled even further when New Line announced in August 1993 that it was being acquired by Turner Broadcasting. In the early 1990s, Ted Turner was desperate for production units to feed his own growing satellite and cable distribution systems. New Line was a stopgap opportunity as Turner continued to seek a major alliance. His ambition culminated in 1996 when he merged with Time Warner for 10 percent of Time Warner stock and the promise that he would continue to assert his power within the Time Warner hierarchy. Time Warner was interested in Turner's cable empire and global news operations. New Line was only an incremental although attractive inducement. New Line was now officially joined with an original major Hollywood studio.

In both the Miramax and New Line cases, the owners and their executive team stayed on to continue doing what they had been doing with autonomy and minimal interference. What did Shaye and the Weinsteins gain? Distribution power. Miramax did not have the power to release a film to a thousand movie theaters at a time, and Disney did. Miramax did not have a video distribution division. It often released the videos through LIVE. LIVE's power over wholesalers and retailers was diluted by its lack of volume. In fact, to gain clout in its dealings with wholesalers, LIVE had agreed to a partnership with Warner Home Video to distribute its product. Therefore, Miramax was

receiving its royalties only after two other companies had skimmed off their 183
distribution fees. An alliance with Disney's Buena Vista, the top home video
distributor, was much better. Miramax could not find a stronger company for
international, domestic, and video distribution. Robert Shaye faced the same
challenges at New Line, and the Turner alliance gave New Line guaranteed
television distribution and a stronger credit line for production and distribution expenses. The subsequent Time Warner merger gave New Line the best
possible access to the video market for its products. Shaye and his team have
responded by producing higher budget movies and spending more on the
theatrical marketing.

This trend continued after 1993 with other independents. The record
company Polygram decided to re-enter the film business by forming Gramercy Studios and acquiring other film production divisions. It joined the top
ten U.S. film suppliers of video product in 1993 and 1994. Gramercy was an
interesting alternative to Miramax, but its independence ended when it was
sold to Seagram/Universal in 1998. At the same time, Seagram/Universal acquired the very small October Films (which did not have a video distribution
arm). The only independent video distributor with significant market share
(above 2 percent as late as 1997) that has survived through 2000 is Artisan,
the successor company to LIVE.[30] In 1998, the LIVE owners received financing from the legendary entertainment investors Allen and Company and
changed the name from LIVE to Artisan Entertainment.[31] They turned the
company back into a private corporation. Although figures are no longer
available, it looks as if they have achieved profitability with the runaway success of *The Blair Witch Project* (1999). Artisan hopes to be well positioned as
the market switches to the new technology of DVD.

Conclusion

This chapter bears out in historical detail that the videocassette business was
defeating the long-term prospects of independence. In Chapter 1, we saw that
independents pioneered new ways of attracting the audience, particularly in
the postwar decades. The video independents continued this pioneering effort only to discover that the numbers no longer added up. Even Vestron, with
its *Dirty Dancing* and other hits, had little chance in this new atmosphere.
As markets proliferated, the theatrical release sucked up all the available
oxygen.

184   New Hollywood responded to a new medium, and at least from a corporate point of view, it resembled the old Hollywood—in fact a much older Hollywood. The relative openness of the film market in the 1960s and 1970s had shut down again. The industry was different now from before video, with few new players permanently admitted to the system and the new video distributors gone or absorbed. Film on video changed the balance of the media environment. Next, we will look at the connections between the corporate landscape, the audience, and the movies.

CHAPTER SEVEN

The Lessons of
the Video Revolution

The narrative of the video revolution culminates around 1993–1994. The years since have not changed the lessons of the revolution, although we can speculate on modifications and further transitions. For example: media corporations merged and grew large in the years following the introduction of the VCR. Now these companies are growing even larger as cultural products are being distributed over the internet. Are the two responses related? Before we speculate on this and what else the video narrative tells us, we must answer the following two-part question: First, what did the media industries learn from the growth of home video into a mass medium? Second, what did home video reveal about the audience?

Media Industries after the VCR

There has been both a general shift in the media landscape in the video age and specific video-driven changes in the individual industries of television, cable, and film. The general shift is the wave of mergers and acquisitions in the video/new media age, which can be explained by the "outflanking" strategy. The absorptions of Miramax, New Line, Gramercy, October, Orion, and Samuel Goldwyn into larger film studios were, in this light, specific instances of a larger trend.

The current wave began with the premature purchase of MGM by Turner Broadcasting in 1985. A more enduring merger in that same year was the takeover of Twentieth Century Fox by Rupert Murdoch's News Corporation. Coca-Cola bought Columbia Pictures the next year and sold it again to Sony in 1989. Warner Communications took over Lorimar in 1988 and merged with Time–Life in 1989 to form Time Warner. Matsushita bought MCA/Uni-

186   versal in 1991 and sold it again to Seagram in 1995. The 1993 takeover of
        Paramount by Viacom was significantly financed by Blockbuster. The trend
        continues to this day with the 1995 purchase of ABC by the Walt Disney Com-
        pany, the 1999 stock swap between CBS and its former subsidiary, Viacom,
        and the 2000 purchase of Time Warner by America Online (AOL). Bertels-
        man is rumored to be looking for a film studio to add to its publishing, Euro-
        pean television, and music operations.

        Video taught film companies to anticipate that they will have to distribute
        their content in new ways. The home video market developed outside the
        flanks of established distribution systems. Video rental ambushed the indus-
        try. The Hollywood establishment had left too many ancillary rights to films
        in the hands of individual producers. They could not impose their rules on
        the video rental market. While rentals did not hurt the established film stu-
        dios, it nonetheless caused executives anxiety because it was uncontrolled.
        Big film distributors allowed newcomers to take the risk and to reap the ini-
        tial profits of the new technology.

        Video also greatly enhanced the value of film distribution. Therefore,
        companies such as Time–Life, Sony, the News Corporation, et al. wanted al-
        liances with major film distributors. Video demonstrated that new technolo-
        gies and even new software would change media markets quickly in the fu-
        ture. In response, media executives now know that they should have all media
        within their corporate tent. It has become a sign of weakness not to own an
        outlet in every medium. A media corporation has to exploit aggressively all
        rights to their shows. This defines the outflanking strategy.

        The top three companies illustrate the point. Disney, Time Warner, and
        Viacom all have strong video distributors and venerable production studios.
        They all have important cable channels. There is the Disney Channel. Time
        Warner's string includes HBO, CNN, and other Turner properties; and Via-
        com owns MTV and Showtime. All three have broadcast networks, such as
        ABC, CBS, and Time Warner's WB network. They and the other media con-
        glomerates have many, many other properties in print and other communi-
        cation modes. These corporations may suffer temporary technological chal-
        lenges such as unauthorized digital transfers of music. Nonetheless, they have
        such complete control of cultural content that they cannot be threatened.
        They will no longer allow individual artists or producers to own "ancillary"
        rights. Digital Distribution is currently giving added impetus to the outflank-
        ing strategy and to multi-media marketing.

There is another level to this analysis, which is the local impact that video-tape has had on television, cable, and film. Television was initially threatened by time shifting. However, the immediate threat (which was always over-stated) receded as television and cable expanded. The expansion has facilitated the re-broadcasting of programs so viewers do not have to feel boxed in to a set schedule. On the broadcast side, there was a 62 percent growth of the number of U.S. television stations from the introduction of the VCR in 1975 through 1994.[1] Of course, cable has added even more program hours to the mix. Shows are syndicated even during their first network run and are pro-grammed into strips (appearing every day of the week instead of the once-a-week format of the first run). The audience has innumerable chances to catch a prime time television show during its first run, its re-broadcast, its syndica-tion, and its appearance on cable channels devoted to old TV shows. The de-sire to time shift will continue for sports programs, continuous soap operas, and other shows. However, programming is saturated, and recording off the air will not be the decisive factor for future technologies that it was with the VCR in the late 1970s.

Other television industry complaints about home video actually created a more favorable policy environment. I have already discussed how the Reagan administration used the emergence of home video as grounds for rescinding enforcement of the 1948 Paramount et al. consent decree. Television policy deregulators also used the video market as evidence of vigorous competition in the filmed entertainment world and as an argument against a "scarcity doc-trine." The scarcity doctrine stated that there was a scarcity of broadcast facilities and was used to justify mandating stations to give response time to viewpoints opposed to the ones aired on the station (fairness doctrine).[2] The fairness doctrine was removed by the Reagan administration. Video and cable's presumed undermining of broadcast scarcity was also the background as the financial and syndication rules of 1972 and 1973 were gradually elim-inated during the Clinton administration. The elimination of these rules al-lowed TV networks to engage in production partnerships and to syndicate their own programs for additional sales after a network run. This deregula-tion may not change television significantly, but it has already smoothed the way for television networks and film production companies to merge and to pursue multi-medium marketing of their shows.

188   A concluding question about the relationship between home video and television is, why did VCR not become an extension of the TV set? In the 1960s Jack Gould, Peter Goldmark, Frank Stanton, et al. thought that it would. Instead, the VCR became the extension of the movie theater. The answer raises issues of the different ways filmed entertainment can become a commodity. Filmed entertainment earns revenues in three ways: direct payment, subscription payment, and as content for advertising. Direct payment is for a ticket at the box office, rental of a videotape, pay per view on television, and purchase of a videotape. Subscription payment is for both basic cable channels such as American Movie Channel (AMC) and premium (additional fees) such as HBO. Film as content for advertising shows up on both advertiser supported cable and broadcast channels and also includes the phenomenon of product placement and product tie-ins.

These three ways represent different balances of risk and reward. The direct payment mode has the highest risk and reward per individual movie. Subscription and advertising modes diffuse the risk since payments are made before the actual size of the audience is known. Subscribers pay their fees before they know how much they will be using the service. Since they pay for a time period, the cable channels are less concerned with the immediate popularity of individual shows and more concerned with the total popularity of their schedule. This fact explains why HBO and other companies in the subscription market often choose to compete on a unique product basis. They want to have programs that the viewer cannot get except through subscribing to their service. Several critics have noticed that recently HBO has been a source of innovative original programs and has taken the time to build the audience for these programs. *The Larry Shandling Show, The Sopranos,* and various made-for-cable movies are meant to attract potential loyal subscribers.

On the other hand, cable is not well suited to the direct payment market. There have been repeated attempts to sell films on cable through a pay per view (PPV) format. The PPV format for films peaked in 1982 with *Star Wars,* though there have been continuing efforts to sell films in this way. The 1993 Goldman Sachs *Movie Industry Update* waxed enthusiastic about Video on Demand (VOD), a computerized PPV system, and was excited about the Time Warner promotion of the system in Queens, New York.[3] However, VOD has since fizzled out. Tapes, box office, and discs continue to be the only major direct payment markets in the United States.

The playing field in direct payment is quite different from that in subscription or advertiser-supported markets. The risk is quite high since there
is a chance that not a single person will pay to see the show (TV and cable always have a minimal audience even for their test patterns). Because the risk
is so high, exhibitors are quick to eliminate a weak movie by either denying
it space on the video wholesalers' shelves or canceling its bookings at the
movie theaters. Distributors now feel that in direct payment arenas they have
little time or space to build an audience. This ruthlessness explains why home
video became primarily a market for high-profile event films. They avoid the
risk of marketing unknown titles. For example, straight-to-video titles (not
receiving any theatrical release) typically account for less than 4 percent of
the cassettes shipped by distributors.[4] TV and cable shows are also a small
part of the cassette market.

In the high-stakes market of direct payment, movie distributors like to add
other modes of competition in addition to product uniqueness. These other
competitive modes are convenience and overwhelming publicity. Convenience competition has resulted in wide releases, staggered starting times for
film showings, depth of copy in video rental stores, and sell-through shelves
in mass market stores and even fast food chains. Convenience and publicity
competition works against building an audience over time. There are occasional slow rollouts of a film, and several films developed reputations that
helped them have successful video releases after modest theatrical performances. Nonetheless, video fits the prevailing logic of New Hollywood marketing better than TV/cable shows' reliance on audience loyalty.

THE IMPACT ON FILMS' PROFIT MARGINS

Convenience and publicity competition has a price. Films earn high revenues, but film profit margins have slipped substantially. Actual statistics are
not published in public records. The clearest study of this slippage comes
from Harold Vogel, who is a high-profile Wall Street analyst of film and other
entertainment industries. Hollywood dealmakers constantly consult him on
various important decisions. Therefore, we can have some faith that the data
he has published reflects an industry consensus (see Table 7.1 and Figure 7.1).

Peter Hoffman, another leading industry figure and the former president
of Carolco Pictures, has warned his colleagues that profit slippage will lead to
long-term weakness in the film industry.[5] Despite such high-level worriers,

TABLE 7.1 Revenue Trends for American Film Distributors, 1980–1993

Year	Total Revenue (billions of dollars)	Percentage Change	Profit Margin	Percentage Change	MPAA Releases	Percentage Change
1980	4.0	n/a	12.20	n/a	161	n/a
1981	3.7	−7.50	8.00	−34.43	173	7.45
1982	4.5	21.62	12.40	55.00	173	no change
1983	5.3	17.78	11.10	−10.48	190	9.83
1984	5.8	9.43	8.80	−20.72	167	−12.11
1985	6.4	10.34	7.30	−17.05	153	−8.38
1986	6.8	6.25	11.70	60.27	139	−9.15
1987	8.3	22.06	11.20	−4.27	129	−7.19
1988	9.1	9.64	12.60	12.50	160	24.03
1989	11.6	27.47	9.80	−22.22	169	5.62
1990	12.7	9.48	8.70	−11.22	169	no change
1991	14.2	11.81	6.70	−22.99	164	−2.96
1992	15.9	11.97	8.10	20.90	150	−8.54
1993	17.4	9.43	5.80	−28.40	161	7.33

*Includes revenues earned from all markets and all territories. Average annual growth rate for revenue 12.29%. Average annual growth rate for profit margin −1.78%.

SOURCES: Harold L. Vogel, *Entertainment Industry Economics: A Guide for Financial Analysis*, 3d ed. (New York: Cambridge University Press, 1994), p. 45; MPAA, *U.S. Economic Review*, 1993.

the deep corporate pockets of multi-marketed multi-media companies reduces the short-term risk of slim profit margins. Hoffman spoke from the perspective of running a single-product company making money only from feature-length movies. Such a company has to live from month to month. Therefore, he warned his audience about the drawback of receiving money from ancillary markets such as video, where a film does not really start earning money until nine to twelve months after its completion. Because of the delay, video money is not as valuable as box office money (which is recovered in half the time). There is a cost associated with delay—inflation of production costs and interest payments on outstanding loans. Hoffman estimated that in 1992 these two factors absorbed at least 12 percent of the video money.[6] His own former company, Carolco, could little afford the cost of waiting for video revenues. Hoffman was already gone by the time Carolco folded in 1996, after the final debacle of its last movie, *Cutthroat Island*.

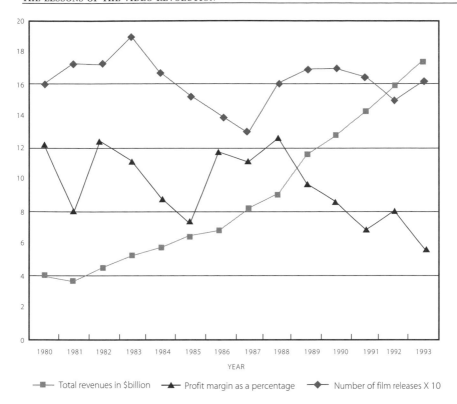

FIGURE 7.1 Revenues, Profit, and Number of Films Released, 1980–1993.

The Disney executives were particularly upset by declining profit margins. In 1989, the profit margin of the studio stopped growing for the first time in three years. Industry reporter Ron Grover charted Disney's problem, noting that in 1989, the margin was 16 percent, and in 1990, it was down to 14 percent.[7] In January 1991, Disney studio head Jeffrey Katzenberg wrote an internal memo about the downward trend that was leaked and attracted wide attention within the Hollywood community. In the memo, he protested the escalating costs and the disappearance of medium-budget films and speculated on the culture of filmmaking. He even grumbled about Disney's high-budget production *Dick Tracy* (1990) despite its substantial earnings—$61 million in North American rentals. Katzenberg reminded everyone that the big blockbusters of the 1950s and 1960s had destabilized Hollywood majors and led to a rise in independent film production at that time.[8] It is perhaps this historical lesson that has since motivated studios to either acquire or create distribution divisions devoted to lower budget films. The typical example of this was Disney's purchase of Miramax. The irony is that over time, these low-budget divisions start to pursue bigger budget productions. This has been true of both New Line and Miramax.

Katzenberg did not link the big-budget "event" movie with the growth of the ancillary markets. He did worry that home video had cheapened the movie-watching experience—literally. He proposed doubling the price of pre-recorded videos in order to force rental stores to charge $5 for a rental. He thought that this would still be "an excellent entertainment bargain" and would somehow increase the audience demand for better stories.[9] Katzenberg's comment about raising rental prices and culture clashes, along with some expressed doubts about Sony and Matsushita,[10] were out of touch. It took others to point out that the new earnings of the ancillary markets were adequately supporting thinner profit margins for the larger companies. Profit slippage becomes part of the post-video media environment. It raises the stakes on every aspect of distribution and makes it difficult for any new company to enter the theatrical market, the enabling condition for entry to the ancillary markets. In the years since, neither Katzenberg nor other studio heads have noticeably reduced publicity or production expenses. Eric Pleskow, former head of Orion Pictures, echoed a sentiment expressed earlier by Austin Furst when he told Peter Bart that "it's almost like theatrical distribution is your loss leader."[11]

Low profit margins are a necessary function of New Hollywood, where instantly recognizable films are crafted for multi-media markets. The splintering of the markets has of course led to an increase in costs, even in the original film production. Executives realize that films cannot be passively sold in just one market. Movies must be heavily advertised and promoted. Vogel observed that video revenues often equaled the same percentage of negative costs as the print and advertising (P&A) budget of major studio films.[12] This suggests that the new Hollywood marketing divisions pegged their increasing P&A costs to video revenues. We should remember that this is an aggregate argument and cannot be applied to individual films, where revenues may fall short or run ahead of P&A. Nonetheless, a large media company has the flexibility to limit its financing of an increasing cost with a specific revenue source.

INTERNATIONAL IMPACT

The symbiotic relation of video and theatrical releases also worked internationally and accounts for the dramatic takeover of the global box office by the U.S. American films earned 92 percent of the German box office in 1992 and 94 percent of the British box office sales in 1993.[13] *Variety* colorfully used the headline "Earth to H'wood: You Win" for an article estimating that U.S. films earned 90 percent of the 1994 global box office.[14] *Variety*'s statistic is probably a bit of a hyperbole. Nevertheless, it is very true that in that year Hollywood took home more money from overseas theaters than it did from its domestic releases. Goldman Sachs estimated that Hollywood earned $2.2 billion from overseas box offices and $3.1 billion from overseas cassette sales in 1994.[15]

How did video lead to global supremacy? There are some direct connections. VCR technology gave television owners an alternative to state-controlled broadcasting. Advertisers and other free market forces used the popularity of this alternative as an additional argument for the breakup of state monopolies, and governments gave way and licensed alternative broadcasters, throughout the eighties. These new broadcasters filled their airtime with the same Hollywood products that were so popular in the video markets. In general, videocassettes heightened the awareness of American films, since international video distributors favored blockbuster films. This could only help the richest film industry in the world, the U.S. On the global scene, just as in the domestic market, the increased revenues from video markets financed high-profile theatrical releases. In a 1995 article, Martine Danan[16] isolated the following improvements in U.S. theatrical distribution in France: (1) The window between the U.S. theatrical release and foreign release dwindled from six months to a few weeks. (2) U.S. companies could flood a country with more than twice as many prints as the local filmmakers could. (3) There was more attention paid to tailoring advertising to various national audiences. (4) U.S. film advertising budgets increased throughout the world. These improvements resonate with the observations made above about convenience competition.

European producers operate in an increasingly hostile investment environment.[17] Many countries, such as the former communist nations, have cut out film subsidies altogether. The most recent European Community initia-

194   tives support a more commercial approach. Coproductions are encouraged. Only film scripts with perceived popular appeal will receive government subsidies. Foreign film distributors, trying to compete with Hollywood distribution, are pressured to produce films that can be pushed through the ancillary markets—that are capable of "selling through."[18]

Media scholar Brian Winston theorizes that there are four general stages of development and adoption of a new technology. The fourth stage is the suppression of the radical potential of a new technology.[19] He explains that no industry will allow a new technology to destroy its very way of doing business. While the overt actions Hollywood took against the VCR were of no avail, the development of sell-through and the emphasis on global blockbuster releases in both theaters and video wholesaling had the desired suppressive effect. The dominant companies before video dominate further now.

    Larger media conglomerates saw that film properties had acquired enhanced sales value. Their elements could be exploited in many global markets. The new multi-market landscape ensured that mass media was the foremost industry in a general "globalizing" of the world economy. The marketing of films is now a variant on the classical Hollywood tiered-release strategy, when film prints worked their way from exclusive first runs to cheap storefront theaters. Now the tiered release begins with the launch of a film from a massive theatrical blitz through to international to video to pay television to "free" television.[20]

Home Video and Changes in the Form of Film

The strong links between home video and media conglomeratization, globalization, and raised entry barriers to distribution means that video is one of the most important catalysts for contemporary Hollywood. In show biz terminology, video may be the biggest thing that has happened to the movies since sound. However, home video has not overtly changed the form and look of feature film, at least not as much as sound. This may account for the relatively slow recognition of its importance. Formal changes may be slower and less apparent than structural changes to the film industry. By 1994, some of the formal changes that are driven by video had already emerged. Other changes are more speculative, and yet other changes have yet to reach the level of a steady trend. The future will bring these to the surface.

I have already argued for the strong mutual reinforcing relationship between high-concept, blockbuster "event" films and video. However, it is difficult to draw lines between specific genres and video. This task is more difficult because the New Hollywood's blockbuster is premised on mixing genres. The linkage of genre trends with home video is obscure, although it seems that video did help both the horror and erotic thriller films. The video market also dramatically caused expansion in two genres with radically different audiences: pornographic tapes and children's shows.

In complete contrast to the mainstream, hard-core movies (featuring explicit shots of actual sex acts) have largely abandoned theatrical releases and are produced and distributed exclusively on videotape. *Adult Video News* estimated that U.S. consumers spent $2.1 billion on this category in 1993.[21] This is 16 percent of the $13 billion that U.S. consumers spent on all videotapes.[22] However, the switch to video has severed the ties that this industry had previously with narrative filmmaking. Earlier sex films were continuous with independent and alternative production and distribution. Noel Bloom and others who used to deal in both no longer do so. It is interesting that just as hard-core tapes allowed distributors to create the infrastructure of video rentals in the late 1970s, so hard-core internet sites were the first profit centers on the World Wide Web.

The children genre includes both feature films and shorter length shows, made for television or video. The entire category is affectionately know as "kidvid," and has now served as an ersatz babysitter to an entire generation. Table 7.2, which shows data for 1992, indicates that kidvid is the only category that came close to general interest feature films in terms of market share.

Table 7.2 (which excludes hard-core) shows that non-feature film videos represented only a small fraction of the market.[23] This has been a general trend since 1986. Children's programming was the only non-feature category that hit double-digit percentages. The perfect fit between children's viewing habits and home video led to the revival of full-length animation at Disney and many other studios. The feature-length animated film for children was once the special province of Walt Disney. After his death in 1966, this type of filmmaking went into decline. The successes of Roy Disney and Jeffrey Katzenberg in reviving this genre led to several studios actively pursuing such productions. The major reason behind Eisner's decision to commit Disney's

TABLE 7.2 Genre Shares of North American Market (Rental and Sell-Through Combined for 1992)

Category	Units Sold (millions)	Percentage of Total Units Sold	Sale Revenues (millions of dollars)	Percentage of Total Sale Revenues
Movies, excluding kid	140.2	47.1	2,665	56
Kid movies	28.9	9.0	398	8
All movies, general and kid	169.1	56.1	3,063	64
Other kidvid	106.2	31.1	1,106	23.3
Fitness	15.0	4.6	195	4.1
Music	8.8	2.8	181	3.8
Sports	9.3	3.0	132	2.8
Miscellaneous "how-to"	5.5	1.8	74	1.6

NOTE: The figures are for all tapes sold. If the figures were only for rental-priced tapes, films would have been 82% of all sales.

SOURCE: *Video Week*, January 11, 1993, p. 2.

resources to such a costly genre was the new revenues of the video market in 1988.

FILM STYLE

The formal impact of home video has not been only on the genre mix; it has also been on the elements of film style. This is not a strictly causal relationship that has been articulated by the film producers, but it can be inferred from looking at how certain patterns fit together. In the world of multimedia marketing, elements that play well on both the small and large screens are more appropriate than ones that give pleasure in only one format. There is a caveat. No one is going to acknowledge that there has been a compromise with big screen effects because the theatrical release is the gateway to all markets.

When Steven Spielberg lamented the disappearance of the epic splendor of *Lawrence of Arabia* (1962) in contemporary movies, he did not dwell on the fact that its visual quality cannot be conveyed in the video medium. Of course, there are many visual wonders that can play on the television, and it is not surprising that today's big-budget movies emphasize these. They can be summarized as those things that give a movie the visceral pleasure of a roller coaster ride, such as powerful camera moves, morphing and other digital enhancements, and quick editing. The eye is never allowed to rest in New Hollywood. The ear has also assumed new importance. Full stereo with surround sound gives a greater dimensional feeling to the film for both the theater audience and to those home viewers who have attached multiple speakers to their VCRs. A handful of movies had surround sound in the mid-1970s; a decade later 90 percent of all films had four channels of sound.[24]

There are attempts to theorize the new style. Jerry Mander argues that "technical events"—"a cut, a zoom, a superimposition, a voice-over, the appearance of words on the [TV] screen . . . each alteration of what would be natural imagery"—have proliferated to compensate for the paucity of the video image.[25] James Bernardoni asserts that this style derives from the "television fallacy."[26] As the shots are simplified so that they play on the small screen, the filmmaker starts adding technical events to compensate for the simplification. This argument was first formulated as television and film started influencing each other in the 1970s. It does not quite capture the frenetic quality of film style in the 1980s and 1990s. Charles Eidsvik hypothesizes a more compelling premise for the frenzy in terms of spectator theory. In the video age, he argues, there has been a transition from gaze esthetics to glance esthetics.[27] An image is not held on the screen for very long because the viewer will not study it but only glance at it. However, the theoretical work on the changes in film style and the rise of the VCR still has a hasty, speculative feeling. It is a relatively neglected area.

Another area for further thought is the role of IMAX films in the video age. IMAX is a super image format that has been used since the mid-1970s for films about natural phenomena, exotic locations, and technical achievements. It finally came of age as a mass medium when the IMAX film *Everest* reached $50 million in theatrical rentals by December 1998. IMAX is shown in special theaters and restores some of the visual splendor that was commonplace in the 1950s widescreen epic. However, IMAX films are still experimenting with dramatic narrative forms. It is often marketed as part of a day at the museum and/or theme park. Is it a reaction to the video "downsizing" of film? Or an extension of the blockbuster event, blurring the distinction between film and other entertainment forms? We should continue to monitor its role in the future.

Filmmakers live in the same media ecology that they help create. There-

198   fore, film style changes are also attributable to the fact that filmmakers increasingly learn their craft by watching films on video. The work of Quentin
Tarantino is illustrative. He did not go to film school but used his time working as a clerk in a video rental shop to educate himself about the medium. He
received financing for his first film, *Reservoir Dogs* (1992), from LIVE Entertainment.[28] The combination of video rental store background and video
distribution financing resonated with his unique style. The linearity of the
Reservoir Dogs narrative was jumbled up, approximating the distractions
of watching a bunch of rented videos in a single evening. The extreme approaches to violence marked the film as a video "nasty" (an English term for
the gory films showing up in the video market). Tarantino is not the only new
director with a video pedigree. Kevin Smith (*Clerks* [1997], *Dogma* [2000])
has also claimed a video education. *Variety* has suggested that video stores are
the film schools for a new generation of filmmakers.[29]

THE LOSS OF MEDIUM SPECIFICITY

The audience's experience of film as both a theatrical and video experience
and the producer's attempt to make a film that serves both experiences leads
to a further conclusion about video's impact. Film has lost medium specificity. The function of film has been expanded in several directions at once—
changes that were triggered by television, accelerated, and were confirmed
with the triumph of the VCR. Both the electronic and photographic versions
of the film are equally authentic. In today's economy of proliferating media,
producers are encouraging the audience to consciously eliminate that part of
the message that is medium specific and to retain only that part of the movie
that can be translated from medium to medium. Few members of the viewing
public will remember or value that part of a film that does not survive its
translations. This explains the new prominence of sound and roller-coaster
effects. These elements survive medium transfer.

This is different from earlier medium transfer. Popular entertainment has
always borrowed from content in one medium to create new forms in another
medium. Shakespeare borrowed the plotlines of his dramas from written histories and sung ballads. Movies have always borrowed freely from dramas,
novels, and newspaper headlines. However, in each case the borrowing involved a translation process where the material was recast to fit the formal
needs of the new medium, whether it was stage or film. The decline of me-

dium specificity results from the translation process sliding into the more mechanical procedure of reformatting.

Obviously, the purest example of this is the film transfer to video with minimal creative intervention. Currently, studios build into the original design of the film (i.e., pre-production scripting and scene design) elements that will lend themselves to reformatting the film as it moves across the various markets. The original design needs little subsequent translation.

Scholars of culture have noticed reformatting as a hallmark of film and other new media. They have labeled it in various ways, with slightly different emphasis. Schatz has spoken of studios creating "not simply films but 'franchises'" to depict the multi-media sale of a film idea.[30] Wasko noticed the coincidence of product placement (pre-production), merchandising (reformatting), and media conglomeratization (multi-media distribution). She unifies these various phenomena with the concept of "cultural synergy."[31] Celia Lury refers to the widespread use of "branding."[32] She emphasizes that this is a general method of selling things with instantly recognizable qualities, in our terms, a universalization of "high concept." These various terms refer to an element—a story, an image, a character—that is placed in the original design of the movie and then can be marketed in a variety of media and places. The media do not just market filmed entertainment, with its binary of film and video venues, but also theme parks, toys and other merchandise, novelizations, and stage shows. *Batman* is sold as both an action model figure and as a videocassette. Pepsi is used in *Top Gun* as both a prop and a positive image association between the soda pop and America's ace pilots.

Home video technology shares a responsibility for ushering in an era when market values have totally subsumed cultural values. Steve Knoll, a reporter for *Variety* who covered the video beat in the early years, made a comment suggesting something similar when summarizing a conference. "For a reporter accustomed to covering broadcasting confabs—where pursuit of bucks is tempered by lip service to 'the public interest'—the unabashed devotion of the home video industry to the bottom line stood out in contrast."[33]

It was not home video per se that accounts for this change; it was the reconfiguration of film across several media and markets. When films were still specific to one medium, producers respected films enough to encourage the craft of filmmaking in the hope that the resulting films would ultimately be commercial. Reformatting, franchising, branding, putting film in a cassette box—all of these developments shifted the balance away from craft. A large company, operating in many different media, will spend little energy on maximizing the potential of any one medium. This is a reason to regret the disappearance of small, independent distributors. These companies operated within one medium, such as the theatrical film, and the distributors paid attention to the cultural power of that medium. Vestron and others sometimes demonstrated similar regard for the unique possibilities of the home video medium. Unfortunately, the home video market forced Vestron and others to diversify into other operations and other media and to lose focus.

Images of Audience Time

I opened this chapter with a two-part question. The second part asks, what did home video reveal about the audience? A review of the changes that the industry made after home video allows this question to be rephrased. Do branding, cultural synergy, franchising, multi-marketing, selling-through, and reformatting reflect anything new about the audience? Such strategies are a result of the constant profit motive of corporations. However, the scale of these strategies suggests a new opportunity—a change in the audience's lifestyle. This is the harried leisure referred to in Chapter 3. There, I described Robinson and Godbey, Harris, and Schor reporting the subjective feeling of lost leisure time and its importance for Sony's time-shifting campaign. However, harried leisure not only accounts for the resolution of the format wars, it shapes the entire relationship between home video and the multi-marketed movie. It is time to briefly revisit the harried leisure model and to link it to multi-marketing.

Women working added to a leisure time squeeze for men and children as well. The division of family labor was renegotiated. Families now often approached non-work time with tools that they had learned at work.[34] Tasks and even play activities became compartmentalized into time slots and often bureaucratized. For example, parents began putting children into organized sports leagues instead of relying on neighborhood pick-up games. This both ensured that the child would be supervised by a responsible adult on a routine basis and fit into the parents' work schedules.

This suggests a theory about the social desire for leisure time efficiency. This theory states that families gradually moved into a polychronic world in the 1970s. Polychronicity is combining several activities in the same "clock block." The post-1970s time crunch brought on a new wave of time-saving devices as people sought out technologies that either freed up time or allowed several tasks to be accomplished at once. Consumerist advertising now promoted appliances that facilitated efficient time use. Flexibility over time spread from just-in-time manufacturing to "just-in-time home keeping."

Pushing a film across different media markets becomes an integral part of "just-in-time home keeping." Single elements of the film can be used in different times, in different contexts. Going out to the film is romantic time, or social time. On the other hand, watching film on video is an alternative to TV time. Buying the film is gift time. Allowing the children to watch the film at home several times is mechanical baby-sitting. The audience can maximize leisure efficiency by seeking the same content in other media. Consuming music or books associated with the film is a sure way to derive additional pleasure from a known cultural artifact. Purchasing items that feature elements of the film such as mugs, books, or T-shirts is a quick way to derive meaning from commonplace objects. Can one film lend itself to all these uses? Think of *Star Wars, E.T., Jurassic Park, Titanic,* and so on. Do all members of the audience behave this way? No, probably not even a majority. Just enough do so that companies tip their resources toward this kind of cultural distribution.

The corporate formations of the 1980s began a new multi-marketing period in film/audience relationships. There are tantalizing hints that the audience itself responded in new ways. For instance, there was an unprecedented spurt of consumer spending on mass media. Newspaper executive Charles Scripps observed that Americans always spend the same percentage of their income on mass media. Media scholar Maxwell McCombs tested Scripps' principle of relative constancy of media spending and found it to be true from 1929 through 1970.[35] Other updates confirmed the principle until William Wood and Sharon O'Hare extended McCombs' data through 1988. They concluded that cable and home video spending was a significant exception to McCombs' principle.[36] Americans were spending more in order to "stay in" and watch their movies at home.

Multi-marketing helped stabilize the theatrical attendance of grown-ups. "Stay-ins" who maintained their interest in film through video and cable are now increasingly tempted to try "going out." Vestron's Peisinger tells the anecdote of his parents, who had lost the moviegoing habit until they saw *Lethal Weapon* (1987) on video and decided to see the sequel in the theater.[37] The return to the theater is partially supported by MPAA statistics. After 1948, as people assumed the responsibilities of age, that generation stopped going to the movies. Therefore, the audiences of the 1960s and 1970s were heavily skewed toward teenagers and youth. By 1995, adults reversed the 1970s trend by continuing to go to the multiplexes even as they entered their thirties. The increase has not been dramatic, but it has been significant.[38] Starting in the early eighties, U.S. theater attendance remained steady with an average of 1.1 billion admissions from 1982 to 1992 and fluctuations averaging 4.5 percent up or down in any given year. In that period, ticket price increases account fully for box office revenue increases.[39]

A Philosophic View of Film and Audience

The film industry was organized around the concept of a mass audience, particularly around the time of the nickelodeon boom a century ago. A large number of people, only vaguely aware of each other, watched an identical filmed performance in many different locations around the world. Early distribution systems achieved an economy of scale through national and international networks. Mass audience revenue supported lavish productions that could not be duplicated in less efficient media such as theater, which is tied to one location at a time. The mass audience expanded when broadcasting was able to reach millions simultaneously. The nature of the mass audience was debated and theorized if only because the broadcast audience was practically invisible. Were they passive recipients of centralized entertainment, or were they active interpreters of popular culture, deriving positive and diverse benefits from television, film, and radio, et al.?

It should be stated that the positions are not mutually exclusive. Indeed, I do not see that much is gained by trying to resolve the positions. Models of "empowered audiences" or "passive audiences" both set up formulas for seeing other people—the audience—as a separate object of study, as a mass. There is a plausible critique that these formulas trap the social analyst into overly romantic or overly pessimistic views of this "separated" mass. We should reflect on the full implications of Raymond Williams' work on mass audience. In the conclusion of his book *Culture and Society*, he writes about the natural tendency never to include oneself in a mass but to see the masses as other people. He points out that objectively speaking, "There are in fact no masses; there are only ways of seeing people as masses."[40] In this study, we are looking directly at those in power (cultural producers) treating audiences as masses. We are not looking directly at the audience. Therefore we can sharpen the chapter opening question by asking, do cultural producers treat the mass audience as active interpreters or passive recipients? How so?

The actual history of video distribution to date gives a complex answer (as all histories do). The defeat of playback-only systems forced the American entertainment industries to recognize the active role of the consumers. Entrepreneurs acted upon this recognition by developing the infrastructure of video rental and creating new independent distribution companies. Other entrepreneurs continued to treat the audience as passive by producing high-concept films, financing expensive theatrical releases, and pressuring stores to buy many copies of the same video title (depth). Other activities that, I feel, presumed a less active audience were mass volume "selling-through" of selected titles and designing blockbuster movies to be reformatted for many different media markets.

However, the passive audience marketing does not explain the major studios' acquisitions of smaller producers and distributors, such as Disney's purchase of Miramax. These acquisitions may be a visible sign that smaller distributors could reach more engaged parts of the audience who are willing to explore films that resist the easy summations of the high-concept formula, reformatting, and cultural synergy. The major studios wanted to spread their bets. Nonetheless, the big-budget, multi-media marketing mentality penetrated even the specialty divisions of the majors. The Weinstein brothers' willingness to join Disney indicated that they wanted vast distribution resources that could sell their films to the largest possible audience. Both the Weinsteins of Miramax and Shaye of New Line became less willing to support quirky, modestly profitable projects after their respective mergers. This was not a sign of bad faith; it was the structural result of operating within media conglomerates.

In the course of this study, I have often gone into the details of corporate fighting and number crunching to make visible the complex way distributors put together large film audiences. The future will revisit many of the historic-corporate issues of video as music, literature, and film come to be distributed over the internet. Home video was the opening wedge in the digital era that I call "flexible home entertainment." This label is a deliberate nod to the style of manufacturing that is called "flexible specialization" and that emphasizes just-in-time inventories. Hochschild suggests this connection in her portrayal of families applying the principles used in their organization of work time to their cultural activities at home. Corporations are already re-

204   combining in anticipation of these new technologies of cultural distribution. This time the media corporations are ahead of the audience in contrast to their catch-up during the emergence of video.

Whither the Mass Audience?

As video rental becomes the formative experience of filmmakers, it also re-shapes the audience's experience of film culture. It is as significant as the development of neighborhood movie theaters during the first decade of the twentieth century. From one perspective, it performed the same function as the nickelodeon, bringing the film to the audience whether they are at home or in the theater. This is obvious despite the headlines proclaiming that there has been a fragmentation of the audience since the advent of new media. Media theorists ask if this is the breakup of the mass audience. There is a certain tone of expectancy, since the breakup of the mass audience promises diversity and democratic access. Particularly exciting is the technical possibility of desktop moviemaking with digital cameras, with editing and distribution over the internet via personal computers.

There will be desktop movies and undoubtedly a few will grab the attention of the mass audience, leading to overblown proclamations that the era of grass-roots filmmaking is upon us. If history serves as any guide, these films will simply be "calling cards" that will enable the desktop film director to move on to a career of making big-budget movies. No one will sustain a successful career at his or her personal computer. Digital filmmaking will be incorporated into centralized production. It is highly unlikely that we will find a silicon-era Roger Corman sustaining a forty-year-long career, working at the I-Mac cranking out a new digital "slasher" every two weeks. This is because the economies of scale have changed since the 1950s. Now that the media conglomerates have learned the lesson of home video, it is clear that they will be able to bring those economies to new media.

Declarations of the breakup of the mass audience and the advent of grass-roots filmmaking are premature. The audience has changed in several ways, while centralized production and distribution continue to thrive. The stress on leisure time that ordinary people experience gives an edge to large multi-faceted companies that can market films across media. Channels and venues may multiply, but audience time cannot expand. Realization of the utopian hope for diverse markets and product proliferation rests more on the reduction of stressed leisure than on new technologies of distribution. If people feel that they are prosperous enough to work less, they will take the time to search for obscure films off the beaten track.

The technology of home video resonated with the blockbuster strategy of New Hollywood. This was neither foreseen nor foreordained. However, there were more determinative results of the VCR. The VCR is directly responsible for the enhanced revenues that New Hollywood enjoyed. It led the revival of the global market for Hollywood products. It taught the media companies the lessons of pushing a cultural product across various media markets. It directly caused the loss of medium specificity, far more than the previously assigned culprit, network television, did.

The VCR is now a part of history, although its moment of departure has not yet arrived. The lessons of Hollywood's response to the VCR may be long term or not, depending on the future. The film form itself has proven to be tough. It conquered the home video market despite the foot-dragging of its master, the Hollywood establishment. The longest running lesson of film history is that feature narrative film is as flexible as the celluloid on which it is shot. It can be distributed in any medium in any and all parts of the globe. It has traveled through sound and from black and white to color. It has been helically scanned onto magnetic tape, beamed onto the small screen, and through the digital pipeline. It has been transmitted by satellites to digital theaters. Perhaps one day, when the audience and corporate landscape are different from today, film will once again be handled by small boutique distributors just as it once was in the opening stage of the video revolution.

Notes

Introduction: Signs of the Time

1. Harold L. Vogel, *Entertainment Industry Economics*, 3d ed. (New York: Cambridge University Press, 1994), p. 45.

2. The consumer price index stood at .54 in 1975 and at 1.458 in 1993, with 1983 equal to 1.0.

3. See Frederick Wasser, "Four Walling Exhibition: Regional Resistance to Hollywood," *Cinema Journal* 34, no. 2 (February 1995): 56–57.

4. Biskind's entire book is devoted to this theme, as is the final chapter of Bordwell, Staiger, and Thompson. Peter Biskind, *Easy Riders, Raging Bulls: How the Sex-Drugs-and-Rock 'n' Roll Generation Saved Hollywood* (New York: Simon and Schuster, 1998), and David Bordwell, Janet Staiger, and Kirstin Thompson, *The Classical Hollywood Cinema: Film Style and Mode of Production to 1960* (New York: Columbia University Press, 1985).

5. Wide release is the practice of having many theaters play the same film on the first weekend of the release. This is contrasted with "tiered" or "limited" release. This occurs when the film plays only a few theaters on the first weekend and goes on in subsequent weeks to other theaters.

6. "Independent" is a slippery term. Here it is used to denote those companies that are outside the Hollywood establishment. The establishment may be defined as members of the Motion Picture Association of America. A more accurate definition is the top six film companies: Disney, Warner, Paramount, Twentieth Century Fox, Columbia, and Universal.

7. See Janet Wasko, *Hollywood in the Information Age: Beyond the Silver Screen* (Austin: University of Texas Press, 1994).

8. *Hoover's Guide to Media Companies* (Austin, Tex.: Hoover's Business Press, 1996), p. 24.

9. W. Russell Neuman, *The Future of the Mass Audience* (Cambridge: Cambridge University Press, 1991).

208   10. R. S. Goald, "Observations on the American Independent Feature Film Movement: 1983–93" (paper presented at the University Film and Video Association Conference, Bozeman, Mont., August 1994).

11. Ann Gray, *Video Playtime: The Gendering of a Leisure Technology* (London: Routledge, 1992).

12. Mark R. Levy, ed., *The VCR Age: Home Video and Mass Communication* (Newbury Park, Calif.: Sage, 1989), and Julia R. Dobrow, ed., *Social and Cultural Aspects of VCR Use* (Hillsdale, N.J.: Erlbaum, 1990).

13. Morry Roth, "Home Video Hypes CES Show," *Variety*, May 27, 1981, p. 61.

14. Timothy Corrigan, *A Cinema without Walls: Movies and Culture after Vietnam* (New Brunswick, N.J.: Rutgers University Press 1991), p. 12.

15. Broadcast date January 12, 2000.

Chapter 1. Film Distribution and Home Viewing before the VCR

1. "United States of America versus The Motion Pictures Patent Company: Brief for the United States. October 1914." Reprinted in *Film History* 1, no. 3 (1987): 196, 296.

2. Russell Merritt, "Nickelodeon Theaters, 1905–1914: Building an Audience for the Movies," in *The American Film Industry*, rev. ed., ed. Tino Balio, pp. 83–102 (Madison: University of Wisconsin Press, 1985), p. 86.

3. European companies developed larger production and distribution facilities although they lagged from the start in exhibition outlets. In 1911, various U.S. consuls reported that European theaters (France, Germany, Great Britain, etc.) per capita were significantly behind the United States (*New York Clipper*, January 20, 1912, p. 12; January 27, 1912, p. 5).

4. Georges Sadoul, *Histoire du cinéma mondial: des origines a nos jours*, 8th ed. (Paris: Flammarion, 1949), p. 54.

5. The most important decision against the MPPC was announced in October 1915 by the District Court of the United States for the Eastern District of Pennsylvania.

6. See Janet Staiger, "Combination and Litigation: Structures of US Film Distribution, 1896–1917," in *Early Cinema: Space-Frame-Narrative*, ed. Thomas Elsaesser and Adam Barker (London: British Film Institute, 1990).

7. Both W. K. L. Dickson (the inventor of the Edison movie camera) and Edwin Porter (one of the earliest filmmakers to use continuity editing) left the company to seek broader horizons.

8. The standard 35mm gauge was generally not used on home projectors since 35mm was expensive and also highly flammable, requiring the attention of an experienced projectionist.

9. Ben Singer, "Early Home Cinema and the Edison Home Projecting Kinetoscope," *Film History* 2 (1988): 57.

10. Ibid., pp. 41–42.

11. Richard Abel, *The Ciné Goes to Town: French Cinema 1896–1914* (Berkeley: University of California Press, 1994), p. 47.

12. Gleason Archer, *History of Radio to 1926* (New York: American Historical Society, 1938), p. 289.

13. Allen David Larson, "Integration and Attempted Integration between the Motion Picture and Television Industries through 1956" (Ph.D. diss., Ohio University, 1979), p. 117.

14. The Dumont network went off the air in 1955, ending an increasingly difficult relation between Paramount and Alan DuMont.

15. See Chapters 2 and 4 in Christopher Anderson, *Hollywood TV: The Studio System in the Fifties* (Austin: University of Texas Press, 1994).

16. Ibid., p. 134.

17. Orrin E. Dunlap Jr.'s monograph, *The Future of Television*, rev. ed. (New York: Harper and Brothers, 1947), is a good example of this rhetoric.

18. As quoted in Amy Schnapper, "The Distribution of Theatrical Feature Films to Television" (Ph.D. diss., University of Wisconsin–Madison, 1975), p. 123.

19. Ibid., p. 118.

20. Ibid., p. 49.

21. Ibid., pp. 67–68.

22. Garth Jowett, *Film: The Democratic Art* (Boston: Little, Brown, 1976), p. 359.

23. Motion Picture Association of America, *U.S. Theatrical Statistics 1946–1995* (Encino, Calif.: MPAA).

24. Jowett, *Film*, pp. 483–484.

25. John Belton, *Widescreen Cinema* (Cambridge, Mass.: Harvard University Press, 1992), p. 66.

26. Jowett, *Film*, pp. 483–484.

27. See Peter Lev, *The Euro-American Cinema* (Austin: University of Texas Press, 1993).

28. Nicholas Garnham, *Capitalism and Communication: Global Culture and the Economics of Information* (London: Sage, 1990), pp. 184–185.

29. Phone conversation with Dick Beesemyer, former general manager of ABC, January 1997.

30. Thomas Schatz, "The New Hollywood," in *Film Theory Goes to the Movies*, ed. Jim Collins et al., pp. 8–36 (New York: Routledge, 1993), p. 16.

31. Newspaper advertising was 88 percent of the total in 1971. By 1988 it had dropped to 69 percent. MPAA, various handouts.

32. Biskind, *Easy Riders*, p. 277.

33. Harold L. Vogel, *Entertainment Industry Economics: A Guide for Financial Analysis*, 2d ed. (New York: Cambridge University Press, 1990), p. 86.

34. Biskind, *Easy Riders*, pp. 264–268.

35. David Newman, a screenwriter on *Superman* (1978), mentioned that great care was taken with the flying effects that were used in an advertising campaign targeted at adults. The ads assured this potential crossover audience that these and other

210   well-crafted special visual effects would "make [them] believe." Personal conversation, December 28, 1992.

36. Schatz, "The New Hollywood," p. 16.

37. Bruce A. Austin, "Home Video: The Second-Run Theater of the 1990s," in *Hollywood in the Age of Television*, ed. Tino Balio, pp. 319–349 (Boston: Unwin Hyman, 1990).

Chapter 2. The Development of Video Recording

1. These forty-five years included a mythic episode when young Sarnoff was one of the first wireless operators to receive the news of the *Titanic* disaster in 1912.

2. Margaret Graham, *RCA and the Videodisc: The Business of Research* (New York: Cambridge University Press, 1986), p. 67.

3. This follows Michael Cusumano's research team's description of the video format wars, published as *Strategic Maneuvering and Mass Market Dynamics: The Triumph of VHS over Beta* (Harvard Business School Working Paper 91-048, 1991), pp. 24–25.

4. Bruce Carl Klopfenstein, "Forecasting the Market for Home Video Players: A Retrospective Analysis" (Ph.D. diss., Ohio State University, 1985), p. 157.

5. Gleason Archer, *History of Radio to 1926* (New York: American Historical Society, 1938), p. 112.

6. For an example of the range of proposals, see "Radio's Big Issue—Who Is to Pay the Artist?" *New York Times*, May 18, 1924, sec. 8, p. 3.

7. Julius Weinberger, "Economic Aspects of Recreation," *Harvard Business Review* 15 (Summer 1937): 452.

8. Francis Hampton, "New Leisure: How Is It Spent?" (master's thesis, University of North Carolina, 1935), pp. 61–62.

9. Roland Gelatt, *The Fabulous Phonograph: From Tin Foil to High Fidelity* (Philadelphia: J. P. Lippincott, 1955), p. 247.

10. "Aylesworth Assails Recordings in Chicago Speech," *Broadcast Advertising* 3, no. 9 (December 1930): 7.

11. Erik Barnouw, *The Golden Web: A History of Broadcasting in the United States. Volume 2: 1933–1953* (New York: Oxford University Press, 1968), p. 218, n. 7.

12. Federal Communications Commission, *Public Service Responsibility of Broadcast Licensees* (Washington D.C.: Federal Communications Commission, March 7, 1946), p. 36.

13. Mark Clark, "Suppressing Innovation: Bell Laboratories and Magnetic Recording," *Technology and Culture* 34, no. 3 (July 1993): 517.

14. Ibid., pp. 534–535.

15. Federal Communications Commission, *Report on Chain Broadcasting* (Commission Order no. 37, Docket no. 5060, May 1941), p. 17.

16. Barnouw, *The Golden Web*, p. 171.

17. See John T. Mullin, "Creating the Craft of Tape Recording," *High Fidelity*

Magazine 26, no. 4 (April 1976): 62–67. The U.S. Armed Forces Radio Service had used wire magnetic recorders built in Chicago, but their use was limited in quality and length. Therefore, it is not surprising that German recordings had the army stumped.

18. A new network that was formed in 1943 when the government forced RCA to sell its NBC Blue network.

19. Mullin, "Creating the Craft," p. 64.

20. Brian Winston, *Media, Technology, and Society* (New York: Routledge, 1998), p. 267.

21. Dunlap, *The Future of Television*, p. 79.

22. William Boddy, *Fifties Television: The Industry and Its Critics* (Urbana: University of Illinois Press, 1990), p. 24.

23. Albert William Bluem, "The Influence of Medium upon Dramaturgical Method in Selected Television Plays" (Ph.D. diss., Ohio State University, 1959), p. 36.

24. *Variety*, May 25, 1983, p. 33.

25. "General Sarnoff: The Twentieth Century Practical Prophet," *Sponsor* (October 1, 1956): 111.

26. Graham, *RCA and the Videodisc*, p. 20.

27. Mark Schubin, "An Overview and History of Video Disc Technologies," in *Video Discs: The Technology, the Applications and the Future*, ed. Efrem Sigel et al., pp. 7–52 (White Plains, N.Y.: Knowledge Industry Publications, 1980), p. 13.

28. Sally Bedell Smith, *In All His Glory: The Life of William S. Paley* (New York: Simon and Schuster, 1990), p. 469.

29. James Lardner points out the misuse of the word "recording" for this playback-only unit in his book, *Fast Forward: Hollywood, the Japanese and the Onslaught of the VCR* (New York: W. W. Norton and Company, 1987), p. 75.

30. Ibid., p. 76.

31. Jack Gould, "Soon You'll Collect TV Reels, Like LP's," *New York Times*, September 3, 1967, p. D13.

32. Jack Gould, "Renting a Movie or a Professor to Take Home," *New York Times*, April 5, 1970, sec. 2, p. 15.

33. Jack Gould, "The Great Day Isn't Exactly at Hand," *New York Times*, November 15, 1970, sec. 2, p. 21.

34. Lardner, *Fast Forward*, p. 84.

35. Avco Industries, *10-K Report* (1973), p. 3.

36. MCA, *Annual Report* (1972), p. 11.

37. Lardner, *Fast Forward*, p. 28.

38. Steve Knoll reported this in "See Vidisk Hour of Truth Approaching," *Variety*, February 17, 1982, p. 43. My own research shows that MCA lumped R&D money into a category entitled "Corporate General Expenses."

39. Efrem Sigel, "The Consumer Market for Video Discs," in *Video Discs: The Technology, the Applications and the Future*, ed. Efrem Sigel et al., pp. 53–68 (White Plains, N.Y.: Knowledge Industry Publications, 1980), p. 54.

40. *Variety*, July 14, 1982, p. 84.

212 41. Since the end of the 1980s, the laser system has gained somewhat in popularity, and other manufacturers (Sony, Philips) have gotten back in. They are packaging the laser system with CD and CD-ROM players; see Michael Rogers, "A New Spin on Videodiscs," *Newsweek*, June 5, 1989, pp. 68–69. In the United States, laser disc households (HH) had grown to 1.2 million by 1993 (1.6 percent of U.S. VCR HH). In the same year, Japan had more than four times as many laser disc owners, or 16 percent of Japanese VCR HH (*Screen Digest*, August 1994, p. 182). Digital video discs (DVDs) are now supplanting Laservision.

42. Graham, *RCA and the Videodisc*, p. 100.

43. Ibid., p. 53.

44. Ibid., p. 112.

45. David Lachenbruch, "The Videoplayer Era," *Journal of the Producers Guild of America* 13, no. 1 (March 1971): 7–12.

46. *Variety*, January 7, 1981, p. 32.

47. *Variety*, May 20, 1981, p. 80.

48. *Variety*, February 25, 1981, p. 82.

49. Graham, *RCA and the Videodisc*, p. 213.

50. Peter Guber, "Is There a Cassette in Your Future—Is There a Future in Cassettes?" *Journal of the Producers Guild of America* 12, no. 3 (September 1970): 6.

51. Steve Chapple and Reebee Garofalo, *Rock 'n' Roll Is Here to Pay: The History and Politics of the Music Industry* (Chicago: Nelson-Hall, 1977), p. 97.

52. Eugene Marlow and Eugene Secunda, *Shifting Time and Space: The Story of Videotape* (New York: Praeger, 1991), p. 110.

53. Lardner, *Fast Forward*, p. 65.

54. Craig T. Norback and Peter G. Norback, *TV Guide Almanac* (New York: Ballantine, 1980), p. 397.

55. Lardner, *Fast Forward*, p. 82.

56. Akio Morita et al., *Made in Japan: Akio Morita and Sony* (New York: E. P. Dutton, 1986), pp. 208–209.

57. P. Rangunath Nayak and John M. Ketteringham, *Breakthroughs* (New York: Rawson Associates, 1986), pp. 23–24.

58. Lardner, *Fast Forward*, p. 160; Nayak and Ketteringham, *Breakthroughs*, p. 45.

59. RCA's eight-track cartridge gained initial market momentum over its rival four-track audiocassette because it had a longer playing time in 1965. Philips' audiocassette eventually eliminated the eight-track advantage. It would be a nice historic coincidence if the RCA executives had this in mind when they talked to the Matsushita representatives.

60. *Variety*, April 7, 1982, p. 37.

61. *Screen Digest*, June 1991, p. 129.

62. Electronic Industries Association of Japan, *Facts and Figures on the Japanese Electronics Industry* (Tokyo: Electronic Industries Association of Japan, 1993), p. 27.

63. Cusumano et al., *Strategic Maneuvering*, p. 9.

Chapter 3. Home Video: The Early Years

1. Gary Becker, "A Theory of the Allocation of Time," *Economic Journal* 75 (1965): 493–517, and Staffan Burenstam Linder, *The Harried Leisure Class* (New York: Columbia University Press, 1970).

2. Juliet B. Schor, *The Overworked American: The Unexpected Decline of Leisure* (New York: Basic Books, 1991), p. 29.

3. John P. Robinson and Geoffrey Godbey, "Are Average Americans Really Overworked?" *The American Enterprise* 6 (September/October 1995): 43.

4. Lou Harris Poll no. 68, November 6, 1995, p. 4.

5. U.S. Bureau of the Census, *Statistical Abstract of the United States* (Washington, D.C.: U.S. Government Printing Office, 1995).

6. Joseph A. Morein, "Shift from Brand to Product Line Marketing," *Harvard Business Review* (September 1975): 161.

7. See William M. Weilbacher, *Brand Marketing: Building Winning Brand Strategies That Deliver Value and Consumer Satisfaction* (Lincolnwood, Ill.: NTC Business Books, 1993), pp. 51–62.

8. Ann Gray's entire *Video Playtime* is devoted to the separate uses of the VCR, particularly by gender, in Great Britain. This use also reminds one of Joshua Meyrowitz's observation that the family room is now the place to go to watch TV in order to escape the rest of the family.

9. Vogel, *Entertainment*, 2d ed., p. 377.

10. Ibid., p. 186.

11. Eugene Marlow and Eugene Secunda, *Shifting Time and Space: The Story of Videotape* (New York: Praeger, 1991), p. 124.

12. This was not a class action suit (464 U.S. 434). Sheinberg solicited and received some financial support from Warner Brothers Studios, and the goodwill of the other major studios as expressed by an *amicus curiae* (friend of the court) brief filed by the MPAA. But Universal was definitely taking the lead while the others had a wait-and-see attitude.

13. See respective annual reports and Thomas Guback, "Theatrical Film," in *Who Owns the Media?* 2d ed., ed. Benjamin M. Compaine, pp. 199–298 (White Plains, N.Y.: Knowledge Industry Publications, 1982), p. 293.

14. Paul Goldstein, *Copyright's Highway: From Gutenberg to the Celestial Jukebox* (New York: Hill and Wang, 1994), p. 149.

15. Ibid., p. 84.

16. U.S.C.A. § 107.

17. F. Supp. 446.

18. "Trying on the New Media," *Variety*, September 24, 1980, pp. 48, 79.

19. Lardner, *Fast Forward*, p. 115.

20. U.S. Congress, *Video and Audio Home Taping*. Hearing before the Subcommittee on Patents, Copyrights, and Trademarks of the Committee on the Judiciary

214   United States Senate (Washington, D.C.: U.S. Government Printing Office, 1984), p. 294.

21. F. Supp. 468.

22. Marlow and Secunda, *Shifting Time and Space*, p. 40.

23. F. Supp. 467.

24. Gillian Davies and Michèle E. Hung, *Music and Video Private Copying: An International Survey of the Problem and the Law* (London: Sweet and Maxwell, 1993), p. 130.

25. U.S. 425.

26. Goldstein, *Copyright's Highway*, p. 64.

27. U.S. 57.

28. U.S. pp. 62–63.

29. U.S. 436.

30. Personal conversation with Professor Jane Ginsburg, Columbia University Law School, October 1996.

31. Lardner, *Fast Forward*, pp. 131–132.

32. Russell Sanjek, *American Popular Music and Its Business: The First Four Hundred Years*, vol. 3 (New York: Oxford University Press, 1988), p. 630.

33. In 1984, the FCC decided to no longer require station logging of commercials. It was thought that this easement would relieve advertisers' concerns about zapping. Stephen F. Stander, "The Impact of the VCR on Broadcast Television," in *Video Cassettes: Production, Distribution and Programming for the VCR Marketplace*, ed. E. Gabriel Perle et al., pp. 481–494 (New York: Practising Law Institute, 1985), p. 490.

34. J. Mandese, "Bates Bullies Nets over VCR Erosion," *Adweek* 27 (1986): 1, 4.

35. Barry S. Sapolsky and Edward Forrest, "Measuring VCR Ad-Voidance," in *The VCR Age: Home Video and Mass Communication*, ed. Mark R. Levy, pp. 148–167 (Newbury Park, Calif.: Sage, 1989), p. 149.

36. Jonathan Sims, "VCR Viewing Patterns: An Electronic and Passive Investigation," *Journal of Advertising Research* 29, no. 2. (April 1989): 13.

37. *Screen Digest*, June 1991, p. 130.

38. *Variety*, March 11, 1981, p. 209.

39. See *Variety*, March 7, 1984, p. 355, for an interesting report of the dominance of blue-collar tastes in the West German video rentals.

40. Joseph D. Straubhaar, "Context, Social Class and VCRs: A World Comparison," in *Social and Cultural Aspects of VCR Use*, ed. Julia R. Dobrow, pp. 125–146 (Hillsdale, N.J.: Erlbaum, 1990), p. 129.

41. Roger Watkins, "Scandinavian TV under Gun from Hotshot Video and Satellites," *Variety*, October 7, 1981, p. 80.

42. Gladys D. Ganley and Oswald H. Ganley, *Global Political Fallout: The First Decade of the VCR: 1976–1985* (Norwood, N.J.: Ablex, 1987), p. 7.

43. Yahia Mahamdi, "Television, Globalization, and Cultural Hegemony: The Evolution and Structure of International Television" (Ph.D. diss., University of Texas, 1992), p. 126.

44. Harold Myers, "Hardware Hot, Software Soft in Japan," *Variety*, October 7, 1981, p. 107.

45. *Variety*, March 28, 1984, p. 39.

46. The Meese commission reported testimony that *Deep Throat* had grossed $50 million by 1982. U.S. Department of Justice (USDJ), *Attorney General's Commission on Pornography: Final report* (Washington, D.C.: USDJ, July 1986), p. 1051.

47. *Variety*, January 19, 1976, p. 1.

48. *Wall Street Journal*, May 8, 1985, p. 24.

49. Merrill Lynch, "The Home Video Market: Times of Turbulence and Transition," in *Following the Dollars from Retail to Net Profits—An Examination of the Businesses of Creating and Using Revenues from Motion Pictures and Television Programs*, ed. Keith G. Fleer et al., pp. 111–113 (Eleventh Annual UCLA Entertainment Symposium. Los Angeles: The Regents of the University of California, 1986), p. 113.

50. See various sections in *Variety's First Homevideo Annual*, September 24, 1980.

51. USDJ, *Attorney General's Commission*, p. 1388.

52. Jennifer Steinhauer, "Prosecute Porn? It's on the Decline," *Wall Street Journal*, December 28, 1989, p. A8.

53. Eric Schlosser, "Business and Technology Column," *U.S. News and World Report*, February 10, 1997, pp. 43–50.

54. Steinhauer, "Prosecute Porn?"

55. Personal conversation with James Bryan, 1990.

56. Lardner, *Fast Forward*, p. 172.

57. "Conversation with Andre Blay," *Videography*, June 1979, p. 53.

58. Vogel, *Entertainment*, 2d ed., p. 360.

59. Douglas Gomery, *Shared Pleasures: A History of Movie Presentation in the United States* (Madison: University of Wisconsin Press, 1992), p. 280.

60. "Conversation with Andre Blay," p. 56.

61. *Videography*, June 1980, p. 44.

62. Marge Costello and Vicki Stearn, "Conversation with Jim Jimirro," *Videography*, June 1981, p. 60.

63. The practice of previewing a tape while still on the premises of the store was subsequently found to be a public exhibition by the court and therefore a potential infringement of copyright (*Variety*, August 10, 1983, p. 39). The words "exchanges" and "previews" fell into disuse as the legal status of renting became clarified.

64. *Variety*, March 24, 1982, p. 229.

65. A survey firm, Media Statistics, sampled the U.S. audience in 1982 and found that 24 percent recorded feature films while 21 percent recorded soap operas. Weekly series followed with 20 percent. Sports recording was a surprisingly low 7 percent. *Variety*, January 26, 1983, p. 39.

66. *Variety*, April 7, 1982, p. 77.

67. Paul B. Lindstrom, "Home Video: The Consumer Impact," in *The VCR Age: Home Video and Mass Communication*, ed. Mark R. Levy, pp. 40–49 (Newbury Park, Calif.: Sage, 1989), pp. 46–47.

216   68. The widespread industry belief in the American reluctance to rent was pointed out to me by the prominent entertainment lawyer Frank Gruber, who began his practice in the late 1970s. Personal conversation, October 21, 1995.

69. *Variety*, April 7, 1982, p. 77.

70. There were 22,765 screens in the United States in 1986 according to MPAA, *U.S. Theatrical Statistics 1946–1995.*

71. By the mid-1990s, the number of video stores had stabilized at 27,000 (Video Software Dealers Association, *White Paper,* October 21, 1996, p. 2), while the number of theater screens had grown to 27,805 (MPAA, *U.S. Theatrical Statistics 1946–1995*).

Chapter 4. The Years of Independence: 1981–1986

1. Vogel, *Entertainment,* 2d ed., p. 66.

2. Todd McCarthy, "'Independent' Producers Bruised as Majors Borrow Their Slants." *Variety,* June 16, 1982, p. 22.

3. An important saving in such partnerships was lower labor costs. This was because independent companies had greater flexibility in avoiding union contracts than their major partners.

4. Suzanne Mary Donahue, *American Film Distribution: The Changing Marketplace* (Ann Arbor: UMI Research Press, 1987), p. 191.

5. Morrie Gelman, "Media Home Claims $2mil for Halloween," *Variety,* October 7, 1981, p. 108.

6. Conversation with Noel Bloom, February 7, 1996.

7. *Variety,* July 1, 1981, p. 42.

8. *Screen Digest,* January 1986, p. 2.

9. Tony Seideman, "Slow Start for Sony 'Vid' Singles," *Variety,* August 17, 1983, p. 72.

10. *Variety,* August 19, 1981, p. 52.

11. Frank Segers, "CBS to Distrib ABC Programs for Homevid," *Variety,* June 3, 1981, p. 90.

12. *Television Digest,* January 25 1982, p. 14.

13. Marge Costello and Vicki Stearn, "Conversation with Jim Jimirro," *Videography,* June 1981, pp. 63–65.

14. Lardner, *Fast Forward,* p. 193.

15. Steve Knoll, "Mag Video Launches Cassette Rent Plan," *Variety,* November 18, 1981, p. 34.

16. The more militant VSRA folded into the VSDA in June 1982 as the struggle against studio rental plans was winding down in triumph for the dealers.

17. Morrie Gelman, "Vegas Fracas Hits Major Rent Plans," *Variety,* January 20, 1982, p. 50.

18. Ibid.

19. Vogel, *Entertainment*, 2d ed., p. 139.

20. Gillian Davies and Michèle E. Hung, *Music and Video Private Copying: An International Survey of the Problem and the Law* (London: Sweet and Maxwell, 1993), p. 53.

21. U.S. Congress, Audio and Video First Sale Doctrine. Hearings before the Subcommittee on Courts, Civil Liberties and the Administration of Justice of the Committee on the Judiciary House of Representatives (Washington, D.C.: U.S. Government Printing Office, 1985), p. 33.

22. Ibid., p. 64.

23. Tony Seideman, "Low-Priced Vidtapes as Lure for Big Retail Chains," *Variety*, March 9, 1983, p. 34.

24. *Variety*, October 29, 1980, p. 53.

25. Veronis, Suhler, and Associates, *Communications Industry Forecast 1994–1998* (New York: Veronis, Suhler, and Associates, 1994), pp. 156–157.

26. In 1976, Professor Thomas Guback warned the National Association of Theater Owners that video had the potential to make their business obsolete. *Variety*, October 13, 1976, p. 6.

27. In 1986 the U.S. box office gross was $3.7 billion and admittance was 1.02 billion. See handout from MPAA, *U.S. Theatrical Statistics 1946–1995*.

28. *Screen Digest*, April 1989, p. 81.

29. There were 42.8 million households with VCRs and 41.2 million basic cable subscribers in 1987. Veronis, Suhler and Associates, *Forecast*, pp. 182–183.

30. By "premium cable services" I mean subscriptions that include HBO and other desirable movie channels, as opposed to basic cable subscription, which is usually a package of regular broadcast channels and less valuable cable channels.

31. Vogel, *Entertainment*, 2d ed., p. 47.

32. Robert Lindsay, "Home Box Office Moves in on Hollywood." *New York Times Magazine*, June 12, 1983, p. 36.

33. Goldman Sachs, *Movie Industry Update–1991*.

34. Andre Blay, "Home Video–An Emerging Market." In *Who's Got the Money: The New Financing of Motion Picture and Television Production*, ed. Michael S. Sherman and David R. Ginsburg, pp. 241–242 (Eighth Annual UCLA Entertainment Symposium. Los Angeles: The Regents of the University of California, 1983).

35. Goldman Sachs, *Update–1991*, p. 4.

36. Four MPAA companies–Disney, MCA/Universal, MGM/UA, and Orion–broke out figures for 1984 that give direct comparisons between pay TV revenues and home video revenues (see Table N4.1).
The Disney figures are anomalous because they had stopped outside pay TV sales in order to build an inventory for their own cable channel. The great value of these figures is that they are actual as opposed to the usual guesswork of industry estimates. Even the one studio reporting greater pay TV revenues, MGM/UA, was impressed with the greater one-year growth rate of home video (39 percent) over pay TV (11 per-

TABLE N4.1 Segment Revenues Reported in 1984

Company	Pay TV (thousands of dollars)	Home Video (thousands of dollars)	Pay TV as Percentage of Home Video
Disney	9,100	69,000	13
MCA/Universal	70,296	90,000	78
MGM/UA	102,828	94,420	108
Orion	3,617	7,254	50

SOURCE: Relevant annual reports.

cent) as reported on page 2 of their 1984 annual report. Unfortunately the next year's report did not state if home video had overtaken pay TV in absolute numbers, although industry estimates would support that conclusion.

37. Merrill Lynch, "The Home Video Market: Times of Turbulence and Transition." Reprinted in *Following the Dollars from Retail to Net Profits—An Examination of the Businesses of Creating and Using Revenues from Motion Pictures and Television Programs*, ed. Angeles Keith G. Fleer et al., p. 116 (Eleventh Annual UCLA Entertainment Symposium. Los Angeles: The Regents of the University of California, 1986).

38. Motion Picture Association of America, *U.S. Economic Review* (Encino, Calif.: Motion Picture Association of America, 1993).

39. Seth Goldstein, "Pay Per View in Retrospect: An Apparent Underachiever," *View Magazine*, April 1983, p. 30.

40. "Conversation with Jon Peisinger," *Videography*, September 1984, p. 61.

41. "Vestron Claims Major Status," *Variety*, January 4, 1984, p. 57.

42. *Hollywood Reporter*, December 30, 1983, p. 1.

43. Embassy shipped 100,000 units (86 percent were videocassettes, the remainder were discs) of *Silkwood* and therefore received $4.3 million. If duplication cost $10/unit, Embassy still had $3.3 million with which to pay the advance of $1.6 million ("'Scarface,' 'Silkwood' Video Hit Tape," *Variety*, May 23, 1984, p. 50). The gamble on *Silkwood* had worked. There were 17 million VCRs in the United States at the time and 16,000 video retail stores. *Silkwood* represented 5.4 units sold per store or one unit for every 200 VCR owners. This qualified it as a major hit, earning a platinum certification from RIAA along with about another sixty titles that year.

44. Mark Silverman, "US Homevid Rights Break $3-Mil Barrier," *Variety*, May 16, 1984, p. 3.

45. Of course Fox had already distributed the movie and had other relationships with the producer George Lucas; therefore not all aspects of the deal may be apparent.

46. For the full story see Frederick Wasser, "Is Hollywood America? The Trans-

nationalization of the American Film Industry," *Critical Studies in Mass Communication* 12, no. 4 (Winter 1995), pp. 423–437.

47. Peter Besas, "Homevid Proves Mifed's Busiest Beehive," *Variety*, October 28, 1981, p. 7.

48. *Variety*, November 26, 1986, p. 28.

49. James Melanson, "Homevideo Bucks Fuel AFM as Labels Add Theatrical Rights," *Variety*, March 20, 1985, p. 38.

50. Roger Watkins, "Homevid Balm and Bucks and Mifed," *Variety*, November 7, 1984, p. 47.

51. Andrew Yule, *Hollywood A Go-Go: An Account of the Cannon Phenomenon* (London: Sphere Books, 1987), p. 85.

52. *Variety*, October 4, 1989.

53. Yule, *Hollywood A Go-Go*, p. 33.

54. See Yule, *Hollywood A Go-Go*, and "Indie HV Labels Hang Tough," p. 42.

55. Yule, *Hollywood A Go-Go*, p. 204.

56. Claudia Eller and Marc Berman, "Industryites Nod and Wink," *Variety*, February 4, 1991, pp. 5, 110.

57. Kevin Lally, "Rambo Spurs Carolco Move from Int'l Sales to Production," *Film Journal* 88, no. 5 (May 1985): 7.

58. Carolco Pictures Inc., *Prospectus* (Los Angeles, April 18, 1988), pp. f-48, f-50.

59. DeLaurentiis Entertainment Group, *Prospectus* (Beverly Hills, Calif., 1986), p. 20.

60. Merrill Lynch, "The Home Video Market," p. 129.

61. *Variety*, September 5, 1984, p. 43.

62. *Variety*, May 30, 1984, p. 51, and *Video Week*, December 26, 1988, p. 3.

63. Merrill Lynch, "The Home Video Market," p. 129.

64. James Melanson, "First Sale, Pay-Per-View Dominate VSDA Sessions," *Variety*, September 5, 1984, p. 43.

65. Ken Terry, "Music Vid Mkt. Share Goes Flat," *Variety*, April 1, 1987, p. 92.

66. *Flashdance* earned $36.2 million for the distributor in the North American market. *Footloose* earned $34 million, and *Purple Rain* earned $31.7 million. *Purple Rain* sold 450,000 cassette units (estimated distributor revenue is $8.2 million), *Flashdance* sold 355,000 units ($7.1 million), and *Footloose* sold 250,000 units ($5.2 million). This was an early example of shows performing differently in the video market and the theatrical market. It is difficult to defend any generalization about the differences, particularly in this case, where there is the complicating factor that the *Purple Rain* cassette had a lower list price (Merrill Lynch, "The Home Video Market," p. 129).

67. "Conversation with Jon Peisinger," p. 62.

68. *Variety*, May 18, 1983, p. 34.

69. Conversation with Austin Furst, November 2, 1995.

70. Douglas Gomery, *Shared Pleasures: A History of Movie Presentation in the United States* (Madison: University of Wisconsin Press, 1992), p. 289.

220   Chapter 5. Video Becomes Big Business

1. Merrill Lynch, "The Home Video Market," p. 124.

2. The first *Star Trek* returned $56 million to Paramount from its 1979 domestic theatrical release while returns for *Star Trek II: The Wrath of Khan* reached only $40 million in 1982. Paramount could therefore assume its price experiment compensated for the weaker popularity of the sequel. However, such an argument was not made since the increased video sales of the second title are more adequately explained by the threefold increase in the U.S. video population that occurred between the two video release dates.

3. *Screen Digest*, May 1986, p. 85.

4. *Variety*, June 1, 1983, p. 25.

5. *Variety*, February 22, 1984, p. 43.

6. Joe Flower, *Prince of the Magic Kingdom: Michael Eisner and the Remaking of Disney* (New York: Wiley, 1991), p. 116.

7. Tom Bierbaum, "Paramount Pricing Switcheroo Drops 25 Titles to $24.95 List." *Variety*, September 26, 1984, p. 37.

8. Goldman Sachs, *Update–1991*, p. 17.

9. Veronis, Suhler, and Associates, *Forecast*, pp. 142–143.

10. Kraig G. Fox, "Paramount Revisited: The Resurgence of Vertical Integration in the Motion Picture Industry." *Hofstra Law Review* 21 (Winter 1992), p. 527.

11. Moya Verzhbinsky, "Cineplex Odeon," in *International Directory of Company Histories*, vol. 6, ed. Paula Kepos, pp. 161–163 (Detroit: St. James Press, 1993).

12. Gomery, *Shared Pleasures*, p. 107.

13. *Screen Digest*, February 1994, pp. 37–40.

14. *Video Week*, June 20, 1988, p. 6.

15. Conversation with Bill Burton, president of the National Association of Video Distributors, December 13, 1995.

16. *Variety*, June 15, 1983, p. 31.

17. Adam Sandler, "Count Grossed Out by Exec Oral Agreements," *Variety*, March 24, 1997, p. 50. Also see Pierce O'Donnell and Dennis McDougal, *Fatal Subtraction: The Inside Story of Buchwald v. Paramount* (New York: Doubleday, 1992), p. 382.

18. Vogel, *Entertainment*, 3d ed., p. 79.

19. Garnham, *Capitalism and Communication*, p. 123.

20. Vogel, *Entertainment*, 2d. ed., p. 299.

21. Wei-Na Lee and Helen Katz, "New Media, New Messages: An Initial Inquiry into Audience Reactions to Advertising on Videocassettes," *Journal of Advertising Research* (January 1993), pp. 74–85.

22. Gail DeGeorge, *The Making of a Blockbuster: How Wayne Huizenga Built a Sports and Entertainment Empire for Trash, Grit and Videotape* (New York: Wiley, 1996), p. 96.

23. Blockbuster, *Annual Report* (1991), p. 12.

24. *Video Store*, April 1990, p. 46.

25. *Video Week*, January 13, 1992, p. 12.

26. DeGeorge, *Blockbuster*, p. 146.

27. Ibid., p. 191.

28. *Video Week*, August 15, 1988, p. 5.

29. Van Wallach, "What If Retailers Ran the Studios?" *Video Store*, August 1990, p. 77.

30. Bart Story, "The Big Picture," *Video Store*, December 1990, pp. 8–17.

31. Daniel Loren Moret, "The New Nickelodeons: A Political Economy of the Home Video Industry with Particular Emphasis on Video Software Dealers" (Master's thesis, University of Oregon, 1991).

32. A good example of such a study is Anthony J. Buono's "1992 New England Video Software Dealers Association Customer Satisfaction Study Summary Report" (manuscript, 1992).

33. Tom Bierbaum, "Backlash on Blockbuster Mania . . .," *Variety*, March 12, 1986, pp. 35–36.

34. Diane Garrett, "Video Quest," *Video Store*, May 7, 1995, p. 25.

35. Doug Desjardins, "Many Happy Returns," *Video Store*, June 5, 1994, p. 28.

36. *Video Week*, February 20, 1989, p. 1.

37. Conversation with Kelly Neilson, vice president, Creative Affairs, Prism Home Video, January 1996.

38. *Screen Digest*, February 1998, p. 47.

39. *Variety*, November 2, 1983, p. 40.

40. Conversation with Suzanne Bouchard, vice president, Marketing, Orion Home Video, December 13, 1995.

41. *Video Week*, January 30, 1989, p. 3.

42. Ken Auletta, *Three Blind Mice: How the TV Networks Lost Their Way* (New York: Random House, 1991), p. 349.

Chapter 6. Consolidation and Shakeouts

1. Vestron, *Annual Report* (1986).

2. Justin Wyatt, *High Concept: Movies and Marketing in Hollywood* (Austin: University of Texas Press, 1994), p. 13.

3. Ibid., p. 22.

4. Charles Eidsvik, "Machines of the Invisible: Changes in Film Technology in the Age of Video." *Film Quarterly* 42, no. 2 (Winter 1988): 21.

5. Ron Grover, *The Disney Touch: Disney, ABC and the Quest for the World's Greatest Media Empire* (Chicago: Irwin, 1997), pp. 130–132.

6. Stephen Koepp, "Do You Believe in Magic," *Time*, April 25, 1988, p. 72.

7. The Walt Disney Company, *Annual Report* (1986).

8. Michael Eisner, *Work in Progress: Risking Failure, Surviving Success* (New York: Hyperion, 1998), p. 157.

222

9. There was one such statement in 1981, at the beginning of the video revolution. Francis (Fay) Vincent, the CEO of Columbia Pictures, justified burgeoning production and release costs by telling stockholders that "we believe expanded opportunities for exploitation of our product will more than offset those costs." See Stephen Klain, "Columbia's All-Media Future Will Update Outside Film Financing," *Variety*, November 11, 1981, p. 34.

10. Peter Hoffman, *L'Affaire de cinema aujourd'hui*. Speech delivered at the Cannes Film Festival, May 1992.

11. *Variety*, January 9, 1995, p. 20.

12. Michael E. Ross, "Videocassette Concern to Make Feature Films," *New York Times*, January 8, 1986, p. C22.

13. *Video Week*, various issues in February of each year.

14. Peter Bart, *Final Fade: The Calamitous Last Days of MGM* (New York: Anchor Books, 1990), p. 232.

15. *Video Week*, January 9, 1989, p. 4.

16. *TapeTrack Compendium 1988–February 1995* (Santa Ana, Calif.: Advanstar, 1995).

17. Tom Bierbaum, "Killer 'Bs' Help Vestron Rebound," *Daily Variety*, July 15, 1988, p. 2.

18. Conversation with Jon Peisinger, January 7, 1998.

19. Part of the fire sale of Vestron properties included a script about the transformation of a prostitute. Touchstone, a division of Walt Disney, bought the script for $200,000 and turned it into the 1989 smash hit *Pretty Woman*.

20. He sued Security Pacific. LIVE refused to take over the lawsuit and Furst kept it going on his own until he won a $100 million settlement in 1993, from Bank of America (the company that bought Security Pacific). *Wall Street Journal*, May 24, 1993, p. B4. Furst got out of the video business and now runs "Inovision."

21. Anne Thompson, "Another Indy Bites the Dust," *Los Angeles Weekly*, August 4, 1989.

22. Cannon's P&A was $24.5 million. Net Cannon rentals was $19.3 million. See Yule, *Hollywood A Go-Go*, p. 189.

23. See Yule, *Hollywood A Go-Go*, for a detailed account of this ongoing struggle.

24. William K. Knoedelseder Jr., "DeLaurentiis Producer's Picture Darkens," *Los Angeles Times*, August 30, 1987, part 4, pp. 1–2.

25. LIVE, annual reports (various years).

26. *TapeTrack Compendium*.

27. Jim McCallaugh, "CBS/Fox Video Gets Media Home Titles," *Billboard*, January 5, 1991, p. 6.

28. Heikki Hellman and Martti Soramäki, "Competition and Content in the U.S. Video Market," *Journal of Media Economics* 7, no. 1 (1994): 29–49. This article shows the drawbacks of using benchmark years, especially when dealing with film estimates. Because the revenue figures are not reliably reported for every title, the best use of revenue figures is to determine trends. Unfortunately Hellman and Soramäki do not

use year-by-year trends but instead use benchmarks four years apart; 1990 is anomalous because of the breakaway results of LIVE's sell-through of *TMNT*.

29. LIVE, *10-K Report* (1995).

30. Trimark Pictures consistently claimed 1 percent of the video market during the 1990s (various issues *Video Week*) and is arguably a significant independent distributor. It was formed in 1988 as Vidmark and changed its name to Trimark in 1992. It used to distribute only horror and other low-budget formula films. It has lately handled artistic films such as *Eve's Bayou* (1998).

31. Andrew Hindes and Benedict Carver, "Hollywood Makeover," *Variety*, April 20, 1998, p. 7.

Chapter 7. The Lessons of the Video Revolution

1. There were 706 commercial stations (UHF and VHF) in 1975 and a record 1,145 in 1994. See U.S. Bureau of the Census, *Statistical Abstract of the United States* (Washington, D.C.: U.S. Government Printing Office, 1995).

2. See Stander, "The Impact of the VCR on Broadcast Television," pp. 481–494, for an influential rehearsal of these arguments.

3. Goldman Sachs, *Movie Industry Update–1993*, p. 5.

4. *TapeTrack Compendium* shows that feature film cassettes without a theatrical release accounted for only 2.87 percent of feature film cassette revenues in 1992. However, the survey is skewed. Mail-order distributors were not reported and neither were cassettes shipping below 50,000 units.

5. Hoffman, *L'Affaire*.

6. Ibid.

7. Grover, *The Disney Touch*, p. 226.

8. "The Teachings of Chairman Jeff," *Variety*, February 4, 1991, p. 24.

9. Eller and Berman, "Industryites," p. 110.

10. "The Teachings of Chairman Jeff," p. 26.

11. Peter Bart, "Times Have Changed, but the Rhetoric Lingers On," *Variety*, February 4, 1991, p. 24.

12. Vogel, *Entertainment*, 3d ed., p. 306, n. 44.

13. For purposes of contrast, the United States had a 62 percent share of the British box office and a 66 percent share of the West German market in 1979. The source for the earlier figures is Garnham, *Capitalism and Communication*, p. 175. Only Italy and France held Hollywood to less than 60 percent of the domestic box office in 1992. The source for the 1990 figures is André Lange, ed., *Statistical Yearbook: Cinema, Television, Video and New Media in Europe* (Strasbourg: European Audiovisual Observatory, 1994).

14. *Variety*, February 13, 1995, p. 1.

15. Goldman Sachs, *Movie Industry Update–1997*, p. 3.

16. Martine Danan, "Marketing the Hollywood Blockbuster in France," *Journal of Popular Film and Television* 23, no. 3 (Fall 1995): 131–140.

224

17. Terry Ilott, *Budgets and Markets: A Study of the Budgeting of European Film* (London: Routledge, 1996).

18. See various high-level comments in Office for the Official Publications of the European Communities, *Report by the Think-Tank on the Audiovisual Policy in the European Union* (Luxembourg: Office for the Official Publications of the European Communities, 1994).

19. Brian Winston, *Media, Technology and Society: A History* (New York: Routledge, 1998), pp. 11-13.

20. Bruce Austin elaborates this analogy in "Home Video."

21. John R. Wilke, "A Publicly Held Firm Turns X-rated Videos into a Hot Business," *Wall Street Journal*, July 11, 1994, pp. 1-2.

22. Veronis, Suhler, and Associates, *Forecast*, p. 169.

23. *Video Week* based its results on store surveys and decided to exclude adult material.

24. Gomery, *Shared Pleasures*, p. 229.

25. Jerry Mander, *Four Arguments for the Elimination of Television* (New York: William Morrow, 1978), p. 268.

26. James Bernardoni, *The New Hollywood: What the Movies Did with the New Freedoms of the Seventies* (Jefferson, N.C.: McFarland, 1991), p. 15.

27. Charles Eidsvik, "Machines of the Invisible," p. 21.

28. Jeff Dawson, *Quentin Tarantino: The Cinema of Cool* (New York: Applause Books, 1995), p. 59.

29. John Brodie, "'Vidstore' Helmers: Rebels with a Pause," *Variety*, June 13, 1994, pp. 1, 71.

30. Thomas Schatz, "The Return of the Hollywood Studio System," in *Conglomerates and the Media*, ed. Erik Barnouw et al. (New York: New Press, 1997), p. 73.

31. Wasko, *Hollywood in the Information Age*, p. 217.

32. Celia Lury, *Cultural Rights: Technology, Legality, and Personality* (New York: Routledge, 1993), p. 87.

33. Steve Knoll, "Homevid Growth Rides on RCA's Player Pitch: Software Genius Needed." *Variety*, March 25, 1981, p. 124.

34. Ariel Russell Hochschild, *The Time Bind: When Work Becomes Home and Home Becomes Work* (New York: Holt, 1997), pp. 49-52.

35. Maxwell E. McCombs, "Mass Media in the Marketplace," *Journalism Monographs* 24 (August 1972).

36. William C. Wood and Sharon L. O'Hare, "Paying for the Video Revolution: Consumer Spending on the Mass Media." *Journal of Communication* 41, no. 1 (Winter 1991): 24-30. Wood and O'Hare do not break out cable versus home video spending, but figures from Veronis, Suhler, and Associates (*Forecast*) and the Electronic Industries Association (*The U.S. Consumer Electronics Industry in Review*) would indicate that home video (both on cassettes and VCRs) contributed an average of 45 percent of the total consumer spending on new video in the relatively mature period of

1987–1993. We should remember that the film industry captures much more of the   225
home video spending than cable.

37. Conversation with Jon Peisinger, January 7, 1998.

38. MPAA, *Incidence of Motion Picture Attendance*, various years.

39. Wasko, *Hollywood in the Information Age*, p. 176.

40. Raymond Williams, *Culture and Society 1780–1950* (London: Chatto and Windus, 1960), p. 300.

Bibliography

Abel, Richard. *The Ciné Goes to Town: French Cinema 1896–1914.* Berkeley: University of California Press, 1994.

Anderson, Christopher. *Hollywood TV: The Studio System in the Fifties.* Austin: University of Texas Press, 1994.

Archer, Gleason. *History of Radio to 1926.* New York: American Historical Society, 1938.

Auletta, Ken. *Three Blind Mice: How the TV Networks Lost Their Way.* New York: Random House, 1991.

Austin, Bruce A. "Home Video: The Second-Run Theater of the 1990s." In *Hollywood in the Age of Television,* ed. Tino Balio, pp. 319–349. Boston: Unwin Hyman, 1990.

Avco Industries. *10-K Report.* 1973.

"Aylesworth Assails Recordings in Chicago Speech." *Broadcast Advertising* 3, no. 9 (December 1930): 7.

Barnouw, Erik. *The Golden Web: A History of Broadcasting in the United States. Volume 2: 1933–1953.* New York: Oxford University Press, 1968.

Bart, Peter. *Final Fade: The Calamitous Last Days of MGM.* New York: Anchor Books, 1990.

———. "Times Have Changed, but the Rhetoric Lingers On." *Variety* (February 4, 1991): 24.

Becker, Gary. "A Theory of the Allocation of Time." *Economic Journal* 75 (1965): 493–517.

Belton, John. *Widescreen Cinema.* Cambridge, Mass.: Harvard University Press, 1992.

Bernardoni, James. *The New Hollywood: What the Movies Did with the New Freedoms of the Seventies.* Jefferson, N.C.: McFarland, 1991.

Besas, Peter. "Homevid Proves Mifed's Busiest Beehive." *Variety* (October 28, 1981): 7.

Bierbaum, Tom. "Backlash on Blockbuster Mania . . ." *Variety* (March 12, 1986): 35–36.

———. "Killer 'Bs' Help Vestron Rebound." *Daily Variety* (July 15, 1988): 2.

———. "Paramount Pricing Switcheroo Drops 25 Titles to $24.95 List." *Variety* (September 26, 1984): 37.

228   Biskind, Peter. *Easy Riders, Raging Bulls: How the Sex-Drugs-and-Rock 'n' Roll Generation Saved Hollywood*. New York: Simon and Schuster, 1998.

Blay, Andre. "Home Video—An Emerging Market." In *Who's Got the Money: The New Financing of Motion Picture and Television Production*, ed. Michael S. Sherman and David R. Ginsburg, pp. 241–281. Eighth Annual UCLA Entertainment Symposium. Los Angeles: The Regents of the University of California, 1983.

Blockbuster. *Annual Report*. 1991.

Bluem, Albert William. "The Influence of Medium upon Dramaturgical Method in Selected Television Plays." Ph.D. diss., Ohio State University, 1959.

Boddy, William. *Fifties Television: The Industry and Its Critics*. Urbana: University of Illinois Press, 1990.

Bordwell, David, Janet Staiger, and Kirstin Thompson. *The Classical Hollywood Cinema: Film Style and Mode of Production to 1960*. New York: Columbia University Press, 1985.

Brodie, John. "'Vidstore' Helmers: Rebels with a Pause." *Variety* (June 13, 1994): 1, 71.

Buono, Anthony J. "1992 New England Video Software Dealers Association Customer Satisfaction Study Summary Report." Manuscript. 1992.

Carolco Pictures, Inc. *Prospectus*. April 18, 1988.

Chapple, Steve, and Reebee Garofalo. *Rock 'n' Roll Is Here to Pay: The History and Politics of the Music Industry*. Chicago: Nelson-Hall, 1977.

Clark, Mark. "Suppressing Innovation: Bell Laboratories and Magnetic Recording." *Technology and Culture* 34, no. 3 (July 1993).

Cohn, Lawrence. "WB Biggest Pic Supplier—Again." *Variety* (December 21, 1992): 6.

"Conversation with Jon Peisinger." *Videography* 9, no. 9 (September 1984): 60–73.

Corrigan, Timothy. *A Cinema without Walls: Movies and Culture after Vietnam*. New Brunswick, N.J.: Rutgers University Press, 1991.

Costello, Marge, and Vicki Stearn. "Conversation with Jim Jimirro." *Videography* 6, no. 6 (June, 1981): 60–73.

Cusumano, Michael, et al. *Strategic Maneuvering and Mass Market Dynamics: The Triumph of VHS over Beta*. Harvard Business School Working Paper 91-048, 1991.

Danan, Martine. "Marketing the Hollywood Blockbuster in France." *Journal of Popular Film and Television* 23, no. 3 (Fall 1995): 131–140.

Davies, Gillian, and Michèle E. Hung. *Music and Video Private Copying: An International Survey of the Problem and the Law*. London: Sweet and Maxwell, 1993.

Dawson, Jeff. *Quentin Tarantino: The Cinema of Cool*. New York: Applause Books, 1995.

DeGeorge, Gail. *The Making of a Blockbuster: How Wayne Huizenga Built a Sports and Entertainment Empire for Trash, Grit and Videotape*. New York: Wiley, 1996.

DeLaurentiis Entertainment Group. *Prospectus*. 1986.

Desjardins, Doug. "Many Happy Returns." *Video Store* (June 5, 1994): 28.

Dobrow, Julia R., ed. *Social and Cultural Aspects of VCR Use*. Hillsdale, N.J.: Erlbaum, 1990.

Donahue, Suzanne Mary. *American Film Distribution: The Changing Marketplace.* 229
Ann Arbor: UMI Research Press, 1987.

Dunlap, Orrin E. Jr. *The Future of Television.* Rev. ed. New York: Harper and Brothers, 1947.

Eidsvik, Charles. "Machines of the Invisible: Changes in Film Technology in the Age of Video." *Film Quarterly* 42, no. 2 (Winter 1988): 18–23.

Eisner, Michael. *Work in Progress: Risking Failure, Surviving Success.* New York: Hyperion, 1998.

Electronics Industries Association. *The U.S. Consumer Electronics Industry in Review.* Washington, D.C.: Electronics Industries Association, 1993.

Electronic Industries Association of Japan. *Facts and Figures on the Japanese Electronics Industry.* Tokyo: Electronic Industries Association of Japan, 1993.

Eller, Claudia, and Marc Berman. "Industryites Nod and Wink." *Variety* (February 4, 1991): 110.

Federal Communications Commission. *Public Service Responsibility of Broadcast Licensees.* Washington D.C.: Federal Communications Commission. March 7, 1946.

———. *Report on Chain Broadcasting.* Commission Order no. 37. Docket no. 5060. May 1941.

Flower, Joe. *Prince of the Magic Kingdom: Michael Eisner and the Remaking of Disney.* New York: Wiley, 1991.

Fox, Kraig G. "Paramount Revisited: The Resurgence of Vertical Integration in the Motion Picture Industry." *Hofstra Law Review* 21 (Winter 1992): 505–536.

Ganley, Gladys D., and Oswald H. Ganley. *Global Political Fallout: The First Decade of the VCR: 1976–1985.* Norwood, N.J.: Ablex, 1987.

Garnham, Nicholas. *Capitalism and Communication: Global Culture and the Economics of Information.* London: Sage, 1990.

Garrett, Diane. "Video Quest." *Video Store* (May 7, 1995): 25.

Gelatt, Roland. *The Fabulous Phonograph: From Tin Foil to High Fidelity.* Philadelphia: J. P. Lippincott, 1955.

Gelman, Morrie. "Media Home Claims $2mil for Halloween." *Variety* (October 7, 1981): 108.

———. "Vegas Fracas Hits Major Rent Plans." *Variety* (January 20, 1982): 50.

"General Sarnoff: The Twentieth Century Practical Prophet." *Sponsor* (October 1, 1956): 109–112.

Goald, R. S. "Observations on the American Independent Feature Film Movement: 1983–93." Paper presented at the University Film and Video Association Conference, Bozeman, Montana. August 1994.

Goldman Sachs. *Movie Industry Update.* 1991.

———. *Movie Industry Update.* 1993.

———. *Movie Industry Update.* 1997.

Goldstein, Paul. *Copyright's Highway: From Gutenberg to the Celestial Jukebox.* New York: Hill and Wang, 1994.

230   Goldstein, Seth. "Pay Per View in Retrospect: An Apparent Underachiever." *View Magazine* (April 1983): 30.

Gomery, Douglas. *Shared Pleasures: A History of Movie Presentation in the United States.* Madison: University of Wisconsin Press, 1992.

Gould, Jack. "The Great Day Isn't Exactly at Hand." *New York Times* (November 15, 1970): sec. 2, p. 21.

———. "Renting a Movie or a Professor to Take Home." *New York Times* (April 5, 1970): sec. 2, p. 15.

———. "Soon You'll Collect TV Reels, Like LP's." *New York Times* (September 3, 1967): D13.

Graham, Margaret. *RCA and the Videodisc: The Business of Research.* New York: Cambridge University Press, 1986.

Gray, Ann. *Video Playtime: The Gendering of a Leisure Technology.* London: Routledge, 1992.

Grover, Ron. *The Disney Touch: Disney, ABC and the Quest for the World's Greatest Media Empire.* Chicago: Irwin, 1997.

Guback, Thomas. "Theatrical Film." In *Who Owns the Media?* 2d ed., ed. Benjamin M. Compaine, pp. 199–298. White Plains, N.Y.: Knowledge Industry Publications, 1982.

Guber, Peter. "Is There a Cassette in Your Future—Is There a Future in Cassettes?" *Journal of the Producers Guild of America* 12, no. 3 (September 1970): 3–14.

Hampton, Francis. "New Leisure: How Is It Spent?" M.A. thesis, University of North Carolina, 1935.

Hellman, Heikki, and Martti Soramäki. "Competition and Content in the U.S. Video Market." *The Journal of Media Economics* 7, no. 1 (1994): 29–49.

Hindes, Andrew, and Benedict Carver, "Hollywood Makeover." *Variety* (April 20, 1998): 7.

Hochschild, Ariel Russell. *The Time Bind: When Work Becomes Home and Home Becomes Work.* New York: Holt, 1997.

Hoffman, Peter. "L'Affaire de cinema aujourd'hui." Speech delivered at the Cannes Film Festival in France. May 1992.

Hoover's Guide to Media Companies. Austin, Tex.: Hoover's Business Press, 1996.

Ilott, Terry. *Budgets and Markets: A Study of the Budgeting of European Film.* London: Routledge, 1996.

Jowett, Garth. *Film: The Democratic Art.* Boston: Little, Brown, 1976.

Klain, Stephen. "Columbia's All-Media Future Will Update Outside Film Financing." *Variety* (November 11, 1981): 34.

Klopfenstein, Bruce Carl. "Forecasting the Market for Home Video Players: A Retrospective Analysis." Ph.D. diss., Ohio State University, 1985.

Knoedelseder Jr., William K. "DeLaurentiis Producer's Picture Darkens." *Los Angeles Times* (August 30, 1987): part 4, pp. 1–2.

Knoll, Steve. "Homevid Growth Rides on RCA's Player Pitch: Software Genius Needed." *Variety* (March 25, 1981): 24.

―――. "Mag Video Launches Cassette Rent Plan." *Variety* (November 18, 1981): 34.   231

―――. "See Vidisk Hour of Truth Approaching." *Variety* (February 17, 1982): 43.

Koepp, Stephen. "Do You Believe in Magic." *Time* (April 25, 1988): 72.

Lachenbruch, David. "The Videoplayer Era." *Journal of the Producers Guild of America* 13, no. 1 (March 1971): 7–12.

Lally, Kevin. "Rambo Spurs Carolco Move from Int'l Sales to Production." *Film Journal* 88, no. 5 (May 1985): 7, 26.

Lange, André, ed. *Statistical Yearbook: Cinema, Television, Video and New Media in Europe.* Strausbourg: European Audiovisual Observatory, 1994.

Lardner, James. *Fast Forward: Hollywood, the Japanese and the Onslaught of the VCR.* New York: W. W. Norton, 1987.

Larson, Allen David. "Integration and Attempted Integration between the Motion Picture and Television Industries through 1956." Ph.D. diss., Ohio University, 1979.

Lee, Wei-Na, and Helen Katz. "New Media, New Messages: An Initial Inquiry into Audience Reactions to Advertising on Videocassettes." *Journal of Advertising Research* (January 1993): 74–85.

Lev, Peter. *The Euro-American Cinema.* Austin: University of Texas Press, 1993.

Levy, Mark R., ed. *The VCR Age: Home Video and Mass Communication.* Newbury Park, Calif.: Sage, 1989.

Linder, Staffan Burenstam. *The Harried Leisure Class.* New York: Columbia University Press, 1970.

Lindsay, Robert. "Home Box Office Moves in on Hollywood." *New York Times Magazine* (June 12, 1983).

Lindstrom, Paul B. "Home Video: The Consumer Impact." In *The VCR Age: Home Video and Mass Communication,* ed. Mark R. Levy, pp. 40–49. Newbury Park, Calif.: Sage, 1989.

LIVE. *Annual Reports.* Various years.

―――. *10-K Report.* 1995.

Lou Harris Poll no. 68, November 6, 1995, p. 4.

Lury, Celia. *Cultural Rights: Technology, Legality and Personality.* New York: Routledge Press, 1993.

Mahamdi, Yahia. "Television, Globalization, and Cultural Hegemony: The Evolution and Structure of International Television." Ph.D. diss., University of Texas, 1992.

Mander, Jerry. *Four Arguments for the Elimination of Television.* New York: William Morrow, 1978.

Mandese, J. "Bates Bullies Nets over VCR Erosion." *Adweek* 27 (1986): 1, 4.

Marlow, Eugene, and Eugene Secunda. *Shifting Time and Space: The Story of Videotape.* New York: Praeger, 1991.

MCA. *Annual Report.* 1972.

McCallaugh, Jim. "CBS/Fox Video Gets Media Home Titles." *Billboard* (January 5, 1991): 6.

McCarthy, Todd. "'Independent' Producers Bruised as Majors Borrow Their Slants." *Variety* (June 16, 1982): 22.

232   ———. "Indie Share of Mkt. Hits 6-Year High." _Variety_ (June 18, 1986): 5.

McCombs, Maxwell E. "Mass Media in the Marketplace." _Journalism Monographs_ (August 24, 1972).

Melanson, James. "First Sale, Pay-Per-View Dominate VSDA Sessions." _Variety_ (September 5, 1984): 43.

———. "Homevideo Bucks Fuel AFM as Labels Add Theatrical Rights." _Variety_ (March 20, 1985): 38.

Merrill Lynch. "The Home Video Market: Times of Turbulence and Transition." In _Following the Dollars from Retail to Net Profits—An Examination of the Businesses of Creating and Using Revenues from Motion Pictures and Television Programs_, ed. Keith G. Fleer et al., pp. 111–133. Eleventh Annual UCLA Entertainment Symposium. Los Angeles: Regents of the University of California, 1986.

Merritt, Russell. "Nickelodeon Theaters, 1905–1914: Building an Audience for the Movies." In _The American Film Industry_, rev. ed., ed. Tino Balio, pp. 83–102. Madison: University of Wisconsin Press, 1985.

Morein, Joseph A. "Shift from Brand to Product Line Marketing." _Harvard Business Review_ (September 1975).

Moret, Daniel Loren. "The New Nickelodeons: A Political Economy of the Home Video Industry with Particular Emphasis on Video Software Dealers." M.S. thesis, University of Oregon, 1991.

Morita, Akio, et al. _Made in Japan: Akio Morita and Sony._ New York: E. P. Dutton, 1986.

Motion Picture Association of America. _U.S. Economic Review._ Encino, Calif.: Motion Picture Association of America, 1993.

———. _U.S. Theatrical Statistics 1946–1995._

Mullin, John T. "Creating the Craft of Tape Recording." _High Fidelity Magazine_ 26, no. 4 (April 1976): 62–67.

Myers, Harold. "Hardware Hot, Software Soft in Japan." _Variety_ (October 7, 1981): 107.

Nayak, P. Rangunath, and John M. Ketteringham. _Breakthroughs._ New York: Rawson Associates, 1986.

Neuman, W. Russell. _The Future of the Mass Audience._ Cambridge: Cambridge University Press, 1991.

Norback, Craig T., and Peter G. Norback. _TV Guide Almanac._ New York: Ballantine, 1980.

O'Donnell, Pierce, and Dennis McDougal. _Fatal Subtraction: The Inside Story of Buchwald v. Paramount._ New York: Doubleday, 1992.

Office for the Official Publications of the European Communities. _Report by the Think-Tank on the Audiovisual Policy in the European Union._ Luxembourg: Office for the Official Publications of the European Communities, 1994.

"Radio's Big Issue—Who Is to Pay the Artist?" _New York Times_ (May 18, 1924): sec. 8, p. 3.

Robinson, John P., and Geoffrey Godbey. "Are Average Americans Really Overworked?" _The American Enterprise_ 6 (September/October 1995): 43.

Rogers, Michael. "A New Spin on Videodiscs." *Newsweek* (June 5, 1989): 68–69.   233

Ross, Michael E. "Videocassette Concern to Make Feature Films." *New York Times* (January 8, 1986): C22.

Roth, Morry. "Home Video Hypes CES Show." *Variety* (May 27, 1981): 61.

Sadoul, Georges. *Histoire du cinéma mondial: des origines a nos jours.* 8th ed. Paris: Flammarion, 1949.

Sandler, Adam. "Count Grossed Out by Exec Oral Agreements." *Variety* (March 24, 1997): 50.

Sanjek, Russell. *American Popular Music and Its Business: The First Four Hundred Years.* Vol. 3. New York: Oxford University Press, 1988.

Sapolsky, Barry S., and Edward Forrest. "Measuring VCR Ad-Voidance." In *The VCR Age: Home Video and Mass Communication,* ed. Mark R. Levy, pp. 148–167. Newbury Park, Calif.: Sage, 1989.

"'Scarface,' 'Silkwood' Video Hit Tape," *Variety* (May 23, 1984): 47–48, 50.

Schatz, Thomas. "The New Hollywood." In *Film Theory Goes to the Movies,* ed. Jim Collins et al., pp. 8–36. New York: Routledge, 1993.

———. "The Return of the Hollywood Studio System." In *Conglomerates and the Media,* ed. Erik Barnouw et al. New York: New Press, 1997.

Schlosser, Eric. "Business and Technology Column." *U.S. News and World Report* (February 10, 1997): 43–50.

Schnapper, Amy. "The Distribution of Theatrical Feature Films to Television." Ph.D. diss., University of Wisconsin–Madison, 1975.

Schor, Juliet B. *The Overworked American: The Unexpected Decline of Leisure.* New York: Basic Books, 1991.

Schubin, Mark. "An Overview and History of Video Disc Technologies." In *Video Discs: The Technology, the Applications and the Future,* ed. Efrem Sigel et al., pp. 7–52. White Plains, N.Y.: Knowledge Industry Publications, 1980.

Segers, Frank. "CBS to Distrib ABC Programs for Homevid." *Variety* (June 3, 1981): 90.

Seideman, Tony. "Low-Priced Vidtapes as Lure for Big Retail Chains." *Variety* (March 9, 1983): 34.

———. "Slow Start for Sony 'Vid' Singles." *Variety* (August 17, 1983): 72.

Sigel, Efrem. "The Consumer Market for Video Discs." In *Video Discs: The Technology, the Applications and the Future,* ed. Efrem Sigel et al., pp. 53–68. White Plains, N.Y.: Knowledge Industry Publications, 1980.

Silverman, Mark. "US Homevid Rights Break $3-Mil Barrier." *Variety* (May 16, 1984): 3.

Sims, Jonathan. "VCR Viewing Patterns: An Electronic and Passive Investigation." *Journal of Advertising Research* 29, no. 2 (April 1989): 13.

Singer, Ben. "Early Home Cinema and the Edison Home Projecting Kinetoscope." *Film History* 2 (1988): 37–69.

Smith, Sally Bedell. *In All His Glory: The Life of William S. Paley.* New York: Simon and Schuster, 1990.

234   Staiger, Janet. "Combination and Litigation: Structures of US Film Distribution, 1896–1917." In *Early Cinema: Space-Frame-Narrative*, ed. Thomas Elsaesser and Adam Barker. London: British Film Institute, 1990.

Stander, Stephen F. "The Impact of the VCR on Broadcast Television." In *Video Cassettes: Production, Distribution and Programming for the VCR Marketplace*, ed. E. Gabriel Perle et al., pp. 481–494. New York: Practising Law Institute, 1985.

Steinhauer, Jennifer. "Prosecute Porn? It's on the Decline." *Wall Street Journal* (December 28, 1989): A8.

Story, Bart. "The Big Picture." *Video Store* (December 1990): 8–17.

Straubhaar, Joseph D. "Context, Social Class and VCRs: A World Comparison." *Social and Cultural Aspects of VCR Use*, ed. Julia R. Dobrow, pp. 125–146. Hillsdale, N.J.: Erlbaum, 1990.

TapeTrack Compendium 1988–February 1995. Santa Ana, Calif.: Advanstar, 1995.

"The Teachings of Chairman Jeff." *Variety* (February 4, 1991): 24.

Terry, Ken. "Music Vid Mkt. Share Goes Flat." *Variety* (April 1, 1987): 92.

Thompson, Anne. "Another Indy Bites the Dust." *Los Angeles Weekly* (August 4, 1989).

"Trying on the New Media." *Variety* (September 24, 1980): 48, 79.

United States of America versus The Motion Pictures Patent Company: Brief for the United States. October 1914. Reprinted in *Film History* 1, no. 3 (1987).

U.S. Bureau of the Census. *Statistical Abstract of the United States*. Washington, D.C.: U.S. Government Printing Office, 1995.

U.S. Congress. *Audio and Video First Sale Doctrine. Hearings before the Subcommittee on Courts, Civil Liberties and the Administration of Justice of the Committee on the Judiciary House of Representatives*. Washington D.C.: U.S. Government Printing Office, 1985.

———. *Video and Audio Home Taping. Hearing before the Subcommittee on Patents, Copyrights and Trademarks of the Committee on the Judiciary United States Senate*. Washington, D.C.: U.S. Government Printing Office, 1984.

U.S. Department of Justice. *Attorney General's Commission on Pornography: Final Report*. Washington, D.C.: U.S. Department of Justice. July 1986.

Variety's First Homevideo Annual. September 24, 1980.

Veronis, Suhler, and Associates. *Communications Industry Forecast 1994–1998*. New York: Veronis, Suhler, and Associates, 1994.

Verzhbinsky, Moya. "Cineplex Odeon." In *International Directory of Company Histories*, vol. 6, ed. Paula Kepos, pp. 161–163. Detroit: St. James Press, 1993.

"Vestron Claims Major Status." *Variety* (January 4, 1984): 57.

Vestron. *Annual Report*. 1986.

Video Software Dealers Association. *White Paper*. October 21, 1996.

Vogel, Harold L. *Entertainment Industry Economics: A Guide for Financial Analysis*. 2d ed. New York: Cambridge University Press, 1990.

———. *Entertainment Industry Economics: A Guide for Financial Analysis*. 3d ed. New York: Cambridge University Press, 1994.

Wallach, Van. "What If Retailers Ran the Studios?" *Video Store* (August 1990): 77.

The Walt Disney Company. *Annual Report*. 1986.

Wasko, Janet. *Hollywood in the Information Age: Beyond the Silver Screen*. Austin: University of Texas Press, 1994.

Wasser, Frederick. "Four Walling Exhibition: Regional Resistance to Hollywood." *Cinema Journal* 34, no. 2 (February 1995): 51–65.

———. "Is Hollywood America? The Transnationalization of the American Film Industry." *Critical Studies in Mass Communication* 12, no. 4 (Winter 1995): 423–437.

Watkins, Roger. "Homevid Balm and Bucks and Mifed." *Variety* (November 7, 1984): 47.

———. "Scandinavian TV under Gun from Hotshot Video and Satellites." *Variety* (October 7, 1981): 80.

Weilbacher, William M. *Brand Marketing: Building Winning Brand Strategies That Deliver Value and Consumer Satisfaction*. Lincolnwood, Ill.: NTC Business Books, 1993.

Weinberger, Julius. "Economic Aspects of Recreation." *Harvard Business Review* 15 (Summer 1937): 448–463.

Wilke, John R. "A Publicly Held Firm Turns X-rated Videos into a Hot Business." *Wall Street Journal* (July 11, 1994): 1–2.

Williams, Raymond. *Culture and Society 1780–1950*. London: Chatto and Windus, 1960.

Winston, Brian. *Media, Technology and Society: A History*. New York: Routledge, 1998.

Wood, William C., and Sharon L. O'Hare. "Paying for the Video Revolution: Consumer Spending on the Mass Media." *Journal of Communication* 41, no. 1 (Winter 1991): 24–30.

Wyatt, Justin. *High Concept: Movies and Marketing in Hollywood*. Austin: University of Texas Press, 1994.

Yule, Andrew. *Hollywood A Go-Go: An Account of the Cannon Phenomenon*. London: Sphere Books, 1987.

Index